QuickieChick's
Cheat Sheet

to ☑ Life,
   ☑ Love,
   ☑ Food,
   ☑ Fitness,
   ☑ Fashion, and
   ☑ Finance

on a Less-Than-Fabulous Budget

QuickieChick's Cheat Sheet

to ☑ Life,
☑ Love,
☑ Food,
☑ Fitness,
☑ Fashion, and
☑ Finance

on a Less-Than-Fabulous Budget

Laurel House

St. Martin's Griffin 🜲 New York

QUICKIECHICK'S CHEAT SHEET TO LIFE, LOVE, FOOD, FITNESS, FASHION, AND FINANCE
—ON A LESS-THAN-FABULOUS BUDGET. Copyright © 2012 by Laurel House. Illustrations copyright © 2012 by Jennifer Cotterill. Photography copyright © 2012 by Megan McCarthy. All rights reserved. Printed in the United States of America. For information, address St. Martin's Press, 175 Fifth Avenue, New York, N.Y. 10010.

www.stmartins.com

House, Laurel.

  QuickieChick's cheat sheet to life, love, food, fitness, fashion—and finance on a less-than-fabulous budget--fixed layout / Laurel House. -- 1st ed.

      p. cm.

ISBN 978-0-312-56456-8 (trade paperback)

ISBN 978-1-4668-0783-9 (e-book)

1. Self-actualization (Psychology) 2. Finance, Personal. 3. Life skills. 4. Self-help techniques. I. Title.

  BF637.S4H67 2012

  646.70082--dc23

                          2012004629

First Edition: May 2012

10 9 8 7 6 5 4 3 2 1

To Julia and Julia

Contents

x

Acknowledgments

THANK-YOUS

Thank you to all of the amazing chicks who have inspired, taught, and believed in me:

Sally Richardson and Matthew Shear, for believing in me, my brand, and this book. Sally, you are an inspiration and the ultimate original Quickie-Chick! Dan Weiss, for believing in and allowing *QuickieChick* to come to be and for being just so awesome. Eileen Rothschild, for seeing the potential of my idea and helping to make it marketable. Nadea Mina and Olga Grlic, your touch and creativity are invaluable. Sarah Jae Jones and Jasmine Faustino, for allowing me to take my idea from YouTube and online and putting it in print (and Jasmine, for loving my Oatmeal and Egg with Sriracha ;). The chicks at FreshID, for creating a seriously awesome online presence and logo. Marcy Posner, for your unwavering belief in me and my potential as a writer. Much and House Public Relations and the entire team of amazing chicks—especially Amanda Molina, Laura Ackermann, and Alana Littler, for being my cheerleaders, but beyond that, for believing in me. Kacey Welch, for being my go-to hair guru and pretty much my therapist, too. Megan McCarthy, for capturing my essence in an image with your amazing photographic eye. Allison Wehrley, for giving me a chance with ExerciseTV to be an "expert" and for posting that first Quickie Workout in Bed that started this whole Quickie concept. Rita Trieger, for seeing something in me and giving me my very first shot as a writer—we all need that one person who gives us our very first chance. Julia Austin, for your words, wisdom, and reminding me to step out of my box on occasion. Kim Kessler, for being my best friend no matter what and supporting me and my happiness, even when my choices weren't so fab . . . Oy! Julia House, for being wise beyond your years, true to yourself, and always honest with me . . . even when honesty hurts. Alex Cafferty, for being awesome. I'm proud of you and all you do. Love you, A! Wendy Wilkinson, for being there for me and paving the writing path in the family. Elvira and Grandma, for your strength. Dad (Anderson House) and Garth, for being strong, stubborn, sensitive, fiercely dedicated, and good men—you are role models. Sang, for helping me focus on what's important, guiding and advising me in areas where I felt uneasy, inspiring and motivating me to take controlled risks, and letting me feel how true and safe love can be . . . and "thanks for bringing the water Sang." Mom (Sharon House)... for always being there, supporting me (moods, crazy life choices—except one, and my unyielding determination), for being my rock, my go-to, my shoulder, my reality checker.

xii

So Who Is This QuickieChick?

First, to address the elephant in the room: Yes, we all know what a "quickie" is (and that's in here, too), but this is more than that; it's a lifestyle. Just as "quickies" are fun, exciting, sometimes unconventional, efficient, sexy, in the moment, and always (or almost always) instantly gratifying . . . so are LifeQuickies. These aren't long, overdrawn processes that require prep work, expensive equipment, patience, and perseverance. They are right now, getting the most out of every moment. Oh, and it's all done on a budget (because you don't need to be wined, dined, and stay in a five-star hotel to have a quickie . . . do you?). Really, there's a Quickie solution for anything life throws your way.

Upping your metabolism or your sex drive, easing a bad mood or a hangover, feeling better after a heartbreak or a hard workout, even faking a perfect body before a big date or faking confidence before a big meeting—there's pretty much a Quickie for every facet of life. The idea is this: Everything from game-changing career decisions to whether you should stick it out with your boyfriend can be boiled down into the essence of the idea, a nugget of information that you can pass on to someone else. In the end, you may be a do-everything chick who lacks patience as a virtue and doesn't have a lot of time to get a lot done, but you still need those extracts of information to help you achieve a better, more-fulfilled, and fabulous life. That's where I come in. Since you don't have enough time, patience, or energy to have all of the full lesson-revealing life experiences yourself, I've done the dirty work for you, and now, in a nutshell, here they are—Quickie tips for fast-paced chicks—like you and me, too.

So who am I? I'm Laurel House—your QuickieChick—and I'm a real chick with a tad too many lived and learned experiences for being thirty-four years old, but my young age gives me an advantage, too: I can still see things from your point of view. From relationship drama to body issues, living paycheck to paycheck to figuring out how to create a kick-ass career, I've been there and done that, made a ton of mistakes, and thankfully learned from most of them. I've also been considered an "expert" in "lifestyle" in general, but specifically in fitness, diet, beauty, trends, spas, luxury, eco-living, and sex. Beyond writing about lifestyle, I have been hired by reputable companies as their "in the know" expert, representing and talking about their brands on TV. And now I'm here to share all my know-how with you—in the form of Quickie tips.

This is your cheat sheet to life.

Your Future Is in Good Hands . . . Yours

GOOD-BYE DIRT-INFESTED DORMS, finals, frat parties, dingy lecture halls, keggers, and waiting in line, on the phone, or online in hopes of getting into your desired classes. The "carpe diem" speech is done. You marched down the family-lined path, up the steps, onto the stage, across to the podium, pausing to smile for the camera as you were handed the rolled and ribboned piece of paper symbolizing your graduation from college . . . sealing the deal when it comes to your future success. You even got a job, and you're living on your own (well, without your parents). Life's great! Right? While, yes, life is certainly great, it might not exactly feel that way . . . yet. Being "independent" means, really, that you can't screw around anymore. Why? Because your livelihood, your happiness, your success is dependent on you. Which is why it's time to get your life in order—stat!

AFTER THE "CARPE DIEM" SPEECH

The transition from college to career can be a tad intimidating if you don't feel equipped with the information that you need to actually succeed. It's like the concept of "think rich and you will be." Really? Come on now, you can *think* as hard as you want, but that's not going to miraculously make you rich. *Thinking* is great, and, yes, an essential step, but then you need to take action, following the path from A (thinking rich) to B (being rich) by putting in the work (detailed in this book) it takes to make it happen. In this book each "QuickieChick's Cheat Sheet" will lay out those steps. It will help you transition from student to adult. (Don't shudder at the thought, this is exciting!)

This is your cheat sheet—your guide to everything you never learned in school about life and how to live it. And since you don't have to worry about selling this book back to the used-books college bookstore, feel free to fill in the "Note to Self" sections, highlight, comment, even scribble if it helps you focus.

What They Don't Teach in School or Anywhere Else

Unlike in college, in the real world we don't simply select our preferred course load, get handed a daily structured list of to-dos, show up before the bell rings, study the textbook at night, and pass with an A if we just go a little bit above and beyond. Obvious, right? There's no textbook, no tutor to help you figure out how to navigate what comes next. In the real world, you aren't handed the step-by-step map to life. Instead you are exposed to a slew of amazing, eye-opening, confusing, frustrating, overstimulating, engaging, brain-numbing, inspiring experiences that, like a thousand-piece puzzle board, somehow fit, forming this incredible, convoluted, but oddly totally sensible life story—yours. But, like braille for beginners, it's a totally different way of thinking.

For your entire life you've been a rule follower (well, mostly), taking all the prereq steps that guaranteed to get you that great job out of college. But now you're out of college and all you can find are low-level positions paying little more than minimum wage to answer some egomaniacal boss's phones or bussing tables. And you, apparently, are one of the *lucky* few. Lucky? How do I figure? Well, considering that the majority of your graduating class is only being offered unpaid internships—and even those positions they are forced to beg for—you're actually being paid . . . maybe! I know you're probably wondering just what was the point of paying for college if the job it afforded you can hardly pay the bills?

Before you get your panties in a twist or call your mom in another tear-fest hissy fit (believe me, we've all been there . . .), know that you're just paying your dues. In time (which may feel like a lifetime) you will climb to a higher rung on the ladder, and even become the boss someday—if that's the goal anyway. Until then, don't let your annual salary get you down. Why be miserable when you can be fabulous (I promise), even on a not-so-fabulous budget.

I know, the commencement address during your college graduation probably threw around statements that yield a lot of power like "claim the success you deserve," "the world is your oyster," "you have the ability to change the world," "if you dream big, you will achieve great things." You tossed your cap into the air and expected your future to fall into place. Many of you then moved to another, a bigger, or simply an unfamiliarly daunting town, with your dreams so clear, your future so bright, your path so specifically laid out in front of you that the possibility of success *not* landing in your lap was almost laughable. But here's the thing: Sometimes reality doesn't end up aligning with your expectations. I mean, even if you *do* score your dream job, if you find an amazing apartment, and if you and your college boyfriend seem destined for a fairy-tale ending, *even if* all of that pans out, reality can really bite. How is that possible? Read on.

Note to Self

Facing Your Fears

Tools

Think about what you are afraid of about postcollege life. Really think about it. Write down your fears.

_____

_____

Think of people whom you admire or whose careers you admire. Why? And what intimidates you about them?

_____

_____

Starter Sentence

Through reading this book, I am going to lessen my fears of (what are your fears?)

_____

_____

so I can emulate the life/career of (name of person or career that you admire)

_____

_____

in these ways (list the steps you will take to make that happen, e.g., get a mentor, research, find an internship, increase confidence, fake it, etc.)

_____

_____

Now that we know the high-level goals, bottoms up—let's start with the reality. Not to be a Debbie Downer, because that's truly not the intention here but . . .

That dream job of yours could very well end up being a huge time and energy vampire, sucking the hours out of each day. And any ounce of reserve energy you want to, well, reserve so that you are physically capable to make it through the week and maintain a social life come Saturday? That could be nonexistent at your "dream job."

Social life? Not so much.

Your apartment—yes it might be exactly what you pictured and more, but all of the unexpected expenses and bills are adding up. . . .

That boyfriend of yours—is he needy and suddenly seriously immature, now that your priorities and lifestyles no longer puzzle-piece together? Is he

out partying at keggers while you are attempting to save enough money to buy a decent suit?

With a new job and a new life you have new priorities and interests that take up any extracurricular space in your life. But your life can still be fabulous . . . I promise. Just keep reading, and we'll get through it together.

How to Get a Grip When You Can Barely Get By

So how do you achieve this so-called fabulous life despite the fact that you are struggling to just get by? By following a few trade tricks, the kind not learned in school. Nope, these are tricks passed down from insiders and older sisters who, through time and practice, learned the loopholes and don't feel the need to hoard the hard-earned insight. Hazing is for sororities; this is the real world. It's time to get down to business!

Initial postgrad life can be head-spinningly stressful and out-of-breath overwhelming, as you feel like you're speeding around in this odd Tasmanian-devil fashion in, ironically, an attempt to just get a grip. . . .

Well, take a deep breath.

Come on, big-belly inhale through your nose. Expand your stomach. Let some oxygen return to your brain. Now let it all out with an open-mouth exhale and a guttural sigh of relief.

I'll help you get through this rough patch . . . without eliciting an anxiety attack. Suddenly you'll realize that you're living the high life, albeit from a tiny apartment and on a shoestring budget.

Edit Your Expectations . . . for Now

The average chick graduates from college and pretty much expects everything to just fall into place. Up until then, life has been mapped, thanks to an annual schedule of an educational grade-based hierarchy, organized by elementary, middle school, high school, and finally, college. Some chicks continue to grad or trade school, extending their education in an attempt to land a higher paying job (hopefully), follow their "destiny" to be a doctor/lawyer/chef/environmentalist . . . while others simply don't feel ready to take that leap from the nest to test their wings in the real world quite yet. If you were lucky enough to have parents support you through school—aside from maybe a lame job at the corner café, providing a little spare change to keep you just above broke (though you tended to spend most of it on café mochas from the café anyway)—the postgraduation cutoff can be a very scary thing. Snip! That's when reality sets in and it's time to figure it out. Find a job. Get an apartment. You're on your own, sweetheart! But that's the exciting thing! It is!

What It Really Takes to Make It on Your Own!

Your whole life you've dreamed about being independent and self-sufficient. For years you've done your best to prove that you can provide for yourself, that you "don't need" your parents, and that you can make it on your own. And you can. I promise you. How? The perfect integration of the three Gs—gumption + grace + guidance—all of which will get you exactly where you want to go (even if you're not exactly sure where that is yet): Fulfilling your dreams in your ideal career surrounded by emotionally and intellectually stimulating, comforting, and inspiring people who authentically care about you. All in all, an honestly pretty fab life.

Wait, hold on, I need to make sure you got that sentence about exactly what it takes, so I'm going to say it again for the sake of it sinking in: All you need is a little gumption, grace, and guidance. What's the point of the repeat? Sometimes hearing something twice is the best way to have it sink in, as opposed to just skimming over it. So let me break it down for you:

Gumption

> *Defined:* Courage, spunk, guts, resourceful

> *Why:* You're not afraid to stick your neck out, take risks, and make your mark. You have the self-assured knowledge that you can and

You're *Not* Carrie Bradshaw

Charlotte, 23, Magazine Writer: "Leave all of your fantasies behind. Don't be an idealist about your job. Work is called work for a reason. Suck it up, pay your dues, and when you have the clout to do something better, you will. Everyone thinks they can be Carrie Bradshaw—but she's a *character.*"

When Is It Time to Finally Detach from Your Parents' Clutches?

Felicia, 23, Television and Commercial Art Department Coordinator: "When I felt like it was stunting my independence. When you are able to afford it, moving out can make you feel more confident and shock you into getting your life organized and focusing on your career. Other motivating factors: the thought of being able to decorate to my taste and have my friends over for dinner, night-out prep, or TV watching . . . without being in my parents' way."

will succeed . . . which can come across as arrogant, so it needs to be tempered with:

Grace

Defined: Seemingly effortless charm, refinement, elegance

Why: In order to successfully carry that headstrong, self-propelled attitude without seeming like a bull-headed egomaniac, you've got to do it with grace, being careful not to be totally offensive and therefore isolating yourself. Be kind, yet strong. Self-assured, yet just slightly self-deprecating (in order not to be hated for being "too perfect"). Driven, yet accommodating. It's a definite high wire to walk, but you'll get the hang of it. Which is why you also need:

Guidance

Defined: Leadership, instruction, direction, insight

Why: You may think you "know it all." I remember when I "knew it all." But just because you are well-read and know a whole lot about learned-in-school lessons doesn't mean you know the ins and outs of life quite yet. Of course, the most effective way to learn a lesson is "the hard way," but guidance from a mentor/sister/wiser one is the less-excruciating way to learn.

Since you weren't taught this stuff in school, I'm going to lay out the details on the basic get-your-life-in-gear essentials, while filling you in on how to be fabulous on your, yes, pitiful pay.

6

What to Expect (Not from Life, Just from This Book)

Here's the basic breakdown so you understand the ins and outs of the book. Each chapter will have:

QUICKIECHICK QUIZ

Quick! Answer each question with the first thing that comes to mind. That's often the best way to get a gut response, sometimes a response so real and honest that even your critical, self-correcting, opinion-editing, "appropriate" side might be surprised by it. Why? Because you don't allow yourself the opportunity to think through the question long enough to place a strategic slant on your answer. Plus, let's face it, quizzes that just might shed a glimmer of enlightenment about ourselves are fun. And not to worry: The questions posed will be addressed within the chapter so that you can better understand your answers and maybe shed light on a few alternate approaches that might better suit the new empowered you!

NOTE TO SELF

Take notes! You know that pulling out the highlighter and jotting "notes to self" along the sides of your books helps you remember useful insight. That's what this section is for. Plus it's a way for you to add your two cents. Sometimes blips of brilliance come at the most random times. If something in these chapters speaks to you or sparks a blip, write it down before you forget it!

EXPERT INSIGHT

One essential component to success in the real world is knowing what you know and knowing what you don't. That's why I contacted some of the best experts in their respective fields to fill in the holes of my knowledge, giving you more in-depth insight that I simply can't. Fact is, I know a little about a lot of things. Some things I know more about, others less. While it's important to put yourself out there as an informed and experienced authority, you can't know all there is to know about everything. You just can't. Oh, and the experts—all of them are successful chicks who, at one time, were just like you, trying to carve out their own self-defined paths to success, happiness, respect, and fabulousness. Not that it was always this flower-lined, yellow brick road. Many of the life-envying chicks arrived at success through lots of trial and error, even mid-course corrections—in other words, they were on a specific path, positive that they were headed in their dream-destined direction, only to realize halfway there that this was not the path for them. Instead of an "oh darn, I guess I'll just deal" attitude, they began to carve a fork in their road, facing an altered, new, or totally seemingly backward direction. A mid-course correction takes guts, as it can look and feel like you're

7

backtracking. But you're not. You're simply constantly reevaluating, going over effectiveness, taking real-time feedback, and altering the strategy based on conditions and influences. After all, it's better to change mid-course and put yourself on a better path than to stubbornly force your way down maybe not the best path just because that's the one you're on right now.

BEEN THERE, DONE THAT

You're not alone. Even if you feel like you're the only one in the world going through whatever crisis/frustration/breakdown/thrill . . . you're still not alone. And that's actually a good thing, because that means that there are other chicks out there who have lived through it already. This is where you can read insight from other chicks who have learned the lessons the hard way—by experience. Why not learn from them?

QUICKIECHICK'S CHEAT SHEET

Kind of like CliffsNotes, each QuickieChick's Cheat Sheet lists the most important components of the chapter, creating a bullet list out of the need-to-know snippets that will make it seem as though you read the chapter in its entirety, even if you didn't.

Mommy and Daddy's Little Girl

Tools

Look at photos from your childhood, at toys, or visit old playgrounds, etc.

Starter Sentence

I am going to *seriously* miss this aspect of living at home because

_____

_____.

(It's OK. Admit it! You'll probably find ways to remedy that feeling of loss in this book.)

Reality Will Check You, but It Doesn't Have to Suck

So what's the point of this novel-length diatribe on how to live your life? To help you not just survive those difficult postgrad years (like your entire twenties and, for some, your thirties, too), but live them fabulously. Because the fact is that despite the pomp, circumstance, hoopla, and fairy tales, when

Life Can Take Longer to Figure Out

Lindsay, 28, Works for a Nonprofit: "I thought I would know who I was going to be and have life figured out by twenty-eight. I'm not sure why that is the magic number, but it has stuck with me."

What was the reality? "The reality was that twenty-eight came and went, and I was not any closer to figuring 'it' out. The only thing I know for sure is that the version of myself that I had in my head at twenty-two is not the person I want to become now. It's no longer about becoming someone, but about figuring out how to be happy now."

reality checks you (and it will), you'll want to be ready for it. Sure, you may be digging your red-soled heels into the dirt and hanging on to your sanity with a string, but you will still be fabulous, yes, even on a budget.

The great thing is that reality doesn't necessarily have to "suck." It just may be different from what you were taught (in school), told (by your parents), and expected (that's your own fault). Now it's time to reposition your perspective and view your future in a more realistic way. Onward and, yes—upward!

9

Postcollege Expectations vs. Reality

Tools

What were your built-up expectations of life in general when you graduated college?

_____

_____

What was the reality?

_____

_____

2

Rent, Bills, Insurance, Roommates & Other Things That Stress You Out

FACT: Once the graduation afterglow has worn off and the reality of the real world sets in, it's not uncommon to be overtaken by a sudden fear, a homesickness (even if your parents are mere miles away). You may feel alone and ill-prepared for the unknown that's ahead. Sure, you may be unprepared, but you are definitely *not* alone. Forget about the full picture for a second and instead hone in on the little steps to make the transition less daunting and more doable.

QuickieChick Quiz

1. The first thing you unpack in your new place is . . .

A. All things kitchen

B. Clothes and shoes and makeup!

C. Favorite magazines, books, CDs, DVDs

Answer A means . . . You're setting up a home! You are tending to the most central and social part of your apartment. You're ready to make dinners for friends and feel at home in your new space.

Answer B means . . . This is just where you crash. You've unpacked everything you need to *leave* your new place. Try unpacking things that go in the house, not just on your body, to make it more welcoming.

Answer C means . . . Don't feel like going out much, huh? While moving into a new place can be scary, you have to break that barrier someday. The longer you wait, the scarier it will be when you realize you haven't gotten out to see your new town, meet neighbors, and make friends!

2. **You want you and your roommate to . . .**

   A. Debrief one another at the end of each day while sharing a bowl of popcorn
   B. Be courteous when you see one another, but home is your quiet place where you can be alone
   C. Invite one another out occasionally, but you would be seriously *weirded out* if your roommate was suddenly texting *your* best friend

   Answer A means . . . Move in with a friend you are already close with or do some serious interview/hangout time with potential roommates before sealing the deal. Make sure they also want a roommate they can be buddies with.

   Answer B means . . . Maybe live alone; certainly don't live with your best friend, as she'll think it is weird that you guys used to meet up for drinks and movies and now you don't even speak in the kitchen you share.

   Answer C means . . . Be sure to lay down boundaries. You don't have to invite your roommate to *every* event you go to, but do it occasionally, and hopefully she'll return the favor! Especially if you're living in a new town, it would be nice to network.

3. **You get your first paycheck. It is *triple* what your monthly allowance was in college. You . . .**

   A. Spend! You worked *hard* for this money, and you have plenty of it now! You no longer have to watch every penny like your parents made you do.
   B. Save, save, save. The apocalypse (OK, maybe a tad dramatic) might be coming. But seriously, you *never* know when you could be down-and-out or when some huge, unexpected expense might pop up! You're opting out of weekly nights out with your girlfriends this month; they add up.

   The correct answer is . . . neither!

   It's true, your paycheck is a big beautiful number, but think of what expenses you did *not* have to pay for with your college allowance. Maybe groceries, car insurance, a phone plan?

   But still, you have worked hard, and if you opt out of ALL of the fun this month, your spirits are going to be *way* down and your quality of work in the office might go down, too! Always be looking out for yourself, otherwise you won't be able to do the work that needs to get done.

Moving Out of Your Parents' House . . . for Good This Time

My postgrad mentality was laser-focused on my career. Everything else I had strategically checked off my list:

- Solid relationship with a great guy—check

- My own (well, with my guy) place—check

- Fast-tracked career—check

And then the guy and I broke up, and I definitely couldn't afford to live alone. So, yes, I did, for the interim, move back home with my parents with my tail between my legs, feeling like a bird that jumped from the nest, figured out how to fly . . . right into a tree branch, forcing me to move back home until I found a roommate I could cohabitate with. When I moved out of my parent's house (this time for good), I made sure to set myself up in a way that would minimize my chances of ever having to move home again. How can you make the move from your parents' house for the last time?

5 STEPS TO MOVING OUT OF YOUR PARENTS' HOME & INTO YOUR OWN

1. Hone in on the neighborhood that you would want to live in for a while.

2. Find an apartment that suits both your lifestyle and budget.

3. Start a savings account and start putting some money aside . . . just in case.

4. Ask co-workers and friends if they know of anyone looking for a roommate.

5. Write up a contract between you and your new roomie agreeing on how rent, bills, and other expenses will be paid, and, in case it doesn't work out between you two, a plan that addresses who moves out and notice time before moving out (so that you can find another roomie to split the rent with). I know it sucks to have to do it. But, like my dad says, "contracts are for worst-case scenarios," because it's easier to discuss them now (even if there is a little arguing or some bruised feelings) than later when you can hardly look at each other let alone speak to one another—a fate, I know, you can't imagine at this moment . . . but, *believe me*, it can happen. I am still thanking my dad for a contract he forced me to write and sign despite my "till death" surety . . . one that ended up, sadly and heartbreakingly, having to be enforced. It's not just marriages that end (hence, pre-

nups), friendships and BFFs break up, too. Sucks but true. Better to be prepared and have that awkward conversation now than, in the off and unfortunate chance, get screwed over later.

HOW TO MAKE A HOUSE, APARTMENT, OR ROOM YOUR HOME

You may just be renting, but you want to feel at home . . . or else you are up-ping your chances of moving back "home." Once you're out of your parents' house, you've got to make the decision to make your new place your own. How?

Smudge. Smudging is an old Native American tradition of taking a wad of dried sage, lighting the tip, then walking around the entire space—every corner and cabinet—allowing the smoke to "clean" out the "evil spirits" and negative energy. Not a believer? Not everyone is. But believing in ridding the evil spirits isn't the important part. What I like about the idea of smudging is that you are walking around your new digs, in silence, burning herbally pungent–smelling sage, and thinking good thoughts. You're setting intentions for the different spaces. So in the living room you might be thinking, *This is a place where friends will laugh, where I will have deep conversations and fun times.* Walk into the kitchen and think, *This is a place where I will make and eat tasty and healthy foods to fill my body and feed my soul.* Walk into the bedroom and think . . . well, whatever your intention is for the bedroom.

A Space of Your Own. Even if you're sharing the space with a roommate, or five, make sure that you make at least some areas of the place your own. But here's the key—don't make it all new or all old. Combine a couple of things from your parents house that make you feel "at home," with a couple of things that help define who you are today and who you want to become.

Throw a cocktail party. *No,* not a house party. This is not about trashing your new place or destroying the carpets or hardwood floors. It's about celebrating your new digs with your close-ish friends, with wine, decent beer (not a keg), cocktails, and snacks (to temper the drunkenness), maybe even serve a dinner! Do up the whole thing—send out an Evite, create a Facebook event, light the candles, dress decently, and elevate the average house party to a more dignified level that celebrates your new life as an . . . adult. After all, if you throw the party and make the statement of being out on your own, it's kind of hard to change your mind, turn around, and move back to your parents' house, your pride following a few feet behind, just because you couldn't hack it. Of course, if it's not an issue of not being able to hack it, and instead an issue of

13

losing your job, having seriously insane roommates, or going through a breakup (with your live-in significant other)—that's a totally different story. Then it's OK to bunk up with the parents until you are able to get back on your feet again. I did it.

Building Your Own Nest

Tools

Walk through the rooms of your parents' house. Which rooms make you feel relaxed/inspired/comforted?

_____

_____

Starter Sentence

A style of room that makes me feel relaxed is (bohemian, shabby chic, contemporary, sparse, art deco, etc.):

_____

_____ ,

and I can create that look with some of these items/colors:

_____

_____ .

How to Avoid Paying a Fortune on Rent

It's so easy to go out apartment hunting with a set-in-stone budget in mind but then see an even better one that's just $250 more, so you raise the budget to accommodate—after all, $250 is only a few nights out with your girlfriends, and you can get a guy to foot the bill for dinner any day. And then you stumble on "the perfect" place in your ideal neighborhood that's within walking distance of work and, and, and . . . *And* it's $175 more than your now-adjusted budget. I know, it's so easy to rationalize another measly $175, but *it's not*. It's in fact $425 more. That's substantial. So before you even allow yourself to get carried away and sign a one-year lease on an apartment that strains you to the point of struggling, *stop*. Get a piece of paper and write down your expenses. I mean realistically, no bullshit: How much money do I spend a month? *Not* how much money do I need to get by. Because "getting by" isn't the point. The point is living fabulously . . . within your realistic budget.

In an economy where salaries have fallen flat yet the monthly fee for a decent apartment has skyrocketed, it's easy to get carried away when it comes to the apartment part of your budget. Realistically, plan on budgeting about 25 percent of your pretax income for rent. Then expect to pay another 5 percent-ish for utilities, like water, gas, and electric.

NEGOTIATION IS KEY

Before you sign a rent or lease agreement with a landlord, negotiate the best deal you possibly can. Why? Because if you end up staying there for a year or more, that monthly $50, $100, or $150 adds up! Don't worry, it's all part of the game. Landlords expect to be haggled with. The longer the place has been on the market, the better your bargaining power. Remember: Each month the place is empty, money is being lost. Here are a few ways to get a better deal:

- **1 Month Free:** Ask for your first month free. (That's the best deal since, broken up across the year, you get a discount each month, which is pretty sweet.)

- **$100 Off:** Ask for a $100 monthly reduction due to "the economy."

- **Add a Room:** With your landlord's permission, you can add a removable wall through the center of a bigger room, allowing you to get another roommate who can pay part of the rent.

- **Sublet:** Oftentimes people have to ditch their digs because of financial issues or last-minute changes, but they can't get out of their ironclad lease. You can often "help them out" by taking over their lease at, occasionally, a discount.

If none of those strategies work and you simply can't afford the upgrade, find another less-expensive spot (one that fits your initial budget) that has been on the market for a while. Use your negotiating power to ask them to fancy the place up for you—refinishing the hardwood floors, replacing the nasty carpet, updating the appliances. Those steps may be something they had intended to do anyway, they just hoped they could rent it out one last time before having to. Suddenly, you have the upgraded apartment that you wanted, without paying the "up" charge.

Snip! Cutting Financial Ties with Parents

Every parent has a different way of going about it. In fact, some parents have a different way of going about it for each of their children. Example (Disclaimer: This is just an example! Certainly not every three-kid family is like this):

- **Child #1.** The first child might be cut off the second she's accepted into college in an attempt to instill a hardworking mentality that harks back to when the parents were in college and had to "work two jobs, trek five miles by foot in the snow to class, and still maintained a GPA of 4.0. . . . " She struggles but gets by with zero social life and a constant pile of stress on her shoulders. Still, in college, she lines up a postgrad mentor and a high-paying job. As if she were a windup toy, her college years were like fingers holding her in the air, her feet spinning just above the ground so she could be ready to run full steam ahead the moment she was allowed to touch down, diving wholly into her career, taking on full responsibility for her bills, and getting by just fine on her own . . . despite the ample amounts of stress and few opportunities for outlet. She even gets married. And then divorced. She was bred to believe that her career and making money were her priority (which was why she got the whole marriage thing—and apparently the divorce, too—out of the way).

- **Child #2.** Upon seeing that maybe that wasn't the most effective methodology, the second child is fully supported through her college years, but upon graduating, her room is turned into an office, at which point she is cut off—almost completely—except for her apartment, oh, and that "gas" credit card. She's not so keen on throwing herself into any strict routine quite yet (and doesn't have pressure from the parentals to do so based on child #1's postgrad choices) and instead decides to take a postcollege trek around the world for a few months. She learns about herself (but doesn't yet "find" herself), explores the world—its food, fashion, religions, people, attitudes, and men. About a year later she is finally able to focus and lands a low-paying but stable job as she continues to try to find her passion in life, the passion that will dictate her career.

16

Getting a Smaller Room in a Shared House/Apartment? Pay a Smaller Rent!

Molly, 22, Program Coordinator for an Animal-Rights-Awareness Nonprofit

"If you're looking at a place and see a grand disparity in room quality, it may be a good idea to ask up front what everyone else is paying. I don't know if this would make you a less-attractive tenant, but at least you won't have to deal with the issue later (after paying an unfair price for a long time). Maybe a less-direct way of getting at the issue is asking what the rent of the entire house/apartment is, so you can kind of calculate your portion of the rent and see if it seems fair."

Your First Paycheck—Where (and Where Not) to Spend It

Tiffany, 26, Clerk at a Law Firm: "Saving is more important than spending. The first big paycheck you get, you want to reward yourself with a shopping trip. This doesn't help! Only saving money does. Before you know it, your entire paycheck goes to bills and food, and you're not saving nearly as much as you thought you would."

- **Child #3.** After having learned a few lessons with #1 and then #2, the parents decide that the third child should have a part-time job to pay for frivolous things during the semester (as opposed to having access to that "gas" card), a full-time job each summer, then, upon graduating, she has to pay her rent and all bills . . . except for the health and car insurance (which are still tied to her parents'), oh, and the cell phone bill (which is still hooked into the "family plan"), and her room stays exactly as she left it . . . just in case she wants to spend a couple of nights at "home." Can you say "threading the last one along in order to not completely feel like empty nesters"? Anyway, the third graduates with honors, moves home for a few months as she tries to get her finances in order, and applies for jobs. She finds a great one! A job that impassions her and stimulates both her creative and financial juices. After a few months as a postgrad career girl, having saved a decent amount of money, she moves out, gets her own place with a roommate, balances social life and work, keeps her finances in check, and, yes, sleeps at "home" at least two nights a week, where she eats to her stomach's content and does her laundry without having to pay the $2.50 in her apartment's overused, underserviced washer and dryer.

Regardless of your parent's snip-it style, it's your responsibility to make sure that you have a plan that will carry you from college to adulthood, an all-inclusive concept comprised of:

- **Your home.** Yes "your" home. This is no longer your parents' home.

- **A job.** One that might even have career potential. One job requirement, however, is its ability to pay ALL of your bills and expenses.

- **A social life.** You don't want to just throw yourself into your work. Balance is key to happiness. I said balance—different from partying and socializing to the point that your job suffers. *Balance.*

17

All of that said, it's not always easy to just go out and find a high-enough paying job that covers your apartment, bills, and life. If you need a little help, it's OK to lean on your parents. After all, when you first learn how to ride a bike, you're going to fall a couple of times. You might even skin your knee and bruise your ego. But eventually you will get it, and the next thing you know, you're taking a hundred-mile ride, speeding down the bike path with the wind on your back and a smile on your face. OK . . . so that might be an extreme example, but you get the picture.

The Comforts of a Credit Card Without the Headache

Another postgrad crutch? Credit cards. *But* that doesn't mean you can rack up thousands of dollars that you can't pay off. Credit card bills come with responsibility—like paying them. If you can't pay your bill in full at the end of the month, be prepared to really pay. Yes, you will have to pay an interest fee, one that can rack up fast if you keep paying only your minimum payment. But the possibility of interest fees shouldn't scare you away from getting a credit card. You want to start building up your credit. "Good credit" is what you will need if you want to buy or lease a car, get a cell phone, buy a house, even get cable hooked up in your apartment. Why? Because companies need to know that you are responsible with money, that you will pay your bills on time, and that you are worth the risk and investment.

Now, to clarify, a credit card is different from an ATM card that you get from your bank, which lets you immediately access your cash, or denies you cash to cover an expense. An ATM card is best used to withdraw cash from your bank account. But if you want to buy things with your credit card, then you should pay off the balance at the end of the month. Why should you at least try to pay off your credit cards at the end of each month when you receive your bill? Because it's not play money, and the more months that you put off paying, the more money will be racked up, and if you don't pay it, it will result in the exact opposite goal of getting a credit card: It will hurt your credit, eventually giving you "bad credit." Not good.

Why You Need Insurance More Than Ever

I know, living with a worst-case scenario mind-set sucks. BUT in some very few cases, you have to. Like what?

- Contracts (which we already discussed on page 12)

- Insurance—both car (because you simply have to have it) and health (because you'd be stupid not to have it)—are two of those possible-worst-case instances you should be prepared for. Yes, they cost a lot of money. And if your parents aren't footing the bill, you might be

inclined to cut out that expense. But *believe me*—that's a bad, bad idea! If you don't protect yourself (by paying up each month), you could end up screwing yourself.

Here is a crazy, random, personal experience of mine, when I needed (and was thrilled to have) health insurance:

YEAST INFECTION TURNS INTO A KIDNEY INFECTION

I was twenty-three years old and working insane hours. I had a slight yeast infection. In fact I was getting them often. My gyno said it was caused by stress. I didn't have time to go in and see him to confirm it this one time, so I wasn't able to get the one-day prescription pill that always eliminated the problem. Instead, I went to the store and bought some over-the-counter cream that was supposed to work in seven agonizing days. Ten days later, I still had it. But I still didn't have time to see the doctor. One morning I had these bizarre pains in what felt like my ovary or stomach. I mean shooting pains. But of course I went to work anyway. A few hours into my day the pain was insane. The next thing I knew, I was doubled over in my chair and in tears. Someone came into my office to ask about a meeting that was about to start and saw me. She could see that this was not normal. I tend to be a machine, work through the pain, refuse to admit weakness. Impossible. I did not, under any circumstances, want to take an ambulance, but I knew I needed to go to the hospital. She drove me. My gyno met us there. I had a kidney infection. It was pretty bad. Apparently untreated yeast infections can turn into kidney infections. The bill was seven thousand dollars! Thankfully, my insurance footed the majority of it.

Lesson learned: If I think I have a yeast infection—I go to the gyno.

Sure, you can attempt to rationalize it, justifying your reason for *not* getting insured: You will be spending money every single month that at the end of the year adds up to *a lot,* and if you ever *do* get into that accident, break a leg, or have a kidney infection, the money you would have spent each month for insurance will about equal the money you have to pay up right now to fix the problem. Not necessarily so. Why? Paramedics, anesthesia, ultrasound, X-rays, injections, IV—they all cost a lot of money. I mean a lot! And the reality is that you likely won't be putting a lump chunk of "just in case I have a medical emergency" money aside, while your monthly health insurance will become a built-in, expected, recurring payment, like your rent. If something does happen to you, the last thing you will want is to realize *I can't afford the treatment I need,* because all you will be thinking is *I will do absolutely anything to rid my body of this pain!* Get insurance.

Because It Doesn't Matter Who Started It: Avoid Roommate Hell

You've likely lived with a roommate in college, so you understand the basics of rooming together. But back then life wasn't taken quite as seriously. Nor was your definition of personal space, clutter, and lifestyle. Back then it was OK to wake up and find some random person passed out on your sofa or floor. It's a friend or "friend" of your roommate. It's college. It happens. . . .

Postcollege you take more pride in your place. Suddenly it's *your* bank account that's on the line if anything in the apartment gets damaged or stolen. You don't have the time (or mental space) to get to know or make pancakes for the random "friend" passed out on the couch. You need your space; you need your routine. Not to say you become more of a tight-ass after college. It's more that the demands of life become more tight-ass. Plus, after a loooong and haaaarrrrd day at work, the last thing you want to come home to is a mess, random drunks on your sofa, and *your* towel in a wet ball in the corner of the bathroom floor despite the fact that you know you hung a fresh, clean one on the towel rack that morning. You're not amused. And you learned enough about staph infections, the flu, crabs, herpes, etc. (either from personal or through-the-grapevine experience) to know that germs are just *waiting* to manifest themselves in some horrible way when you have multiple people cohabitating. Now might be the time to think about what type of roommate you want to live with in your new life.

HOW CLOSE DO YOU WANT TO BE WITH YOUR ROOMIE?

So how do you avoid roommate hell? First, make sure you have a roommate with whom you are compatible but not necessarily BFFs.

If you can find that perfect balance between a friend and just a housemate— fantastic! But since that perfect balance is *very* hard to find, on page 22 are the pros and cons of having a roommate be a friend or just a roommate:

Note to Self

Learn from Your Mistakes

Tools

Think about the worst/most stressful/annoying situations you encountered with your college roommates. Write them down.

_____

_____

What could you have done differently to make everyone happier (or at least make yourself happier)?

_____

_____

Do you always have to be "right," or sometimes is it OK to agree in order to have peace at home?

_____

_____

What compromises are you willing to make?

_____

_____

What issues are you not willing to bend on?

_____

_____

Starter Sentence

In college, it drove me _nuts_ when my roommate would

_____

_____ ,

but if I would have simply said/made the compromise of

_____

_____ ,

I could have been happier in my living situation.
(Have this phrase prepared in case your next roomy does the same thing!)

Just a Roommate?

Pros

- Sometimes you come home and you Just. Dont. Want. To. Talk . . . to anyone. If you and your roommate *aren't* friends, you won't be expected to have a lengthy chat session, and she won't be offended in the slightest if you wave *Hi* and head straight to your room.

- A roommate won't feel as comfortable hitting you up for money if she is short on rent.

- Your apartment is not a social place, so you don't have to worry about coming home to find random people gathering in your living room when you're getting home from the gym with sweaty clothes and no makeup on.

- It's easier to make your opinion known to your roommate because you don't have to tap-dance around emotions—it's more like a business relationship/partnership. You are partners in this apartment.

- They are less likely to eat your food/borrow your clothes or car.

Cons

- Sometimes you come home extremely stressed/depressed/excited/ angry, your best friend isn't answering her phone, and you just don't feel comfortable venting/sharing with your roommate.

- You can't hit up your roommate for money if you are short on rent.

- Going on a trip one weekend and missing your cleaning turn? You can text your roommate to give her a heads-up about the sink full of dishes, but don't expect her to make any efforts to hide her scornful face or cold shoulder when you get home. You're not friends. She's

Should You Be Friends or Just Friend/y with Roomies?

Anne, 25, Teacher: "We're friends, but not close friends. I prefer to have someone I'm comfortable living with but not my best friend whom I spend all my time with. We both have our own groups of friends and occasionally hang out outside the house, but that's rare. I think it's best to keep some distance so that we don't get sick of or annoyed with each other."

not excited for you because you got to go on some fun trip (that results in a dirty kitchen for her); you just owe her a cleaning turn.

- You'll feel uncomfortable having friends over, constantly worrying about making noise and cleaning up every ten minutes.

- You can't eat her food/borrow her clothes or car.

Roommate & Friend?

Pros

- It's like coming home to Mom again: You know she'll listen to you vent about every grueling detail of your day. She knows she has to, because if she doesn't, you won't do the same for her next time. . . . Oh, and she wants to listen—she's your friend.

- You can easily negotiate/make compromises when it comes to house duties. Example: You're going out of town last minute . . . on the day of your cleaning duties. Your roommate/friend agrees to take over the cleaning so long as you clean the week after you get back. She is more excited for you and this trip you're going on than she is annoyed about a little extra cleaning.

- Two closets! You trust each other and know each other, and let's face it, wherever you are wearing your roommate's clothes, she is probably coming with you so she can keep an eye on her favorite little black dress/satin blouse or whatever.

- You can share food! You'll probably even end up cooking a lot together, so keeping track of who owes who what will be just too complicated. Also, it's not healthy to eat alone, emotionally or physically. You may overeat out of loneliness or just because you eat too fast when there is no one to talk to. If you and your roomy/friend share schedules, you can be a healthier, happier eater.

Cons

- Your roommate/friend will probably get offended if you don't invite her to a party/movie or to have drink one night while you go out with other friends. (And YOU might get offended if she does the same to you.)

- Your home will inevitably be a social place. I mean, hey, the two people living there are friends, so it's already a place to socialize. Your roommate/friend will feel comfortable enough to have friends over maybe more than you are comfortable with.

- Privacy lines are seriously blurred. Your roommate may have no problem fighting with her boyfriend in the middle of the living room rather than taking it outside. You will have to take on the drama/stresses/concerns (and, of course, celebrations) of another person's life.

- You might come home, rushing to get ready for a date, only to realize the dress you wanted to wear is currently out on another date—your roommate's.

These are all things to consider in establishing what exactly your relationship is with a roommate. If you've got enough close friends already, always ready to listen to you and support you at the end of the day, you can afford to keep the distance from the roomy. If you do decide to buddy up, make sure there is enough respect between both of you so that your roommate doesn't feel entitled to slacking on her responsibilities as just that—a roommate.

Furnishing Your New Digs
Without Going Broke

Felicia, 23, Television and Commercial Art Department Coordinator: "I got a leg up because I asked family to give me furniture for my college graduation and birthday. Then I splurged on one piece that I loved—a really cool cabinet made out of old post-office boxes."

Funky, Formal, or Just Plain Filthy: What Does Your Home Say About You?

More than a place to crash, your environment tells your story. It's an expression of your inner self. Look around your home, your office (or cubicle), your spaces; imagine that what you are seeing is a painting illuminating a certain aspect of your life, of who you are. What story does the painting tell you? Is it colorful? Patterned? Messy? Organized? Is it disciplined or chaotic? How does your space make you feel? How does it come across to others? That is your visual biography.

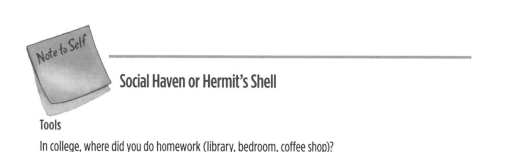

Social Haven or Hermit's Shell

25

Tools

In college, where did you do homework (library, bedroom, coffee shop)?

_____

_____

Where did you have most of your meals?

_____

_____

How did you get exercise, and where did you do it?

_____

_____

Starter Sentence

Based on my answers, I want my apartment to be a (e.g., social haven or hermit's shell)

_____

_____ ,

because

_____

_____ .

Note to Self

What Is Your Home Saying About You?

EXAMPLE

What? My apartment always has fresh-cut herbs from the grocery store in a vase on the kitchen counter.

Saying? I love to cook, infuse the room with the scent of herbs, make a pretty bouquet without spending a pretty penny.

EXAMPLE

What? I have unopened newspapers and stacks of gossip magazines strewn all around the living room.

Saying? I'm a bit of a slob, with intentions of keeping up with world and celeb news, but I haven't had much time lately.

Take Note

What? _____

Saying? _____

What? _____

Saying? _____

What do you *want* your home to say about you?

EXAMPLE

What? I have an adventurous spirit.

How? Mount photos from my travels on foam core and hang them on the wall in my living room. Place several "hip hotels" books in a stack on the coffee table.

EXAMPLE

What? I am introspective.

How? All of my coffee mugs are different, each with a mantra, quote, or thought to ponder, so that each morning when I sit and have my coffee, I can read the saying and think about how it pertains to my life and will help motivate me through my day.

Take Note

What? _____

How? _____

What? _____

How? _____

Because You Can't Always Use Paper Plates

Can't afford a full set of brand-spanking-new dishware? That might actually be for the better. Stock up on an eclection (yes, that's a made-up word meaning "an eclectic collection") of dishes, including maybe a plate from Mom and Dad's (for nostalgia's sake), a few found at local yard sales, vintage pieces, hand-me-downs, maybe even one or two fabulous finds from favorite design stores. The point? Eat on different dishes depending on your mood. When entertaining, for an extra serving of eye candy, serve each guest's dish on a different plate. Okay, so I admit that I am a bit of a plate purist—it comes with the food-snob territory—and I have to say that I believe that food is optimally displayed on plain white plates. But sometimes you have to change it up in order to keep it interesting . . . kind of like sex. So go ahead, live a little! Take a trip to an antique shop and pick up a random collection of retro plates (or whatever style suits your fancy) and let the colors come to life as your guests consume their meal.

Living Paycheck to Paycheck . . . Doesn't Have to Mean Living Miserably & Broke

Unless you get the luck of the draw and score an extremely cushy job making a windfall of cash, don't expect to be raking it in right after college. Which isn't something to stress about! Even if you're working your ass off to heave-ho and drag in a measly paycheck that forces you to live on a strict, no-frills budget, you don't have to live a no-thrills lifestyle. Of course, if you're always looking forward with the "when, then" attitude (when I have more money, then I can have fun), you won't allow yourself to have that fun that you honestly can be having right at this very moment. Here's how to save your money while still having a whole lot of fun:

Save some money. Have a money drawer where you put a few dollars and cents here and a couple more there whenever you have spare change. When it adds up, treat yourself to something sweet (like low-fat ice cream), or even a fab shopping spree to a secondhand store, where you pick out just the coolest used handbag. If you know there are expenditures that you can shave some money from here and there—do it. You need to allow yourself a few occasional splurges on things that simply make you happy so that you don't feel like you're neglecting yourself (kind of like when you're on a strict diet and always craving cookies).

Adjust your attitude. Happiness doesn't come from money. *Believe me.* I've tried to extract happiness from money. It does not work. Happiness

comes from attitude. Just stop the bitching for a second and look around you. What is fabulous in your life right now? What truly makes you smile? What makes you honestly deeply happy? Now remember that during your moments of "I wish I could . . . but I can't because I can't afford it."

Know what's worth splurging on. I look forward to my morning cup of coffee even before I fall asleep at night. I bought myself a slightly more expensive coffeemaker because it makes just the best coffee. Was the extra forty dollars worth it? Absolutely! Why? Because every single morning as I am making my coffee I am so happy. Sometimes it's the little things that make your day. This special cup of coffee makes mine. If there is a pair of shoes that you covet, and you know that every time you put them on you will look and feel damn sexy . . . buy them. Spend the extra little bit and treat yourself this one time. Don't make a habit of it, but sometimes you have to do the little things that will go a long way.

Go kayaking. Even in Manhattan, New York, you can rent and take out a kayak for an afternoon adventure (in New York you kayak along the Hudson—which is actually fabulous).

Take an architectural tour. Churches (even if you aren't religious), famous people's homes, landmarks, even cemeteries are great places to spend the day not only seeing another side to your town but also appreciating architecture and history.

Get in touch with nature! Forget the BlackBerry at home for a few hours and go berry picking, apple picking, wine tasting, or on a garden tour. Most cities and towns have some type of activity opportunities that allow you to be one with nature by enjoying the fruits of your labor. Love fresh fruit, hate the high supermarket prices? If you live near fields, there are likely pick-your-own places where you pay a nominal fee then are set free to pick as many blueberries, strawberries, oranges as you'd like. In any proximity to wine country? Drink for cheap! Tote around a picnic basket of cheese and bread, and enjoy the day (believe me, it feels super luxurious but without the luxury price tag attached).

Find a festival. Street fairs, music in the park, art walks, even farmers' markets are great places to enjoy culture, people-watch, and get out of your box for little to no money. Plus they are super fun!

Eat out! Set a date with your girlfriends to dine at some fab new upscale spot, then order appetizers and have a drink. Take it from someone who has dined out *a lot*—the apps tend to be the best part of most restaurant meals. Not always, but generally. It's those little bites filled with amazing flavor that I most savor. The entrée is more about filling you up. Trick: Eat *some*thing at home before going out—like a chicken breast, a cup of fat-free Greek yogurt, even a couple of eggs. Protein takes longer to digest, so it will keep you fuller longer (which is also why you shouldn't late-night-snack on protein). Then go out and indulge on the tasty appetizer bites. You will leave satisfied and fulfilled!

Happy hour. Search online for the best happy-hour spots near you. Some of the most "it" restaurants and bars become that way because they have a happening happy hour that drives people in early for cheap booze and food (then keeps them there late for expensive booze and food). Just watch the clock!

Camping . . . is not just for hippies or high school. Get a group together and find a cool spot to camp. Designate each couple/person responsible for two or three items (in addition to each person being responsible for his/her own sleeping gear and other basic necessities). Campfire food is some of the best food I've had (which is saying a lot!). Food needs: S'mores ingredients, booze, tinfoil, tofu/steak/chicken/shrimp, onions, peppers, zucchini, BBQ sauce, butter, salt and pepper, potatoes, instant coffee, muffins, fruit. Dinner: Make a thick bowl out of the tinfoil. Fill it with the chopped-up veggies and meat. Put it over the fire. Take the potatoes and wrap them in the foil. Put them in the fire. You've got dinner. Dessert: S'mores. Easy.

Do You Really _Need_ 100 Rolls of Toilet Paper? When to Buy in Bulk

There's definitely an art to buying in bulk, whether it's your parents taking you out on a random home-stocking spree, or you planned a trek to your closest discount bulk-buying megastore. Here's something to keep in mind: Sometimes more is better, and sometimes more is worse, and sometimes more is just a space-taker and an eyesore that infringes on your daily life. Let me explain. . . .

More is better when . . . you purchase items that make sense in bulk. So, for example, if you live in a house with ten roommates, almost everything in a quantity of "more" is better. When it comes to small items with long lives (like canned soup), and you happen to enjoy and eat a decent amount of canned soup, more is better, especially if you have a roomie who wants to split everything with you—including taking five of the ten bulk tooth-brushes!

More is worse when . . . it comes to bulk items that quickly go bad, like certain fruits, fresh meats, and eggs. Those five-pound candy jars of your favorite, totally irresistible treats . . . and you're trying to lose weight (or at least maintain weight), but, as I said, they are irresistible and so you give in—well, after a night of gorging then getting mad at yourself for overindulging and carrying the candy to the outdoor garbage bin, saying good-bye to that ass-enlarging indulgence forever . . . more is worse.

More is a space-taking eyesore when . . . you live in a teeny apartment that seriously lacks storage space, yet you stuff your car with that seriously discounted box of hundred rolls of paper towels. You lug the thing up the stairs and down the hall to your front door, push the sucker inside, then end up having to store paper towels in every unused space—like under the sofa, along the wall in the bathroom, and in the corner behind the kitchen table. Eyesore.

If you want to save hundreds of dollars a year, there are tricks to shopping at discount stores. Here's how:

Make a List, Then Stick to It!

One of the issues with shopping at bulk-item stores is that they are *huge*, and it is easy to get carried away thinking you "need" an insane amount of stuff just because it's so inexpensive. But remember, impulse buys at bulk stores are not the same as impulse buys at your average grocery store. We're talking about two hundred packs of gum vs. one pack of gum. Really, do you need two hundred packs *just* because it's your favorite flavor? Chances are once you get past pack fifty, the rest will be stale and hard, dissolving into a chalky mess in your mouth. I've done it. I know. Remember, it's only a deal if you use it.

Compare "Unit" Pricing

Since it's being presented to you as a "discount," it's easy to just assume that it is. Not necessarily so. To ensure that you're not paying more on every single one of the five bottles of soy sauce than you would have spent on the one at your local grocery store, check the unit price—that's the price that each of the soy sauces would go for if they were sold individually instead of in a five-pack. I'm not saying that you should go to the bulk store, write down prices, then phone a friend awaiting your call at the grocery store and send him or her on a wild-goose chase for that one specific size and type of soy sauce. But since you do have a list in hand, know about how much each item on that list costs at your local grocery store before braving the bulk store.

Don't Shop Hungry

One of the absolute worst things you can do when it comes to grocery shopping—at any grocery store but even worse (because you're buying in bulk) at a bulk store—is shopping when you're hungry. Why? Because everything looks good to you. Even the pool table–size sheet cake that reads "Happy 75th Anniversary!" The other issue with shopping at bulk stores when hungry? Samples. So, maybe it's not bad if you are looking at it from the angle of "now I don't have to spend money on lunch," but from a skinny-jeans point of view, those samples that they give out in mass tend not to be the healthiest. In fact, the sweet "do you want to try one?" ladies handing out freshly nuked or toasted, piping-hot whatevers, attempting to trap you into *needing* more and therefore buying the dinner party–size frozen pizza, can be very dangerous when it comes to your diet. Go when you're full and let your brain, not your stomach, do the shopping.

Clear Out Space in the Pantry, Fridge & Storage Shelves First

Before you go, go through your pantry, fridge, and storage shelves, dumping old, bad, never-used-and-never-will-use space-wasting items that will make room for the bulk items that you really do *need* and *will* use. Um, notice the emphasis on *need* and *will,* as opposed to *want* and *might.* Now that you've cleared out, know how much room you have. No need to measure, but take a mental note. Try and figure out in your head, based on your shopping list, about how many of each bulky item you have space for.

WHAT'S *BETTER* TO BUY IN BULK?

Olive oil. Olive oil is a good fat. Of course, moderation is key, but if you sauté often and tend to stick to olive oil, you could easily start to go through it pretty quickly, and it can be pretty expensive. Instead of buying the teeny bottles at the grocery store because they are the least expensive, only to have to buy another in a month, buy a big one at a bulk store. No, not five. Buy one big one. The problem with buying five is that oil does go bad and will, after a while, smell and taste rancid. If you want you can keep one of your smaller bottles from the grocery store and use the big guy to refill the little guy for easier handling.

Toothbrushes. Just an FYI, the American Dental Association suggests changing your toothbrush every three to four months. If you have a cold, you should really switch it as soon as you're better. Unless of course you are interested in harboring that bacteria on the bristles and then sticking them in your mouth and exposing yourself to your own germs again. Toothbrushes (and toothbrush heads if you use an electric one) are small. They take up a minimal amount of space thanks to their ability to be stacked or stand. Buy them in bulk.

Cereal and oatmeal. Yes, it is the most important meal of the day. It just is. You can't argue it. Many people have tried. The purpose of breakfast is to break your fast—breakfast. It gets your metabolism going so that your body doesn't go into starvation mode, holding on hard and tight to any food and fat that it is storing. If you think you don't like breakfast because you're not hungry in the morning, you actually trained yourself to not be hungry in the morning. Retrain yourself. It will take a couple of weeks, but pretty soon you will be hungry in the morning, you will experience an increase of energy, and you will then eat less food, calories, and fat in the afternoon—since you won't be starving from not eating all day. Loooong story short: Buying cereal and breakfast foods in bulk is a great idea! Just make sure they are a brands you know you like. Bulk buys are not the way to test out new flavors.

Canned soup and tuna. If you're a fan of canned tuna or soup for meals (you know, you can really dress them up and make them taste fresh-ish), then buying them in bulk is a brilliant idea. Again, check the expiration dates, make sure there isn't rust on the can (which could mean the can has been punctured and the innards are now uneatable), and stack them up in your pantry. I like to add oatmeal or bread crumbs to my canned tomato soup, sometimes a little fresh basil, and a drizzle of olive oil.

Dog food. If you have a dog, you know how expensive it can be to properly feed it. You also know how much it sucks when you're late for work and you suddenly realize that you don't have enough dog food for your pooch's breakfast, forcing you to resort to serving up a mix of your cereal (remember, sugar is bad for dogs) and last night's leftovers, making you feel like a bad mom. Instead, stock up! Also buy an airtight bin and pour the food in there. You can store the big bin somewhere other than in the kitchen; that way you always have enough but it doesn't have to get in your way.

Beer, soda, wine. You would be shocked by some of the deals on wine at bulk-shopping stores! And you never know when a couple of friends are going to stop by to hang out or when you will decide to throw a last-minute dinner party. Beer and soda—also deeply discounted in bulk (like one-third the price). If you have the room and you like that kind of thing, you may as well stock up.

WHAT'S *WORSE* TO BUY IN BULK?

Brown rice. Definitely, if you're going to eat rice, brown rice is the much better option since it isn't stripped of all its fiber and still holds nutrients while simultaneously filling you up, like any good carb should. But brown rice doesn't last even close to as long as white rice does on the shelf. If you eat mass amounts of brown rice, go for the bulk buy. But if it's an occasional thing, buy it at the grocery store in a smaller-size bag. No reason to waste food (and money) by allowing it to go bad.

Candy. As mentioned in the "more is worse" rant, buying candy in bulk, unless it's for the purpose of giving out on Halloween or giving it away at a party, is *completely* unnecessary and will just tempt you to the point of totally negating your diet and ultimately ending up feeling guilty the next A.M.—every next A.M.—until it is thrown in the trash. What a waste (but you'll keep your waist!).

Paper towels and toilet paper. When it comes to buying paper towels and toilet paper in bulk, yes, they could in the end save you a couple (or even several) bucks. But if you don't have the space to store them, you end up attempting to squeeze them into every possible available spot as you replace any nook of comfortable living space with a puffy (albeit less-expensive) roll. Instead, buy an eight-pack and restock when you have two rolls left. But if you happen to have the extra storage space, stock up!

Nuts. You might be inclined to go nuts over a big container of nuts. Stop yourself. Nuts go bad. Sure, they don't take up a lot of space, and, yes, you can get great deals on them at bulk stores. However, similar to olive oil, your average nut starts to go rancid, taking on a bitter flavor and scent, after a few months. Why? Nuts are filled with natural fat. When exposed to elements (like air, from opening and closing the container repeatedly, and light), the fat starts to turn bad. Of course, if you are having a party, like to keep nuts out for the hoards of friends constantly streaming through your place, or you tend to eat a few handfuls of nuts a day (not great for your weight), buying nuts in bulk is OK. The same concept applies when it comes to sesame seeds, flaxseeds, and pine nuts. Best bet—buy a normal-size container of nuts.

33

Mayo, ketchup, salad dressing. Make sure to look at the expiration date before you go and buy a gigantic vat of your fave condiment. Unless you are, as I have said over and over again like a broken record, having a party or you are a huge condiment person, buy condiments in normal-size containers. On a side note, when it comes to fat and calories, check the nutrition label! Some condiments are stuffed with sodium, while others are soooo fatty (like salad dressing; yes, a salad doused in dressing can contain more fat than a burger!). However, there are some great options that add lots of flavor without the fat and calories—a great way to spice up a dish without the guilt—like mustard, hot sauce, horseradish, lemon juice, minced and sliced jalapeños.

Vitamins and nutritional supplements. Sure, you can get them for less at bulk stores, and they generally are a definite deal. But *again,* check the date! If there are 500 One A Day pills, and they expire in six months, do the math. That's 180 days. Even if they expire in a year, you won't finish the bottle. On the other hand, if you have plenty of time prior to expiration, realize that you are committing to over a year of the exact same stuff. If it's a protein powder or fizzy vitamin drink, make sure you in fact want to drink the exact same flavor, day in and day out, for over a year. If you get sick of the taste within a few months and ignore the container until it eventually goes bad, or you simply throw it out, you've just wasted both money and product.

Spices and herbs. Unless you're a restaurant or serving up *a lot* of food flavored with *a lot* of spice and herbs, there is zero need to buy those big plastic bottles. You also don't need to stock your kitchen with lots of little bottles that you will then never use. I know, you "might" use them one day. But even if you cook regularly, chances are you will infrequently come across a recipe requiring most of the drawer full of spices you have (like turmeric, cardamom, allspice). Plus, after about six months spices begin to lose their kick. Again, what a waste. Know your palate. Buy the spices that you like. Me: I keep sea salt, Spike seasoning (it's a cool mix of several spices, which I put on almost everything), cinnamon, cayenne, white pepper (I prefer it to black pepper and I use it a lot), and mustard powder (it brings an interesting depth of flavor to lots of dishes). If your palate changes, or if a fave recipe calls for a spice that you don't have, go and buy it and incorporate it into other dishes, too. When it comes to herbs like thyme, garlic, parsley, rosemary, and oregano, I prefer them fresh and, if a recipe calls for them, I buy them from the produce section of my supermarket. Or I grow them in a little pot in my kitchen next to the window; they add greenery, look gorgeous, and I always have fresh herbs when I need them. Another trick is to buy a little bunch of fresh herbs from the grocery store, then put them in a glass of water—like a flower arrangement—and keep them near your kitchen window for use and display. They don't go bad as fast, and you have something pretty to look at. Bottom line: Unless it's something you will use a LOT, forget the bulk spices and herbs.

Bleach. The big bottle of bleach from the grocery store is fine. But the gigantic size from the bulk store is crazy (unless you and all of your roomies go in on it as a group purchase). Aside from it being very heavy, increasing your chance of accidentally dumping way too much into each load (making it a waste in the end), cleaning products have a shelf life. In fact, every year bleach loses its effectiveness by 20 percent, getting your clothes less and less white while wasting more and more of your money. Really, do you use that much bleach that you need to buy it in bulk anyway?

Frozen foods. Yes, if the expiration date is way out, then it's okay. But, do you really need twenty-five packages of the exact same meal that will take you several months to eat, all the while taking up loads of space in your freezer just so you could save a couple of bucks? That's for you to decide. Or you could use your club card at your regular grocery store to make the frozen-food purchases. You will often find that those items in particular have "buy five save two dollars" type of deals, making them bargain purchases even when not buying in extreme bulk.

QuickieChick's Cheat Sheet

1. You can live paycheck to paycheck and still live well by being cost conscious in all areas except for the few that you choose to splurge on—the areas that make you feel most alive, like going out to dinner or buying fancy cheese at the grocery store.

2. There are ways to get cheaper rent. Ask for the first month free, for renovations, or for one hundred dollars off per month. It all adds up.

3. Get a credit card . . . now! If you ever want to buy a car, a home, anything expensive, you'll be glad you built up the credit.

4. Get health insurance! It's not worth skimping on it just to save a few hundred bucks a month. Some procedures cost thousands of dollars!

5. Think about what kind of relationship you want with a roommate before meeting with potential roomies. Communicate with them what you'll want out of the relationship. Best friends? Or just housemates?

6. Your home says something about you. Consider that in your decorating, your cleanliness, which belongings you display.

7. Decorate on a dime by sifting through thrift stores for easily refurbishable finds, like a chest of drawers that you simply have to paint white.

8. You can save a lot of money by buying certain items in bulk. But be smart about it: Do you have the space? Is the bulk actually less expensive than the unit price? Will it expire before you use it?

9. Remember, you're taking all these steps to make sure you **don't move back with your parents.**

10. Don't freak out. Take each of these steps one at a time.

Making Money 3

JUST A JOB VS. A CAREER

FACT: Most college grads have high expectations when it comes to their career, then feel slapped in the face when the only job they can land has nothing to do with their major, as they find themselves living paycheck to paycheck—and for what? If you want to get out of the job-rut before you slip into it, you've got to focus. But focus on what? Well, the first question is: What's your passion? What drives you? Not sure? Not to worry. Maybe now's the time to test out a few different career paths by dabbling in them, interning for little to zero money (if you can afford that), asking questions, researching . . . soul searching.

Before we begin this focused analysis of what you want to spend the rest of your life doing—the eventual designation of your career, let me clarify the difference between a "job" and a "career."

Job:

A job is purpose-driven (as opposed to passion-driven). A job is shorter term. You can have several during your lifetime.

Career:

A career is passion-driven (which doesn't mean that you can't make money from it; in fact, you can make even more because you put all of you into it—you're passionate about it). A career is a long-term journey that builds upon itself as you ascend the ranks, grow, and expand your presence, reach, and position. It can evolve as your interests and experience matures. A career exhibits your talents, desires, and strengths. Some people never find a career, others take years to discover it, and still others dive into it immediately.

Determining Your Career Potential

Tools

What's your job criteria? Every one of us has a different set of criteria, reasons, goals, ideals, and life pursuits that lead us to select our individual jobs and careers. Before you hone in on a job, fill out the sections below:

1. What do the subjects listed below mean to you?

Balance: _____

Work: _____

Life: _____

Success: _____

2. Rank the importance of each on a scale of 1 to 5, with 5 being the most important.

Money	Respect
Passion	Enrichment
Relationships	Security
Influence	Inspiration
Adventure	Create change
Freedom	Give back

Now What Kind of a Career Will I also Enjoy?

Don't think. Just answer. First thing that comes to your head, write that down. Go!

Take Note

What do you enjoy doing; what makes you happy?

_____

_____

Do you love to sit all day in your head, writing out your thoughts?

_____

_____

Do you love to research?

_____

_____

Do you need social interaction?

_____

_____

Do you enjoy group settings and decisions by committee?

_____

_____

Do you prefer to establish the rules or follow them?

_____

_____

Do you like to follow or lead?

_____

_____

Are you a self-starter, or do you need someone to motivate you?

_____

_____

Do you want to travel?

_____

_____

Do you want to sit at a desk?

_____

_____

Do you like routine?

_____

_____

Do you like to get your hands dirty?

_____

_____

Do you like to constantly be challenged, or do you prefer consistency?

_____

_____

Do you want to have weekends off, when you don't even think about work, then start
each Monday with a clear head, excited about fresh pursuits?

_____

_____

(continued)

Do you prefer ongoing projects?

_____

_____

What kind of advice do people ask you for?

_____

_____

What kind of advice do you like to give?

_____

_____

What topics do you find yourself reading about, engaged in, talking about?

_____

_____

So how do you find a career that you actually like and may lead you to want to spend your life pursuing it?

It's time to start thinking about what you like and the type of day-to-day lifestyle you want to live. Why? Because every career dictates a different type of life.

Once you have pondered and answered the "Note to Self" questions above, start writing down your passions—every day. If you find passion, inspiration, "aha" in anything that you do, say, an activity or even just something that someone you know does or says, write it down in a List of Happiness. At the end of the month, take a look at your List of Happiness and see if your career takes shape.

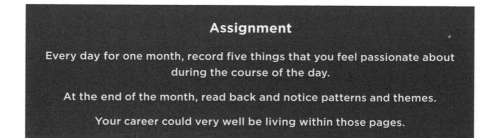

Assignment

Every day for one month, record five things that you feel passionate about during the course of the day.

At the end of the month, read back and notice patterns and themes.

Your career could very well be living within those pages.

Nicole Williams

Nicole is a three-time best-selling author of *Girl on Top: Your Guide to Turning Dating Rules into Career Success.* She is also the founder of WORKS by Nicole Williams—the go-to resource for career-minded chicks, and was responsible for one of *Forbes* magazine's Top 10 Career Web Sites for Women. Yeah, she's fab.

#1 Piece of Career Advice

Own your career. You're going to have to take a very proactive role in managing the direction of your future. If you want something, ask for it. If you think you could be utilized in some way, take action. We'd like to think people are looking out for our best interests and will hold our hands, especially when we're fresh to the work scene, but most of the time that's not the case. Trust your judgment and don't let titles hold you back. If you want a better job, do a better job.

41

QuickieChick Quiz

True or false: It's okay to lie . . . a little . . . on an application.

False. Embellishment is one thing. Sure, highlight experiences and activities that might enhance your skills and illuminate why you are great for the job. For example: If the job is in social media and public relations, slip in a quick fun story about your close friendship with trendsetters and influencers to show that your interest in the job at hand goes beyond work and occupies other areas of your life. The fact is that your potential future employer wants to know that you have something to contribute, that there is a reason to hire you, that you know what you're talking about and aren't merely a blank book looking to be educated. *However,* if you choose to *lie* and you are caught, you're pretty much guaranteeing yourself that you won't be getting that job. If you don't get caught, you will then be carrying that lie throughout your time there, possibly creating more lies to support your lie, strategizing and writing down the lies upon lies in order to ensure that you keep your facts straight.

Keep it simple. Keep it straight.

How to Ace the Job Interview

What to Wear

This is your one and only opportunity to make a first impression. You want to stand out . . . in a good way. Dress your best. Put on the most polished outfit you have in your closet. A suit is best, regardless of the industry or position you're applying for.

What to Do and Not Do

Do be strong, confident, and articulate.

Don't curse, use a lot of slang, or be egotistical.

Do talk about how you are the right fit for the company, what you bring to the table, and what you can contribute—how you will make a positive impact within the position and the company as a whole.

Don't ever answer the question "How are you today?" with "I'm tired." They don't want to know that. You are obviously not responsible enough to get an adequate amount of sleep in preparation for a big and important day like this.

Do be enthusiastic.

Don't be fake.

Do smile.

Don't be too long-winded or rambling with your answers.

Do be yourself, with your real laugh, your authentic smile, your true wit and charm. Just be you—the best you you can be.

Prepping for a Job Interview

Jorie, 23, Registered Marriage- and Family-Counseling Intern: "In order to appear or feel confident, I remember the importance of making a good first impression. Therefore, I research the company and the people working in it. I also make sure that I am dressed for success, give a proper handshake, and maintain eye contact. I genuinely listen to the interviewer or guests in attendance. One thing that I always try to remember is that I wouldn't even be invited to the interview or social business situation if they didn't like me. I also think that people understand that I am just starting out, which allows me to feel more at ease. Sometimes the best thing is just working on building relationships and focusing on commonalities."

The Job Offer: Take the $ or Ask for More?

In this tough market flooded with overqualified, equally hungry applicants, is there room for negotiation? When you are given an offer, is it okay to ask for more money?

According to career expert Nicole Williams, "Yes—and you should. Aim for 20 percent above what you're worth (you'll have to do some research by asking friends with similar jobs and doing some basic Google searches about what others in your position are paid) and then leave it to them to negotiate—but decide on a bottom price before you walk into the interview."

You Got the Job!

TIME TO SET UP YOUR DESK

One of the fun (and oddly daunting) parts of settling into a "real" job is setting up your desk. It's easy to spend loads of money on unnecessary extras that cost a lot and serve little purpose. But we wouldn't expect for you to totally pare down, either, denying yourself the joy of office accessories that put a smile on your face because they are just so darn fab in every way! So we contacted Holly Bohn, founder of See Jane Work, an online office-supply store that equips fast-paced chicks with essential goods that are both functional and stylish. Holly believes that "inspiration comes more easily to those surrounded by beauty, not smoke-colored desk accessories," and we had to know what her top ten desk must-haves are. Here's what she said:

1. **White Stacking Basic Letter Trays.** The simple design allows me to change my accessories without having to invest in all new basics.

2. **Ace Pilot Stapler.** The design hasn't changed since the 1930s. It's well made and priced right. Sometimes the basics are best.

3. **Rubber Band Ball.** It's fun, practical, and a great stress reliever and time killer!

4. **Coccoina Adhesive-Glue Stick.** Almond-scented all-natural adhesive. Why? Come on—it's an adhesive that *also* smells like almonds!

5. **See Jane Work Storage Collection.** Colors and styles of file boxes remain consistent so I can add on as my storage needs grow.

6. **See Jane Work Basic Pencils.** I love a found object for a pencil cup—an old trophy, a silver cup, a piece of pottery, but these items can look messy filled with chewed-up pencils. Simple pencils in one color ties the look together.

43

7. **Small Tray.** Any cute little tray will work to keep small items from taking over your desktop. From business cards to paper clips.

8. **Binders.** I prefer colorful binders to white plastic. I tear out pages from magazines and place them in sheet protectors then into a binder. I have a style binder, a design binder, a decorating binder, etc.

9. **Project Envelopes.** These keep my projects together and organized.

10. **Basic Notebook.** I use one notebook for all my notes, whether it's meetings or tasks, so I know they're all in one place.

Want to splurge on something seriously special and smile-making?

Patent Leather Dictionary & Thesaurus. These are definite splurges, but they are things you will have for a lifetime.

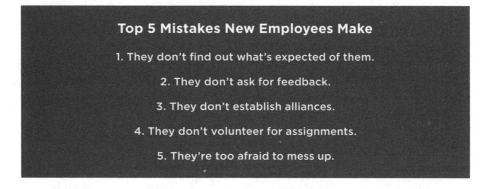

Top 5 Mistakes New Employees Make

1. They don't find out what's expected of them.

2. They don't ask for feedback.

3. They don't establish alliances.

4. They don't volunteer for assignments.

5. They're too afraid to mess up.

WANT A RAISE?

Nicole says that if you want a raise, "Ask for it! Try it today (assuming you haven't gotten one lately and have been at the company longer than a year). The number-one mistake we make is not being proactive about it. People, especially women, wait until the raise is offered to them." No one is going to have your back and best interests in mind more than yourself. If you need, feel you deserve, or just want more money, take the initiative and ask for it! If you want to wait for the "right time," many companies have an annual review. Bring it up then.

Can You Really "Think Rich & You Will Be Rich"?

"The world is at your fingertips!"

"Think rich and you will become rich."

That's what you've been told, right? Yeah . . . it's all great and exciting in theory! The problem is: We're talking about theories. Not reality. There's a difference.

While, yes, the world and all its bounty is out there for you to grasp, and thinking is definitely a component to becoming, there are steps that need to be taken in order to turn theory into reality, your brilliant business idea into a thriving career, your scheme into a success. It doesn't "just happen" because you will it to.

Look, this is a time of transition. I know, many of you are chomping at the bit, anxiously waiting to grab the reins and take control of your lives. You have bigger plans and want to broaden your reach. You see, feel, even taste what it will be like to be happy, fulfilled, and living "the dream." You read dozens of self-help diatribes that explain in great detail how thoughts create our reality and that if we think rich we will be. Problem is: You are *waiting* for the happiness and fulfillment to happen to you instead of taking action and *making* happiness and fulfillment happen.

Sorry to be a bubble burster, but thinking, even tasting success won't magically manifest it. But if you *think* it, *focus* your daily tasks around it, and *take action* by making contacts, doing tireless research, and embodying the person you want to be . . . it *will* happen.

THINK, ACT, SUCCESS

When I was twenty-two years old I got my first paid writing gig. I had no idea what I was doing—which was oddly a good thing. Why? Because I was clueless as to how hard it can be to break in. I just always assumed I could do it. Not that it would just come to me, but that if I worked hard, put in the hours, made the contacts, and worked my a★★ off, I couldn't not be successful at it. Honestly, I would say that I didn't become successful because I was a great writer. I was great at selling myself, working hard, and dedicating my entire self first. And then I learned how to be a great writer.

I had a "may as well ask for what you want; the worst thing that can happen is they will say no" attitude. Maybe it was naïve. Maybe it was arrogant. Maybe it was a little bit of both. But it worked.

That first gig was as the health and beauty editor for a national magazine called *Fit* magazine. I wrote ten articles a month. And at first I wrote for free. It seemed so "easy." So I viewed all of it as easy and proceeded to contact the editors at other magazines to see if I could freelance for them in order to expand my reach. OK, so I didn't simply "ask." I sent e-mails that included "sample" articles, I called, I offered to write for free, I sent e-mails including more sample articles . . . and I landed *Spa* magazine, *FHM, Vegetarian Times, Healing Lifestyles & Spas, Men's Health,* and *Women's Health.* I worked tirelessly. I lived and breathed articles. I would wake up at 4 a.m. with my mind already giving dictation to my fingers, then fall asleep at midnight when my mind would finally go numb.

Translation: As career expert Nicole Williams puts it, "You need to get out of your head and do something—take action. Those that take the leap—make the call, ask for the raise, stay up all night and write the proposal—achieve financial success."

The Lesson: You can't just *think* it, you have to *act* on it, and chances are you *will* achieve success.

Confidence: Be *That Chick*

Are you confident when you walk into a meeting with a higher-up? Do you walk into a room and own it? Are you comfortable in the skin you are in? No? Fake it—just for a little while. How? By embodying "*That Chick.*"

That Chick is the overachiever side of you who desires greatness. You know she's in there somewhere, but for some reason you are struggling to allow her to penetrate the skin, liberating that internal power onto the world. *That Chick* is the outspoken, head-held-high, poised woman within you who isn't afraid to speak before a crowd of hundreds, can calmly yet effervescently appear on live national television without having an anxiety attack, has the ability to walk up to anyone and strike up a stimulating conversation at an event or party, isn't afraid to speak her mind and let herself shine.

My *That Chick* is my stand-in, my stunt double, my security blanket when I am too shy, nervous, or insecure. If I am walking into a situation in which I feel that I need that extra oomph from *That Chick,* I imagine zipping up the full bodysuit, the confidence suit, the *That Chick* suit. Once "she" breaks the ice and I feel comfortable enough to come forward, *That Chick* retreats back inside of me and I take over.

Sometimes you have to create *That Chick* . . . until you actually are able to embody her yourself. That's when you realize that you no longer are faking it, for *you are* strong, confident, in control, and in demand, and you're as real as you're ever going to get!

Expert Insight

Nicole Williams

Top 5 Confidence Tricks to Boost Your Interview/Meeting Success

1. **Research, research, research.** The key to feeling confident is preparation. Learn anything and everything about the industry and company you're interviewing for.

2. **Practice.** There are basic questions that all interviewers ask: "Tell me about yourself? What interests you about this position?" Before you get asked the tough questions in the big leagues, practice with your friend, beau, or mom.

3. **Dress up.** If you want to feel confident, you need to look confident. Find that outfit that makes you feel powerful and in control. Try it on the night before and test that the skirt isn't too short or the jacket too tight. Polish your shoes and clean out your bag.

4. **Pep talk.** One of my tricks is to have a conversation with someone whom I love and who supports me, before I walk into the big meeting.

5. **Listen up.** Another trick is to listen to fast, powerful, fun music before you walk in. Take the energy of the music with you into the interview.

From Scaredy Pants to Hot Pants

Tools

What are terrifying scenarios for you?

_____

_____

Who do you admire?

_____

_____

Why?

_____

_____

Starter Sentence

My _That Chick_ is

_____ ,

and she can tackle that terrifying scenario above by:

_____

without stressing.

You're Not Entitled to Anything . . . & Why That's a Good Thing

There are lots of twenty-somethings entering the workforce bright-eyed and bushy-tailed, excited to sink their teeth into their future, chomping at the bit to work their tail off (to a "reasonable" point) and, as an expected result, be paid a pretty penny.

There are two things in the above sentence that must be tweaked in order for you to get a clear picture of what you need to do to succeed in this workforce that you so completely want to excel in.

1. You will have to work hard. _Hard_. If you want to overachieve and surpass the flock that falls into the average range, then you need to realize that nine-to-five work hours are unrealistic in the real world. Overachieving bottom-rungers often work tear-inducing hours. Want a comparison? Think finals week. That's as close to the real

world as you're going to get within the comfort of college. So why does finals week feel more like hell than anything else? Because you haven't adapted yet. You haven't learned how to find comfort in pain, adjusting your lifestyle, your social expectations, your sleep cycle accordingly. Don't worry. You'll get used to it, and soon it won't be nearly as painful. You'll learn how to cope . . . almost comfortably.

2. You likely won't be paid a pretty penny yet. In fact, your pay will likely be pretty much a penny. And that's just the way it is. If you're lucky enough to get a "real," non-interning job, then, yes, minimum wage is a requisite by law, but sometimes you won't be afforded the luxury of billing overtime hours, because you will find that you are working even during off-hours, after you've technically clocked out. Why? Because those are the hours that count. It's like working out: You can do ten push-ups, but it's those extra two at the end, the two beyond the requisite ten, those are the two that count, that make the difference.

People think that Gen Ys (the fresh-faced teens and twenty-somethings) have been spoon-fed their whole lives. In some cases it may be necessary to take extra steps to prove you're "not one of them." Put in long hours when necessary, mingle with co-workers of all ages, don't complain about getting coffee for the entire office, understand that everyone else has put in their time—and you will, too.

"Pick Their Brain Until It Bleeds"—a Mentor Is Key

The fact is this: You are new to this game. You have zero (or minimal) experience in an industry that you are seriously considering spending the rest of your working days in. So what is the best way to navigate these unknown waters? (Sorry for the cliché.) A mentor—hands down. A mentor will enlighten you on the details, fill you in on the unsaid but well-known politics and policies, and guide you through the straight truth. More than that, though, a mentor will often help you get that job in the first place, then be there when you are having a hard day and don't understand why you have to work for twenty hours straight for a meager pay that can hardly afford you the suit that you have to wear in order to keep that job. More than enlightening you about the daily minutiae, a mentor is there as proof that, if you put in the time, energy, dedication, sleepless nights, sweat, and likely tears, you can and you will succeed. And you know what? Having that mentor may actually help that success happen faster. Why? Because you essentially have a backer. You have someone who believes in you so much that they are willing to dedicate time, energy, and even lend connections to you. And those connections will know that you are backed, that you are, for all intents and purposes, third-party approved, signed off on, sealed, and now delivered. You have a leg up.

FINDING MY MENTOR

There's no cookie-cutter, cut-and-paste way to find that someone to mentor you. But here's how I got mine:

I was in a film-studies class in college, and the professor assigned us the task of getting in touch with and interviewing someone in the entertainment industry whom we admired and who had a biography or autobiography out. That week, superagent Michael Ovitz (who was at the time one of the most powerful and feared men in the industry) was on the cover of *Time* magazine, or maybe it was *Newsweek*. I admired him, he had a best-selling biography on shelves at every bookstore. I wanted to interview Michael! It happened to be on the heels of his now-infamous Disney payoff, a controversy that elicited another book. I proposed Michael as the focus of my paper. My professor's response: "If you even get Michael Ovitz to acknowledge your existence, I will give you an A in this class." Sounded like a challenge to me.

Upon minimal investigation I found out that Ovitz's son went to the same posh high school that my younger brother went to. I got ahold of the student directory, obtained the home address of the powerhouse, and wrote him a letter. A couple of days later, while I was at school, the phone rang in my apartment and my roommate, who I happened to be in a fight with at the time, answered.

"Laurel House please," said a stern voice on the other end of the phone.

"Oh, Laurel's not here," replied my roommate, with just as snippy a tone.

"Is this her assistant?" the voice asked matter-of-factly.

My incensed roommate responded with, "No, you asshole, this is her roommate."

"Well," said the voice, "this is Michael Ovitz."

Gulp! My roommate knew how important this phone call was to me and how HUGE this man was.

"I am her assistant today," she responded.

"Good. Tell Laurel she should be a writer, get a cell phone, and call me back immediately. Here's my number. . . . " And with that, Michael Ovitz hung up.

I bought a cell phone that day and called Ovitz back from my new number, one that my roommate was sure not to answer. We chatted for several minutes and several minutes more the next day. I drove down to L.A. for an in-person visit at his Brentwood home and interviewed him poolside, a few steps from his gym, where he had private daily martial-arts lessons, overlooking the mountains and the ocean. Ovitz mapped my career path on a napkin, then gave me a book, *Man the Manipulator*, from his personal

collection, one that he had clearly used and studied—as was evident by the worn pages and penciled notations throughout. He told me that when I find a person whose path I want to emulate, I should "pick their brain until it bleeds." He became my mentor, and night after night I picked his brain (though I don't think I made it bleed) as I racked up hours on my cell phone.

That summer, Ovitz got me a job at Creative Artists Agency (CAA), the agency that he cocreated and that, in turn, created him. I was a "summer camper"—basically, an unpaid intern who delivered mail and copied scripts, all the while wearing a suit. That is when my life became my work. And I loved it. A few months later it was back to school, a by-then–unfamiliar place that seemed so petty compared to the working world that had saturated my senses, seeped into my bones, and flowed through my blood. I was addicted.

My Mentor: Laurel—Your QuickieChick

Hi. I know Laurel is telling you all about the benefits of having a mentor. But that's just her perspective. I'm Julia—the one she bosses around. . . .

Just kidding! Laurel is my mentor and has been instrumental in helping me actually avoid the whole "Oh my god, what the h★★l am I going to do now?!" moment that comes right after college.

For every little step I've taken, there have been a dozen questions on exactly how to take that step. Like:

- How do I word this e-mail?

- How long do I wait to send a second follow-up e-mail to a potential employer if the first e-mail went unanswered?

- What insider lingo can I use to show (or at least pretend) that I know what I'm talking about?

- And, most important: Do I even *want* to be going in the direction I'm headed in?

A mentor can answer these questions, so, instead of wasting weeks reading books on "how to become a successful x, y, or z," you could be learning all of that in a fraction of the time *and* getting experience *and* making contacts.

And that's where Laurel came in. She was looking for an "intern," so to clarify: someone who would work for her for free. It ended up being much more than just an internship. For both of us, I think. She became my mentor, and now that I have graduated from college, I actually officially work for her (for money). So how did I get that unpaid job in the first place? She posted an ad on Craigslist that was reposted on the UCLA job board. It read:

This is an unpaid internship (school credit is great) with the possibility of eventual pay . . . for a long-term writing/blogging/assistant/social media maven intern to work from my home office in Santa Monica. I am a print and online writer, published author, television and social media fit living spokesperson with way too much on my plate and I need help.

    The job may include (but is not limited to):
- *Writing articles*
- *Tweeting*
- *Facebooking*
- *Blogging*
- *Researching and coming up with articles/tweets/Facebook posts on fitness, diets, healthy living*
- *Running some personal errands*

    I am looking for someone who already has a polished yet sassy writing voice and wants to learn more.

    I am looking for someone who isn't just in it for five months but wants to be mentored.

    I am looking for someone who wants to be in this industry and is interested in learning how to be a freelance, independent, full-time writer.

    I need someone who:
- *Has Experience Writing*
- *Understands and can handle deadlines and working on a time crunch*
- *Is savvy in social media, Facebook, Twitter, blogging*
- *Understands discretion, privacy, and confidentiality*

52

- *Is dedicated, professional, committed to working*
- *Is responsible and trustworthy*
- *Can work at least three days a week for five hours each day*

I am easygoing, but I have high expectations and want things done right and my way.

Please submit:
- *One-paragraph letter as to why you are right for this internship*
- *Bio (written in your writing style)*
- *Résumé*
- *One writing sample (If you have never been published, that's OK. Just write up a quick one-paragraph "article" on how you live a fit life.)*

Laurel had never been a mentor before when I responded to her Craigslist ad and showed up on her doorstep for my interview, and I had no idea what to expect out of the experience as a protégé. Honestly, that was probably for the best, because our relationship just evolved very naturally, neither one of us having any set expectations. Because of the nature of our work (we write from Laurel's home) we spend a *lot* of time together. We have grown very comfortable with each other. Not all mentor-protégé relationships need to be super close, but the communication should be super fluid. Laurel would read me her e-mails from people she was working with and explain to me why exactly they were pissing her off, making her happy, screwing her over . . . whatever. Then she would read me her response, which always seemed to come so quickly and was said so perfectly. She would teach me what kind of language to use when pitching Web sites and magazines. We would totally let ourselves get carried away in conversation about our love lives, body inse-curities, whatever, because, since we write about lifestyle, we knew some of the best article ideas came from those conversations. Every Thursday night she would take me to dinner and let me ask her any and all questions I had about what she does, how she got there, and the ins and outs of how I can do it, too. She sent e-mail introductions to her contacts at magazines to help me get my foot in the door, then helped me word the e-mail pitches that I would send them. She was like training wheels on a bike until I was comfortable enough to do it myself. She put her business calls on speaker so I could listen in (sorry to anyone who didn't know they were on speaker). It was like being the camera crew on a reality show. You see how the person interacts with the outside world, and then when no one is looking, they turn to the camera and tell you what they *really* think about what just happened.

More than anyone else, she also saw and still sees just how badly I want to succeed. No one you ever e-mail a résumé to will really be able to see that. But when you genuinely care about learning about an industry, and your mentor can feel that, a certain energy is created. You get very into helping them with their work, and they start naturally thinking of ways they can help you. More than working for her, Laurel to this day sends me multiple daily e-mails of Web sites she thinks I should pitch or writing jobs she found that she thinks I should apply to. Honestly, we like each other. We've become friends. And that makes my job even more fulfilling.

Funny thing—I almost left Laurel. I know. It sounds like we're married. But we spend basically 24/7 together, and a few months into working for her, I decided I wanted a normal, routine life with a nine-to-five job and co-workers and happy hour and benefits and the whole shebang. Honestly, I'd just been broken up with, and I was feeling lonely, which made the breakup even harder. I mistook this for being unhappy with my career. When I told Laurel my plans to change paths—and although she was clearly a bit annoyed and, I think more than that, a bit hurt—she suggested I try interning at her mother's PR firm. I would get the nine-to-five, co-worker, and office thing. I gave it a try . . . and I wanted OUT within the month. I missed the lifestyle of being a writer. I missed my creative freedom. I told Laurel this, and she said, "I know. I knew you'd come back."

Lesson: A really good mentor will gently guide you in the right direction but won't push you. Laurel could have just dropped me and found another intern who wasn't going through all the head stuff I was. But she saw potential in me. She knew I was on the right path with writing, but she wanted to let me figure that out for myself. She just gently guided me there while helping me get another job working somewhere that she knew I could easily quit (working for her mom) but still provided all of the things I thought I wanted in a work environment.

WHAT A MENTOR CAN TEACH YOU

- From a mentor you can learn how to walk and talk like you've been in the industry for years, in a matter of months, and that is very helpful when applying for jobs.

- A good mentor will be on the lookout for opportunities for you.

- A good mentor will take the time to stop and explain to you what he/she is doing and why.

- A good mentor takes you out to dinner and/or drinks once a week and introduces you to his/her contacts.

- A mentorship is a great way to get an all-inclusive look at the life of a certain professional, which includes his/her life outside of work. Why? Because more than the career, it's also about the lifestyle: Does my boss have a life? Is she a happy person? What kind of hours does she work? What kind of friends does she keep, etc.

In the end, you might come to the realization that what your mentor does for work isn't actually something you want to do at all. And that's OK, too. The great news is that you learned—a lot (hopefully)—and you can use all of that insight in carving your own path and maybe mentoring someone else someday in your chosen profession, just like Laurel did.

Act Savvy . . . Even When You're Clueless

Insecure? Unsure? Honestly, totally clueless? That's OK. Just don't act like it. That's not to say that it's OK to totally fake complete knowledge. Fact is, most high-ups don't know exactly what the job entails until they are actually in it. There is often at least some degree of faking it when it comes to getting a new job or landing a promotion. Example?

When I landed the job as health and beauty editor at *Fit* magazine, I will admit that I bit off much more than I could chew. At least at first. The magazine had gone down for several months, and it was about to relaunch. I happened to know the editor in chief from when I was working as a publicist for healthy lifestyle companies—a job that is based on relationships with editors and writers. I wanted to switch sides, become a magazine editor, be the one publicists called to pitch story ideas to. So I called this editor to feel out her needs. It turned out the magazine was in need of someone to take on a lot—*stat*! In one call I went from receiving one article assignment to becoming the Health and beauty editor. I had no idea what that meant. Unlike editors at other magazines (and the other editors at *Fit* magazine—the office being in New York and me in Los Angeles, I was going to work from my home, never going into an office. I was to create my own hours, come up with my own article ideas and assignments, make my own deadlines, decide what products and people to mention and which would be featured . . . oh, and coordinate every aspect of the photo shoots (including budgeting).

Instead of freaking out, I honestly called my mom. She had been a publicist for many years, was close friends with editors, had relationships with photographers, and even knew other competing publicists who had clients that I could possibly write about—essentially all of the pieces that I needed to put this puzzle together. The writing was easy. I wrote about products and people that I believed in, knew, and used. After all, I had always lived healthfully; I had been drinking that Kool-Aid for a very long time. It was the photo shoots that made me nervous. Despite the fact that I was clueless as to what to do, I reached out to modeling agencies to secure models (for free in order to be budget-conscious); first-time models will work for free in order to have the experience. I was referred to a photographer with magazine experience, who connected me to a makeup artist and a stylist. Then I hired a girlfriend to be my "editorial assistant," who oversaw the details of the shoot, coordinated the location, arrival of the models, and made sure that the products arrived on time.

Somehow the thing went off without a hitch (sure, there were a few little hiccups but no blowups). The pictures looked great. The articles were turned in on time. And the magazine went to print. I was beside myself with pride, and honestly a bit of shock and awe, when I first saw my name in print: "Health and Beauty Editor: Laurel House."

Was I a pro? No. Did I let on that I was clueless? Absolutely not! I was an editor with one success under my belt. I acted savvy without being snotty, paid attention, collected info and insight so that I could become better and more confident in this newly minted position. I started to make more connections, always telling people at parties and events that I wrote for magazines in order to start collecting more contacts, expanding my roster and stable of experts, photographers, models, and even other writers, whom I could hire to help with my workload. Of course, I continued to watch other seasoned editors and writers, taking note of how they did it and making a few mid-course corrections and adjustments based on other ways of doing things that were more efficient, more professional, higher quality . . . whatever it was. I also asked my mom, who had been to countless photo shoots, for insight. Why did I choose my mom instead of a colleague for help? Because my mom would give me advice without judgment. Same goes with a friend or a mentor. It's OK to ask questions and seek guidance; in fact, if you're not sure how to do something, ask! But do some research first to see if you can quickly figure it out on your own. Just keep in mind that there are often lots of solutions to solve the same problem, lots of ways to go about the same thing. Careers don't have to be cookie-cutter. It's OK to have your own way of processing and working. As long as the outcome is quality and timely, the way we get there is less important.

IT MAY BE FASHIONABLE TO SHOW UP LATE . . . BUT DON'T

Take a tip from a top publicist who is paid to get her client's noticed—my mom: Sharon House. When it comes to timeliness at a work function or event, one where the likelihood of knowing people is slim to none, but you know it's a great way to network, make contacts, get your face out there . . . be on time. It may be fashionable to show up late, but if you want to be successful, show up early and show up prepared. The point of your early arrival? You are banking on the classic party thrower's fear that no one is going to show up. Show up first, and everyone will be desperate to talk with you—even if they don't know you, never met you, and wouldn't have noticed you in the hallway. They will care tonight! Why? Because they need someone to talk to and you happen to be there—who cares why! They will notice you and remember you since you will be the first one to ease their "no one is going to show up" angst. Try this tactic, and you will get more face time than almost anyone else who arrives after you. Once you have put in your time and the thrower's attention is taken by other guests who soon begin to circulate, you can relax or leave early.

If your conversation leads to any suggestions or requires follow-up, be sure to either remember exactly what was said or write it down immediately! Then follow up and follow through.

Note to Self

Act and Eventually Be Confident and Successful

Tools

What are your strengths?

_____

_____

Of what are you most proud?

_____

_____

What do you have to contribute to a company?

_____

_____

What are you afraid of?

_____

_____

What is the most you can lose?

_____

_____

They don't return your call? Big deal. It happens to me all the time. It's not necessarily because you suck. It could very well be because they are busy. Honestly. If they *do* return your call, there must be something about you they like. You have something to offer. They have something to offer as well.

Know what you want, what you need, who you are, and *how fabulous you are.*

Get Out of the Way of Your Success

Sometimes the only person standing in the way of your success is you. Think about it for a second. Are you afraid you're not good enough, don't know enough, are not the absolute best for the job, or not ready? Maybe you're not.

57

But here's the thing: Whether you are or you aren't, you're right. In other words, if you think you can't do it, you can't. But if you believe you *can* do it, then do everything you can and put in every second you have to work your butt off, make those contacts, learn, prepare, and be exactly what that job needs. Then suddenly you will discover (and hopefully your boss will, too) that you are exactly perfect for the position.

Even if you approach things with a slightly naïve attitude. Even if everyone is looking at you, thinking that you're crazy for trying, or telling you that your job title requires much more than you have the experience to fill. Even if you have no idea what you're doing or understand the reality of how hard the task at hand is, don't think about it that way. You've got this.

Unsure? Ask questions, study up, look online—that's what Google is for! Put in the sleepless nights and evenings at home instead of out with friends. Really, is yet another Taco Tuesday with friends worth possibly not knowing the answer to the question that your boss is going to pose on Wednesday morning? Of course, life and work is all about balance, so it's time to find some. Here's the thing: If you're new to a position or are unsure about something, research it, ask questions, figure out the ins and outs of what you do before someone asks you a question, a machine breaks, or you find yourself guessing about what you should do . . . and then you're wrong. Sometimes, absolutely, it's about faking it. But the key to faking it is doing it to the best of your knowledge. Like an educated guess, fake it to the best of your ability while you're learning how to do it for real.

Beyond all of that, here are a few essentials when it comes to getting a leg up as opposed to tripping yourself up:

Follow Up

Ask Yourself WHY

Why, when your friend's friend who is in your desired career position gave you her business card and said to call her so you could get together for coffee and constructive conversation, did you stare at that card in awe, then put it in your pocket and didn't call? It's not that you didn't want to call, but maybe you were afraid or intimidated.

Next Time

Be proactive. Make the call. Send the e-mail. Do something to show that you appreciate the outreach and you would like to learn more. But, of course, don't be pushy, nudgy, whiny, or annoying. Be professional.

ALWAYS FOLLOW UP WITH CONTACTS

One thing that I know for sure is the importance of contacts and connections. I would not be here today if it wasn't for Rita at *Fit* magazine and the relationship that I had initially created with her as a publicist. If you make contact with someone whom you think maybe, just maybe, you might be able to do business with someday, follow up. Just send a quick e-mail saying "Great to meet you. . . . " Easy. It's something that I think lots of newbies seriously need to work on.

DON'T BURN BRIDGES

Remember: Bridges are easily and quickly burned. Repairing them is very, very difficult. Make friends, build relationships, and maintain them! Do *not* burn those bridges. You never know when you might need one to cross.

REMEMBER THE RULES OF CONVERSATION

- Avoid rambling language, like "I was wondering . . . " Have a point. Be direct. But don't be abrasive.

- Don't let your eyes wander away from theirs. Look in their eyes without stalker-staring.

- If they are sarcastic, insert a bit of your wit back.

- Ask questions.

- Stand/sit tall.

- Look confident.

- Accept compliments. Don't put yourself down in front of them. There is a time and place for self-deprecation. That time and place is *not* when talking to a higher-up who could possibly hire you.

Why Paying Your Dues Is Worth the Put-Downs, Personal Errands & Tear-Jerking Hours

You show up to the first day of your new job determined to make an impression. You wear a crisp suit, your best new (and insanely *uncomfortable*) heels. You woke up too early and spent too long prepping your hair and makeup to first-impression perfection. You enter your new office, which could easily be swapped out for an elementary school cubby-size desk—you know the kind with blinders on either side to make sure you don't get distracted by visuals around you, kind of like the blinders horses wear to avoid being spooked. And your first order of operation is to pick a fast-food restaurant and go around to all of the other employees taking their orders for lunch. Wow. Major mental stimulation. A definite learning experience. Right? Surprisingly, yes. The theory is this: Once you make it to the top, if you ever have an employee near the bottom who attempts to inform you that "You don't understand what it's like to be at the bottom since you are the one raking it in, making the big bucks, having your lunch delivered piping hot at exactly 1 P.M.," you can say, "Yes, I do." The bottom is the best place to observe behaviors, personalities, office politics, and see the people behind the facade. It's where you learn how you want to be and *not* be. It's where you can judge if you really want to make it to the top, if you like the people up there. I mean, really, do you like who they are, who they became (knowing that they likely started exactly where you are right now)? Do you like what their life looks like—including all of the trappings, the stuff, the friends, and the workload/lifestyle? Like it? Great. Now's the time to pay your dues, run the errands, do the grunt work, because that's how you will truly learn the ropes. That's where the bummers with benefits come in.

Sure, stapling stacks of papers, delivering mail, and picking up the dry cleaning may not, in the end, be teaching you much about the industry in which you are attempting to excel. But there are actually several learning opportunities there for you. Like what?

Business. Learn about the back end. What's this business really like?

Life. Learn about the real life of your boss, your boss's boss, and the people they deal with day in and day out.

Yourself. Learn about yourself—your strengths and weaknesses, your limits, your edge, your comfort levels, your interests, your worst and best. Those are things you need to know.

MY PERSONAL DUES-PAYING EXPERIENCE

My first job out of college was at the hottest entertainment-management company founded by my mentor, who, as you now know from reading the mentor section, "Pick Their Brain Until It Bleeds," (page 49) was at the time considered to be "the most powerful person in Hollywood." Ovitz said that he would "take care of me," which I assumed translated to getting me a cush job at his new company . . . which instead became one of my first (of many) reality-check moments.

You see, I had always wanted to be in "the industry." I knew it from the age of eight. It was a career propelled by passion, and I did everything I could to align myself with industry insiders, score the ideal mentor, create a supportive home life, buy the best power suits that I could afford, and land a job in the mailroom of a management company—the exact right spot to start.

I graduated from college, got married a few weeks later, and dove head-first into my career at Ovitz's new controversial company, Artists Management Group. My career was my priority. I got up at 5:30 A.M., went on a run, and headed to work and stayed there until 11 P.M., sometimes later. After eating a way-too-late dinner and barely able to keep my eyes open, I read scripts and wrote "coverage"—basically reviews of the scripts so that the managers didn't have to waste their time. Essentially, on barely a drop of sleep, I was contributing to the potential life (or death) of a dream—a writer's script. I barely saw, let alone spoke with, my husband. He made me dinner, massaged my feet, and drew my bath: He was wonderful. But I had become a bitch, treating him like I was treated at work—like shit. We grew apart and our marriage quickly disintegrated. My career, though, stayed firmly intact. I was a "trainee," which meant that I wore a suit and delivered mail, but I also made deliveries (like a messenger service) to the homes and offices of actors, producers, directors, and writers, and, lest we forget, got yelled at constantly. I'm not complaining; it's just the way it was. The assistants who generally did the yelling were once in my shoes being yelled at, too. Why? Well, if I happened to be two minutes late, I was wasting their time. Time is money. That's the truth. That's just the way it was in phase 1, the first rung of the industry ladder. It sucked, but, oh well. It was kind of like being hazed, as I got my feet wet and prepared for the big leagues. Can't take the heat? Leave. Go somewhere else. If you want it badly enough, prove it, put up with it, push through it with a smile on your face and fire in your blood until you get to the next rung!

At this point, Ovitz was kind of like my silent mentor. He would acknowledge me in the halls by way of a slight head nod. Sometimes I was called into his office, where he would check on my progress, ask how I was doing, and make sure I was staying on track. "On track" meant that I was doing my job—the mail delivery, etc., plus doing my research, listening in to conversations in the halls and in the offices as I took my time to properly place the packages in the in-boxes, paying attention to alliances, learning about the politics and unsaid policies, reading every deal/contract/memo I could get my hands on, anything to give me more insight, information, a leg up, expand my breadth of knowledge of this industry and its players. It was like a postgraduate class requiring every drop of my energy, attention, and time if I wanted to succeed. It worked for Ovitz when he was in my shoes (yes, he once was a trainee, too).

And so, I followed suit. I read, I studied, I watched, I listened, I ingested the industry into my being—lived, breathed, dreamed it.

After a few months I climbed to the second rung and got "on a desk," which meant that I was promoted from the mailroom to an executive's desk as an assistant. Being an assistant to an executive is not the glamorous job

61

that it may seem to be. What it meant was that I was on call to my boss 24/7. I carried around his phone list, consisting of over twenty 8½ × 11 pages of phone numbers and addresses (this is before smart phones with full contact capacity). But I didn't just carry around this list during work hours; the list went wherever I did—stuffed into each of my purses, in my bedside table, in my car, and in my gym bag. If my boss called in need of a number, whether it was 1:30 P.M. on a Tuesday and I was on my lunch break (which rarely took place anywhere but at my, or rather his, desk), on Easter Sunday, or at 2 A.M. on a Saturday, I had to be able to provide it. If, on a Saturday morning, after having been out partying until 3 A.M., my cell phone rang at 7 A.M. with my boss on the other end of the line saying that he couldn't find his key to the office, but that he wanted to get some work done, it was my job to get up, get dressed, and open the door for him with my spare key—another mandatory accessory that went wherever I did. In the end, for many reasons, the industry that I had for my entire life aspired to one day rule was not for me.

So, were the tear-jerkingly long hours, the hazing, the dues I paid worth it? Well, yes, because I learned about myself, my limits, my interests, needs, and wants when it came to my career. I learned that I didn't want to wear a suit, I wanted to have a more-lax work environment. I didn't want to work for a large corporate-style company. In fact, I wasn't sure that I wanted to work for anyone at all. I learned that I didn't want to wake up so early and get home so late, that I wanted to have both a career *and* a life, and that I wanted to be more creative as opposed to strategic. And so I took what was intended to be a short-term respite at my mom's boutique public relations firm, one with a much more laid-back atmosphere, hours, and dress code. I represented wellness companies like Whole Foods Market, yoga studios, healers, chefs, young entrepreneurs, and authors. Though it was still corporate, I was working with healthy lifestyle companies that I was passionate about promoting and simultaneously learning from. I spent my days communicating with magazine writers, editors, and producers, as well as testing out my clients' offerings—like vegetarian frozen meals or yoga classes. Still, as much as I was learning about the wellness world, I was also learning about myself—my business interests and workplace preferences—and realized that I wanted to be on the other side: I wanted to be a writer. So after two years, having soaked in everything I could about the industry of wellness, I took another leap (and a serious pay cut) and left the PR business to pursue writing. As crazy busy (with hours even more nutty than my first job) as I was trying to forge my own path, I felt like I could finally exhale. I was doing what I loved and what, oddly, didn't feel like work at all. And that's how I knew it was right.

Now, remember back in the "Pick Their Brain Until It Bleeds" section, where I said that Ovitz's first piece of advice was that I should be a writer? He was right. I sold my first book right off the bat, as if I was doing exactly what

I was supposed to be doing. Job opportunities just seemed to appear as my career fell into place. That doesn't mean it was easy. I worked nonstop. *Nonstop.* Sometimes I would wake up totally exhilarated at 4 A.M., so excited to check my e-mail, start conceptualizing ideas, researching and pitching stories, sending e-mails to as many editors whose addresses I could get, and writing—oftentimes for free! Sure, my social life and relationships were at first affected by my long hours. But I was working for myself, paying my "dues" . . . and I didn't mind at all. In fact, I thrived on it. I loved being a workaholic. I felt enlivened by it. It was like the ultimate high! Sure, there were down moments, frustrations, times when I questioned my choices, wondered "what's the point?" felt deflated, and considered giving up and getting a "real" job. But then something great would happen: An editor would e-mail me back, I would get an e-mail from a reader who loved an article I wrote, I would be invited by a publicist to a dinner where I knew lots of big-shot writers would be, or I would write the perfect sentence . . . and suddenly I was right back on track. The great thing about all of the many downers, frustrations, screwups, even being told off by an editor who thought I was too persistent, was that I learned, became stronger, more aware, detail-oriented (which had never been my strong suit), and resilient. Really, what I did was take full advantage of every weakness and failure and turn them into lessons that would help me be a better writer, businesswoman, entrepreneur, even a better person.

The harder you slam a ball into the ground, the higher it bounces back up. A divorce, a breakup, losing a job, or just feeling seriously down can ground you, rough you up a bit, leave calluses on your feet and grit under your fingernails. But more than that, it leaves you wiser and stronger next time. Life is about experiencing opposites, isn't it?

Bottoms Up!

There are at least three ways to take the title of this section:

1. You're starting from the bottom and working your way up.

2. If you want to get through the first few phases of your career—those hazing years when you seriously question if you can stomach another second, except when you think about the end goal—bottoms up, chickadee, you're going to need a stiff drink to survive.

3. You're about to get your butt kicked . . . bottoms up!

Really, it's a combination of all three. If you want to luxuriate in success (unless you have an in, have a lot of luck, or carve your own path), most industries have a pecking order, a corporate ladder, a "brigade system." Take, for example, an executive chef or a restaurateur. It's the brigade system—basically a hierarchy of jobs, an established chain of command, that not only is in place to train and check you on your way up to chefdom, but also to make sure there is organization in the kitchen, so that food can be prepared in a sanitary, flavorful, and timely manner. The brigade includes:

- Dishwasher
- Apprentice
- Line cook
- Sous chef
- Chef de cuisine
- Executive chef

Plus there are several cooks within the "line cook" delineation determining the specific task—pantry, fish, meat, sauté, grill, fry, vegetable, roast, pastry, etc. If you want to become an executive chef, you really have to experience every rung. Why? So that you know how to prep and cook at each station. Why? So that one of your guys doesn't come up to you someday and say, "You don't understand what I am going through." Because you *will* understand it. Because you cooked at that station once, too.

This is not just the way it is when it comes to the restaurant industry. It's the way it is when it comes to most industries. Be diligent! Be proactive! Don't think you're "too good" for a certain rung along the ladder. In order to get up to your ultimate goal of director, CEO, executive chef, president, partner, manager . . . whatever, you might need to get bruised, abused, and mistreated as you work your way up in some career paths, but that's all part of the "fun" of it, the experience of it, the learning curve.

Expert Insight

Candace Nelson

**Founder of Sprinkles Cupcakes, Celebrity Baker,
Host of Food Network's *Cupcake Wars***

How did you transform your passion into a career?

Baking was always a passion of mine and a family tradition. When it came time to turn this passion into my career, I took calculated risks. Opening the world's first-ever cupcake bakery in the height of low-carb mania seemed like an unlikely success story. I made sure to research every angle of the bakery business and know my obstacles. I perfected my recipes over a two-year period, researched real estate for the perfect location, and worked with a designer to create the Sprinkles aesthetic.

Were you afraid to take the leap? What helped you decide to go for it?

Of course there is always the fear of failure. However, before Sprinkles, I operated a custom cake business out of my house and had built up a loyal client list. I knew there were people yearning for freshly baked desserts—a rare find in Los Angeles five years ago! I felt there was an untapped market, and I knew if I didn't give it a try, I would never forgive myself!

What are your top-five tips to other aspiring entrepreneurs who want to turn passion into profit?

1. **Make sure you really know what it is you are passionate about.** Avoid the urge to replicate other people's successes. Your success will grow from your own passion.

2. **Talk to everyone you know in the business!** Talk to business owners, join industry groups, and don't be afraid to ask some dumb questions!

3. **Learn from other people's failures.** Research why business concepts similar to yours did not succeed. Did they overexpand? Choose the wrong location? Fail at providing a differentiated experience?

4. **Be original.** Customers respond to new products and innovative ideas.

5. **Know that you can't do it all alone!** We sold out of cupcakes within a few hours of our first day open. I knew I'd have to hire a larger team, invest in the time to train them properly, and trust they could get the job done so I could focus on growing the business.

Power Panties

Men love power tools. Well, so do we. Ours are just a little different. According to feng shui belief, wearing something red can up your "wow" factor, arouse self-confidence, energetically emit power, and attract luck. But you can't always wear a red outfit, and a red accessory doesn't always match. So . . . wear red underwear. But, more than for reasons of practicality or even for the purpose of feng shui, wearing seriously sexy fire-engine red panties under your basic black suit is like your little secret that takes your confidence to a whole new level.

Don't feel bad if you don't know what feng shui means (by the way, the correct pronunciation is "fung shway"). Ask the average person who tosses the term around what it actually means, and the response will likely be, "Um, doesn't it have to do with organization and spiritual home design?" Well, kind of. In a nutshell, feng shui is a four-thousand-year-old Chinese practice of placement, which originated through the use of math and science, with the intention of creating harmony and balance in the home, office, and living spaces. My first experience with a feng shui consultant was with Hollywood's advisor "to the stars," who wore rather off-putting bright red shoes that didn't seem to go with the rest of the outfit. I assumed it was an oversight. Nope. She explained that, in addition to being the color of passion, wearing red helps attract luck and power in the office place. If a swatch of visible red doesn't befit your outfit, you can actually make the same impact, impressing the pants off your company's conservative board (or whoever you're meeting with), by wearing a pair of red panties, even if they can't see them. No, this has nothing to do with sex appeal. It's all about luck and power. Hey, men get to wear power ties; we get power panties!

How, When & Why to Quit

How do you gracefully quit a job without burning a bridge? The best thing you can do is make sure you've tied up all your loose ends. Delegate unfinished projects, alert clients you're leaving, and help train your replacement until he or she is comfortable, even if that means your "two week's notice" is actually four.

I know, you're thinking *But isn't the point of me quitting that I don't owe* anything *to this crappy, stress-inducing job anymore?* And it's true, you're leaving the job because you have to do what's right for you. But just because you're leaving the job doesn't mean you didn't get anything out of it. You probably have a whole slew of skills you can now add to your résumé, as well as (hopefully) some recommendation letters coming your way. And just as this job has given a lot to you, you should give it something in return (especially if you want that recommendation letter!). Also, you never know when in the future you might need some of those contacts from the job you are leaving.

QuickieChick's Cheat Sheet

1. Don't just *think* it. *Act* on it and you will *become* it.
What is the energy that you want to exude? Who do you "wish" you could present to the world? Think about it. . . . Now write it down, stream-of-conscious style, making a list of who you want to present to this world, what attributes of successful people you want to embody in yourself. Pull those words, images, and attitudes together and start acting and embodying those attributes. Give your new, confident persona a name if it helps. You are her; you just don't know it yet.

2. Making connections from family, friends, and acquaintances is the best way to find a job that you actually like, maybe even a career. Job boards tend to be slim pickings of presifted and passed-over "opportunities."

3. Don't be afraid to ask for . . . anything! A raise, feedback, a meeting with one of your superiors. If you don't ask, somebody else will.

4. There are steps that need to be taken, dots that need to be connected, actions that need to be initiated, lots of them, in order to get from "think"-ing rich to "be"-ing rich. Think it, act on it, it will happen.

5. Prepare to work hard for what you love. If your job has you crying every day, it may be time to spruce up that résumé. . . .

6. Finding a mentor is not only key, it's strategic in most every industry. Not only will you get a full view of a certain lifestyle you'd like to emulate—what will your boss be like? the hours? the projects—but that mentor will get you great connections and maybe even a job, because he or she knows you and trusts your quality of work.

7. At a business meeting or business social event, be sure to: (A) Present a business card. (B) Follow through and follow up with an e-mail or call. Don't wait a week! Do it the next day. (C) If people go out of their way to give you advice, make a call on your behalf, or let you sit and pick their brains for an hour . . . send a thank-you card. They went out of their way for you. Take the time to go out of yours. (D) Use the connections that surround you—friends, parents' friends, friends' parents, etc. (E) Put it out there: Tell people what you do, who you are, who you want to be. Of course . . . without being obnoxious. (F) Listen, contribute, listen, contribute. That's a conversation. It's not just listening or just yammering on and on. (G) Remember: Big shots love to hear themselves speak! In fact, have conversations with big shots and let them speak a fair amount and they will consider it a great conversation (even if you said next to nothing, they won't notice), but they might remember you for being so interested in them!

8. When you meet with someone whose path you want to emulate, "pick their brain until it bleeds." A little extreme? Maybe. But I would rather pick and prod then be paralyzed with intimidation. If you sit down for a meeting with an intimidatingly powerful person, have a goal in mind, hone in on it like a laser, and let that focus force you to forget your fear and instead empower you.

9. Organize your ideas and come up with a concise way to describe what you want to do. You've pushed aside your fear and you're nurturing your network. It's time to start thinking about how to find focus for the idea of your career and direction for pursuing your passion.

10. Sometimes "faking" confidence is the best way to become confidant. Be *That Chick,* channel an ultraconfident, assertive, sexy, clever chick. Even if you feel like you're acting, act away! One day it will just come naturally.

68

Work and Party Balance

HOW TO HAVE A SOCIAL LIFE IN REAL LIFE

FACT: Socializing in unfamiliar social scenes can be stressful, awkward, and embarrassing, leading you to sometimes unknowingly be totally and completely inappropriate. You are no longer in a group of just your peers, and instead are thrown into situations with people of all ages, possible bosses, co-workers, etc. Dress code, attitude, even conversation is different. Learn how to navigate the scene and be seen as interesting and intelligent by following a few steps that I lay out in this chapter.

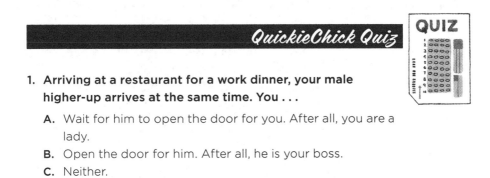

QuickieChick Quiz

1. **Arriving at a restaurant for a work dinner, your male higher-up arrives at the same time. You . . .**

   A. Wait for him to open the door for you. After all, you are a lady.

   B. Open the door for him. After all, he is your boss.

   C. Neither.

   The answer is C. Even if the CEO of *everything* is there ahead of you, and you are just *dying* to show your enthusiasm by opening the door for him, whomever gets to the door first should open it. Dining with coworkers, and even bosses, is gender neutral.

2. **When meeting your boyfriend's parents you . . .**

   A. Ask to see all their photo albums, home videos, etc. You want to collect as much info on your new guy as you can. Plus a little ass-kissing isn't bad either.

B. Bring up political issues. Your guy has informed you that his parents are majorly into politics, and you want to show them that you are knowledgeable, up on current events, and a good conversationalist.

C. Wait for them to ask you questions. Then answer without revealing too much. You don't want to offend, say something inappropriate, or cross any lines.

Honestly, none of the above! Don't look like you're trying to move into your guy's life too quickly by nosing around his family heirlooms. Bringing up political issues is only going to have them judging you before they even know the *real* you. And if you just sit there silently, they may think you came from a home where the motto was "a good child is one who is unseen and unheard." Talk to them! Be yourself. Bring up their favorite hobbies or trips you know they've gone on. This isn't an interview; it's a time to get to know each other.

3. **At a work interview, you are asked what your experience is with a certain computer program.**

True or False: You should tell them all about the experience you've had with that program, a funny story that happened with it once, how you saved your last employer's butt while using it, and then some. If you actually have never worked with that program, lie and say you know it inside and out.

False. The truth is, nobody likes to listen for THAT long, and you'll sound like you're bragging if you go on and on. Give them sufficient information so that they feel confident in your skills, but don't drag it on. If, on the other hand, you've never worked with it, don't lie. Getting caught in that lie could be very bad for their ability to trust and depend on you. Instead say that you are a fast learner and you have a close friend who is very savvy with it and you will be sure to call them when you get home and get a lesson on the ins and outs.

4. **At an after-work party . . .**

Y   N   You arrive fashionably late. You don't want to get there early and stand awkwardly with people you don't know! If you're late, they will already be drunk and no one will notice you anyway.

Y   N   You don't know what to say while standing in a group? You tell a cute story about your pet or that night last week when you were so drunk you accidentally went home with some guy you didn't know. Hey, whatever gets a laugh or an "ahh" response.

N   Y   You see your boss's wife standing alone, looking bored. You go strike up a conversation with her—nothing invasive, just trying to be nice.

A coworker you are attracted to will be there. You wear a dress that shows off your figure nicely and flirt like crazy. You're not "technically" at work. . . .

If most of your answers were in column 1, you *need* this chapter! If most of your answers were in column 2, you may as well read it, too. You could learn something, or at least solidify what you already seemingly know.

To help you figure out what and what not to say, do, and wear, I contacted etiquette expert Jacqueline Whitmore, who is paid serious bucks to coif, train, smooth, and update even the most socially awkward and inappropriate. Her insights are woven throughout this chapter, so pay attention!

I love Jacqueline's definition of etiquette: "strength under control." I mean, with that definition, why *wouldn't* you want to embody it? You can still:

- Have a sense of humor

- Have fun

- Enjoy yourself or others

- Be genuine and sincere and do what is comfortable for you

- Stay true to your morals . . . and others will respect you.

71

Expert Insight

Jacqueline Whitmore

Etiquette 101: The Basics

Dining with Co-Workers

- Eat first, talk business later. It's wise to make small talk and share a few stories with your dining partner before talking about business.

- Dining with co-workers is a gender-neutral event. It is not necessary for a man to pull out a woman's chair. Today, whoever reaches the door first should open it for the other person. Also, whoever does the inviting pays for the bill, regardless of gender.

- If you drop a piece of silverware on the floor while having dinner in a restaurant, leave it and ask the server for another.

- Don't put your handbag, keys, notebook, or cell phone on the table.

- Don't apply lipstick or touch your hair at the table.

- Pass the salt and pepper shakers together, even if someone asks you to pass one or the other.

- The person you are sitting with takes priority over any cell phone calls or text messages. If you are anticipating a very important call, notify the person you are with ahead of time.

- Steer clear of difficult-to-eat foods, foods that easily get caught in your teeth, and foods that leave you with bad breath.

- Don't overindulge in alcohol. One or two glasses of wine should be your limit. If no one else is drinking, you shouldn't either. And *never* drink alcohol on a job interview!

Meeting the Friends/Parents of Your New Guy

- Be sincere and take the time to get to know them. It may take three or four visits before you feel comfortable. Go in with an open mind and know that you may not agree with everything they say or do and vice versa.

- Try to find out as much as you can about your new beau's friends or parents ahead of time. Have a few conversation starters in your head, just in case there is a lull in conversation.

- Don't go overboard trying to impress them. Family and friends want to see who you are naturally.

- Keep the conversation light. Steer clear of controversial topics like politics, religion, etc.

- Don't expect to be best friends overnight.

- Let them know how much you enjoyed meeting them.

- Take the time to set up another meeting.

- Send a note thanking them if they paid for dinner.

Job Interview

An interview is an occasion to represent yourself and make a lasting first impression. However, being a little nervous is natural. Here are some interview strategies that will make you appear more polished and prepared:

Do your homework. Find out as much as you can about the company and the person interviewing you. Go to the company's Web site and read the "newsroom" page and read press releases, PR activities, facts and figures, and company awards. Find out about the company's history, mission statement, and values. Don't be afraid to call someone who works for the company (like a receptionist) and ask her questions about her experience with the company. Know exactly what the job position entails and how you can contribute to the position. Be prepared to talk about your accomplishments, career goals, and volunteer and extracurricular activities. Try to know as much about the company as the person who is interviewing you.

Know when to talk and when to listen. During an interview, try to limit your responses to one minute or less. The worst thing you can do is keep talking until the interviewer cuts you off. Remember, there's power in the pause. When you're asked a question, pause briefly before answering it. This creates anticipation and gives you time to think about what you're going to say next. Ask the interviewer questions about what he/she likes about the company and his/her job.

Be aware of body language. If you see the interviewer starting to gaze away, tap a foot, fidget with a pen, or, worse, check his BlackBerry, these signs may indicate that you no longer have his attention. At that point, stop rambling.

Brag modestly. An interview is your time to shine and talk about your accomplishments. Keep in mind that others will be sharing their accomplishments, too. Talk about what you bring to the table, your transferable skills and how you can benefit the company.

Accentuate the positive. Talk about what you can do instead of what you can't do. A statement such as "To be honest, I've never been in charge of managing an entire division" is a negative response, not to mention it projects insecurity and self-doubt. Instead, you might say, "I'm excited for the new challenge of managing this division. I believe that my fresh perspective will breathe new life and enthusiasm into the group."

Keep it professional. Avoid showing too much skin or wearing too much makeup or perfume. In more conservative industries like law and accounting, neutral, tailored suits are best. Colors like navy blue, dark gray, or black are more appropriate. And get a professional e-mail address. Addresses containing names like Honey Bunny, Princess, or Master Blaster are immature and may sabotage your chances of getting a second interview. Make sure your shoes are shined and in good condition.

Be yourself. Stay true to your hobbies, interests, and morals. You will come across as insincere if you start talking about a topic that you know nothing about. And if you don't know the answer to a question, tell the interviewer that you will find out. Thank the interviewer for his/her time and follow up with a thank-you e-mail within twenty-four hours.

The Rich, Powerful & Wise: How to Talk to Them Without Them Realizing You're Not One of Them

Do you always shy away from the conversation, fearing that you're not good enough, interesting enough, or important enough to chime in? Then you never will be. The fact is that regardless of your age, bank account, or status, your ideas and experiences matter. No, I am definitely not saying that you need to assert yourself wherever you can, adding your two cents to any and all conversations that you happen to know a thing or two about. Being obnoxiously opinionated is totally different from contributing your thoughts. So how do you make yourself known without being perceived as annoying?

If you're younger: Ask someone who is older or more successful for his/her opinion or advice. In general, people love giving advice and feeling helpful. Worst-case scenario? They say no. No big deal. Not sure who to ask? An employee who has been there longer, your mentor, a friend in the same line of work at a different company, even your boss.

If your goal is to be on the same level: Do you share any commonality with the person? Sports, outdoor activities, food faves, vacation spots, hometown. Your bonding glue doesn't have to be about business!

DON'T FORGET

Always Give a Proper Handshake.

That doesn't mean to squeeze the life out of the other's hand. This is not a strength contest. But offer up a firm shake. Practice with a friend if you want (it helps). Ask how he/she perceives your shake—honestly! Remember that if you rotate the other's hand under yours so that the top of your hand is facing the ceiling, that's a sign of aggressive dominance. A limp fish handshake equals weakness. I know, there are many fine lines between meek and aggressive when it comes to the handshake, which is why I suggest to practice. That's how I learned.

Eye Contact Is Essential.

Good eye contact projects confidence. Don't do one of those lame handshakes in which you reach out your hand to shake and as soon as you touch skin you look away. It reads like you are looking for someone more impor-

You Are *Very* Interesting!

Tools

Think of amazing trips you've gone on, unique restaurants/stores you've visited, volunteer programs you've done etc . . .

_____

_____

Pick out the most interesting events, conversations, people, components—the highlights from each experience.

_____

_____

What was your takeaway, what did you learn, how have you grown from those experiences?

_____

_____

Frame those experiences in a story.

_____

_____

Starter Sentence

I actually *do* have interesting things to bring to the table, because I have learned/done/seen/experienced . . .

_____

_____ .

tant to say hi to. Either that or you are embarrassed to be shaking the person's hand. Regardless, it's bad, bad, bad. And rude. Now, the opposite of looking away is looking stalkerlike and freakishly at the person, making it seem like you are actually attempting to look through them instead of at them. Scary. Also not OK. Smile, make eye contact. Be sincere, even if you have to fake sincerity. Eye contact, or a lack thereof, is one of those things that will be remembered after the encounter—for better or worse.

Be Attentive & Engaging.

Being attentive—such as through eye contact—builds credibility and trust. But beyond looking at the person you are talking to, participate in the conversation. *Conversation is give and take.* I say something, you respond. You say something, I respond. I'm not being sarcastic! You have no idea how many people have no idea how rude they are being by either dominating or seemingly ignoring the conversation. It's not a pissing match of who has the better story, who can be more interesting, who has, does, is better, bigger, more. Engage in the conversation. How? Listen to what the others say. Respond to what they say by asking a question or contributing your own thoughts to theirs; share personal stories. *Don't* listen to what they say, all the while having something that you want to make sure you get to say, which causes you to be distracted from what they are saying, forcing you to blurt out your point as soon as they finish theirs. The problem with that? You aren't engaging. You should not be speaking to hear yourself speak. The speaker can tell if you are paying attention or if you're just nodding your head and saying, "That's interesting." Engaging doesn't mean that you can repeat everything I just said. Engaging means that you listen, process the content, think, then contribute, in the form of a statement, question, remark, or similar scenario.

Make Them Feel Interesting.

Another trick? *Shine the spotlight on the other person and less on yourself.* Yes, let them shine! People want to feel interesting. If you make them feel that way, they will then walk away thinking that the conversation was, in fact, very interesting. Even if you were bored to death.

Be Aware of Body Language.

More than what and how much you say, keep in mind that a picture can be worth a thousand words. Same goes for your body language.

- Watch your body language and don't engage in nervous gestures like playing with your jewelry or hair while talking to someone else.

- Don't tilt your head excessively. It's a submissive pose. Keep your head straight up.

- Avoid filler words like *uh, like, you know.*

- Avoid girlish giggling. This signals a lack of authority.

- Look the other person directly in the eye.

Expert Insight

Jacqueline Whitmore

2 Most Common Etiquette Mistakes Chicks Make at Work

1. **Burning bridges.** The potential for arguments and disagreements is always going to be a part of doing business with others. However, how you handle a situation will reveal your character. When you have

a conflict, confront the person face-to-face, if possible, so you can see the other person's body language. Don't talk about people behind their backs. People love to gossip so your words may get back to the person. Remember the saying, "If you can't say anything nice, don't say anything at all." Never send a nasty e-mail. Once you e-mail something, it can be forwarded or saved and it may be held against you. You may think you may never see or need this person again, but don't count on it. Keep in mind that you might someday need this person for a job referral or for networking purposes. Think twice before you burn a bridge; make it a last resort!

2. **Neglecting to admit your mistakes.** If you screw up, admit it. And do it sooner rather than later. Remember that there is a great power in saying, "I'm sorry," if you are in the wrong. Most people will try to cover up or deny their mistakes. Admitting your fault puts you one step closer to dealing with it and can often be the first step toward a successful turnaround. At the least, it shows that you're someone with integrity and courage, even in the face of disastrous consequences. By taking full responsibility for your mistakes and acting appropriately, you'll have set yourself on a path to failing successfully—to learning what there is to learn and moving forward with grace and dignity.

Get Carded

Business cards show that you are serious. They are also much easier (not to mention insanely more professional) to whip out when someone says, "We should exchange information." Digging into your purse for a pen, followed by a scrap of gum wrapper to write your phone number or e-mail address on . . . um, tacky. Even the "I'll just type it into my cell phone" alternative— not the best. Your business card doesn't have to be fancy and it doesn't have to define your profession. If you're an aspiring writer, actor, artist, activist, entrepreneur, designer, etc.—put that. Don't want to be defined by your career? Fine. Put nothing but your name and contact info, or get creative and define yourself some other way. Just remember that you might be handing this out to another professional, potential boss, potential date, potential friend, potential landlord. Be appropriate.

Another benefit of business cards: They help you to really think about how you present yourself and how you want to be perceived.

So what should you include on your business cards?

Necessary

- Name

- Contact info—either e-mail or phone or both.

Optional

- Mailing address (not a good idea to put your home address. I have a UPS box address where all of my mail goes—all of it).

- Profession

- Logo

- Quote or your personal or professional "tagline" (e.g., Nike's "Just Do It" or QuickieChick's "Quickie Tips for Fast-Paced Chicks")

- Image (a drawing or even a photo, if appropriate)

Never Reveal on Facebook . . .

Think about Facebook as the visual résumé of your life—a breakdown of who you really are, what your interests honestly include, and how you conduct yourself in social situations. It is filled with picture-proven facts of your life, unedited commentary from friends on your "wall," and your real interests and extracurricular activities. Now think: Do you want your potential future boss to stumble upon that page and discover the real you, beyond your proofread and professionally structured résumé?

Chances are you are one of millions of social media addicts recording your thoughts, sharing your photos, listing your fave songs and TV shows, and revealing all sorts of info about who you are (or at least who you want to be perceived to be) to all of your "friends," if not anyone who happens to accidentally stumble onto your page. It may seem to be all fun and games, but the fact is that there is some information you really shouldn't be exposing to just anyone—particularly parents, potential suitors, bosses and co-workers, and, worst case, criminals.

Before I even go over the list of "never reveals," let me say one thing loud and clear: Privacy Settings!

Privacy Settings

If you have personal things that you want to share with friends, that maybe you don't want potential employers, your health insurance company (yes, some of them are catching on and checking before making a decision about whether or not to insure you), your parents, potential boyfriends, or unknown (or even known) sickos, make sure you enable the setting that allows friends only to access it. Once you opt for that option, you are responsible for only "friending" people whom you truly trust, people whom you know—for sure—are trustworthy with that information.

7 THINGS NOT TO SHARE ON FACEBOOK

1. **Drunk photos.** Sure, sharing a few funny moments out with friends is normal. But when photo after photo is of you drunk, partying, being vulgar, or—worse—doing drugs, you are painting a picture of who you are to the world. I know, but you're only like that on "special occasions," and those happen to be the same times when the camera comes out to document the festivities. Fine. Just choose your pics wisely. Maybe make a point to also document days when you're out doing cultural, studious, interesting, and different activities. *Who cares?* You will when you don't get a job because your potential boss is savvy enough to go online and do a quick Google search on you, only to discover what appears to be your hard-core partying ways. If you still want to upload your every binge-fest online, fine. Just set your privacy settings to only allow friends to view those photos. Then don't accept just anyone to be a friend.

2. **Your birth date.** If you want to share your birthday—the month and day of your birth—so that you can experience the pleasure of being inundated by wishes, I totally understand and agree. Facebook truly does make birthdays exciting! *However,* you should *not* reveal the year of your birth. Make sure to select "only show month and day in my profile." It's a bit of information that identity thieves need to steal your financial info and potentially wreak havoc on your credit and life. No, it's not a hoax; this stuff really happens.

3. **Your city of birth.** It's another item that identity thieves need to take forced ownership of your life, accessing bank information, bank account codes, etc. How? A study done by Carnegie Mellon researchers showed that people often somehow incorporate their date and place of birth, as well as their social security number, in codes, passwords, and lock combinations.

4. **Vacation plans.** When you post "About to leave for the airport for Mexico!" on your Facebook wall or Twitter page, you are advertising that you won't be home, that you are leaving a house empty, that you will have no idea what's going on back home for an entire week—an ideal opportunity for a burglar to break in and even stay awhile! Want to show off about your fab vaca? Who doesn't? Just do it when you return by posting pics. After all, the pics will give you much more bragging power than a measly written post.

5. **Home address.** If I really need to elaborate on this one, ummm . . . You do not, under any circumstances, even if the page is set for the

viewing pleasure of friends *only,* publish your home address. Why? Because some nonfriends could accidentally slip through the cracks, and you really don't want people who you don't know knowing where you live. If you have a "mailing address" or P.O. box that's not the address at which you actually live, fine, publicize that. But not your home. Too many crazies out there. You never know. . . .

6. **Confessions.** You hate your job; your parent's are awful people; you (or even your friend or boyfriend) stole, cheated, did drugs, broke the law, etc. I know, it feels good to off-load that stuff sometimes . . . but *not* on Facebook! That's what diaries and best friends are for. Don't publicly admit that stuff or—worse—go on and on in a confession-style monologue admitting, detailing, and providing from the horse's mouth proof of your feelings and exploits. Why? You could get fired, dumped, or it could simply be used against you. It has happened before. Don't let it happen to you.

7. **Password clues.** You know how your online banking, credit cards, and other password protectors ask certain questions, to which you supply specific answers that will give you access to your accounts in case you forget your password? E.g., What's your mom's maiden name? What was your first elementary school? What was your first pet's name? Who was the maid of honor at your wedding? Don't reveal the answers to those questions on your Facebook page . . . for obvious reasons.

Expert Insight

Jacqueline Whitmore

5 Facebook Etiquette Tips

So what if your co-worker wants to add you as a friend? Should you mix your professional life with your personal life? With Facebook having such a large role in the business arena these days, it brings about a whole new set of social networking dos and don'ts. Here are a few to consider:

1. **Don't be offended if someone does not respond to a friend request.** A lot of people try to limit their Facebook friends to only those in their personal life. Also, some people may only use Facebook for specific purposes, like finding local events in the area or staying in touch with long-distance friends and relatives. If you'd rather not add a boss or co-worker to your friends list, offer to add them to your LinkedIn list instead.

2. **Customize your privacy settings.** As a Facebook user, you can tailor your privacy settings for persons on your friends list. Therefore, if you don't want your boss to see pictures of you outside of the work setting or you don't want an old flame to see who you are dating, you can block that information from them.

3. **Be careful what you post on Facebook.** You should only include information on your profile that you wouldn't mind seeing on the front page of a newspaper. Once something is posted and written in words, people can save it or send it to others over the Internet. Therefore, avoid posting rants about your boss or racy photos of yourself or others.

4. **Remove a friend as a last resort.** Don't be surprised if some people get offended and/or hurt when they notice that they're missing from your friends list. Try to increase your privacy settings before eliminating a person completely, especially if you share common friends or if you run the risk of running into each other in public.

5. **People will form their opinions and judgments about you from the information on your profile.** While everyone understands that you have a personal life (and a sense of humor), what may be funny on a Saturday night may not be appropriate to display to your co-workers who may have a different perception of you at work.

After-Work-Party Protocol— How to Dress, What to Say & How to Act

Want to connect with the boss outside of work or create alliances with co-workers on your off time? Work parties give you that access in a more personal, less formal environment. They are not only a good idea to attend, they are pretty much essential. Consider them part of the job. Why? The more work functions you make it to, the more opportunities you will have to get some face time with the people who matter, showing them that you are a team player and willing to dedicate not only your day but your off-hours to the company. Think your attendance will go unnoticed? Think again. Why? Just like every other party thrower, your boss also has insecurities that no one will show up to his/her party (despite the fact that he/she pretty much pays everyone to be there).

WHAT IF YOU KNOW NO ONE?

Whatever you do . . . don't be Wendy Wallflower. We've all been there. You go to a party or networking event and you know no one. As you scan the room for a familiar face, your mind scrambling for something, anything to talk about to whomever also happens to be standing completely alone looking desperate for a "hello," your nerves set in and you consider slowly backing up, placing yourself out of sight against the wall. Stop that insecurity-driven response right now! If you're camouflaged with the wall, no one is going to come up and talk to you, which will only make your problem worse, not better!

THINGS TO CONSIDER BEFORE YOU GO

- **Leave the shop talk at the office.**

- **Don't talk about office gossip, sex, or politics.**

- **Go to the party with a genuine interest** in wanting to know more about your boss and co-workers on a more personal level. Jacqueline Whitmore suggests that you find out who will be in attendance and then decide whom you'd like to meet the most. Learn as much as you can about those people ahead of time. Google them. Facebook (but *don't friend-request*) them. You'll be surprised by how much you find out by searching for people on the Internet. Once you find a few interesting facts about them, think about whether you have anything in common, like if they have traveled to places that you have always wanted to go, if they belong to food clubs and you consider yourself to be a "foodie," or if you went to the same college. Keep these insights in mind . . . literally. Inside your head. Don't say, "I saw on Facebook that you traveled to Fiji last month . . . "; that seems stalker-ish. Just take a mental note of their general interests and allow that insight to help direct the flow of conversation.

- **Read the newspaper, watch the news, listen to the radio, or skim the afternoon's headlines** online to brush up on the current events for your own opinions, but realize that not everyone will necessarily share it. Even if you are passionate about a point of view, you don't need to push or even share that passion in public. Knowledge and understanding of the topic are enough.

- **Wear an interesting conversation piece,** such as a colorful pin, a vintage necklace, or a fabulous pair of shoes.

- **To make the conversation flow more smoothly, think ahead about commonalities** between you and your co-workers. Talk about what interests your boss or co-workers (your Facebook/Google search will help give you access to that information). No insight online? Think of the items that your boss and co-workers have in their offices. Usually people display items that reflect their family, hobbies,

and other interests. Do a little research on these hobbies so you can take part in the conversation. Find out if anyone in your office has recently won any awards, had an article published, just competed in a marathon/triathlon, or just returned from an exotic vacation. Most people also like talking about their pets or their children.

MEN NOTICE HANDS; WOMEN NOTICE SHOES

Appearance speaks louder than words. A nice appearance enhances your personal brand and your overall package, as well as pays big dividends. In general, it is always best to look classy and professional. Most women notice shoes, and most men notice hands and feet. Keep hands, feet, and shoes clean, polished, and in good condition. When in doubt, don't wear it.

LISTEN MORE, TALK LESS

Still not sure what commonality you have with any of your colleagues that could possibly lead to an engaging conversation? Practice active listening. Ask open-ended questions, such as "What was it about your profession that initially intrigued you to pursue it?" or "Aside from work, what do you like to do on the weekend?" with the purpose of gathering more information and maybe finally finding common ground. When the information is being revealed, *listen.* Even if what they are saying is of zero interest to you. Don't zone out. Pretend you will tested on what they are saying. People love talking about themselves. In fact, I've had conversations with people whom I just met, and 95 percent of the conversation consists of them yapping on and on about themselves, their interests, their beliefs, vacations, etc., etc. Then I hear through the grapevine that that person liked me so much and so enjoyed our conversation. Remember: Listen more, talk less. If your co-worker's spouse, partner, or significant other is in attendance, make sure to include him/her in the conversation. Why? Because as soon as they get in the car to drive home, or even as soon as you walk away, that significant other will likely voice an opinion about you.

Notice someone sitting alone? You know how awful that feels! Take a minute to go over there and say "hello." Introduce yourself, engage in small talk by talking about the obvious—the food, the music, or decorations.

Expert Insight

Jacqueline Whitmore

Top 5 After-Work-Party Etiquette Rules

1. **Dress professionally.** The main mistake women make at work parties is dressing too sexy. Always keep an air of professionalism in mind when you choose your outfit. A work party is an extension of the office, and this is still a business event, and how you dress reflects your character. Wear something a bit more festive than you might wear to work, but keep it more understated than what you would wear to a nightclub or sports bar. Wearing an overly provocative outfit to a corporate event can even cost you a promotion. You don't want to be labeled as the woman who dressed too sexy or flashy. Save the low-cut, tight, and sparkly dress for an occasion when your co-workers won't be in attendance.

2. **Don't overindulge.** A work party is not the place to take advantage of the free beer or play drinking games, dance on the tables, or see how fast you can get a buzz. After all, you don't want to be the topic of conversation at the watercooler on Monday morning, do you? Your co-workers probably have minds like elephants and will not easily forget what you said or did while you were under the influence. If you see someone who isn't imbibing alcohol, don't call attention to this person's choice of beverage. Doing so will not win you any popularity contests. Drinking is a personal choice, and many people abstain for health or dietary reasons. Also, eat a little something before the event so you don't nosh on too many high-calorie appetizers or drink on an empty stomach. Your goal should be to network, not gorge yourself.

3. **Avoid gossip or off-color jokes.** Don't be surprised if you feel more relaxed and let your guard down at an office party, especially if you decide to drink alcohol. Be mindful of the jokes you tell and the comments you make. What you might think is funny may be offensive to someone else. Think before you speak, because once you

84

say something you can't take it back. Remember the saying, "Loose lips sink ships."

4. **Keep things light and fun.** If there's some gloom and doom in your office as of late (downsizing, bonus cuts, or talk of a takeover), try to banish the dark clouds for the duration of the party with a sunny attitude. It may be tough for co-workers to stay away from these topics, because that's what they hear all day long, but talking about it at a party can really put a damper on everybody's mood. You don't want to be labeled "Debbie Downer," so focus on positive events and the spirit of the season to avoid ruining the party for your colleagues.

5. **Get to know your boss and your boss's boss.** Use the office party as an opportunity to rub elbows with executives at your company with whom you don't usually interact. You can't always get close to senior executives or partners at the office, because they're so busy or inaccessible, but in a social environment, they're accessible and open to small talk. This is a great opportunity to share your ideas and gain exposure. Shake her hand, introduce yourself, and ask about her hobbies or interests, sports or volunteer activities. Smile and act relaxed. Read the person's body language. If the boss is not interested in idle chitchat, thank her for her time and move on. How you behave is more important than what you say. Blabbering for the sake of blabbering signals lack of self-awareness. Never forget that senior leaders are people first; executives second. Small talk can have a big impact on your career.

85

Socializing Outside of School: Different/Same, Better/Worse?

Samantha, 24, Web site Designer: "It's totally different. At school, there were three neighborhood bars, so if you'd go to one, you were bound to know at least 40 percent of its patrons, and well. Now that I'm in a big city, it's more upscale, and I rarely run into people I know. Usually, I talk exclusively with the people I came with. At bars with friends, I feel that people don't talk to you unless they see you as sexual prey. It gets frustrating. At work-related networking events, I feel safer and have a better idea of what to do. For networking or work events, I first try to glam down. I'll leave my highest heels or short dresses home. I also try to take advantage of these situations by doing research on attendees beforehand so I know what to say and ask before I strike up a conversation. I usually have a goal for the evening (meet two new contacts; introduce myself to that hotshot producer) and feel less threatened."

SHOULD I BRING A GIFT—YES OR NO?

Whenever you are invited to someone's house for a party, you should bring a host/hostess gift to show your appreciation for the hospitality. Your gift does not have to be elaborate or expensive. Hostess gifts that are acceptable include flowers in a vase, picture frames, treats for pets, coffee-table books, chocolates, coffee, tea, or hot chocolate. If you decide to bring wine or something edible, the hostess is not required to open it during the party. Simply say, "This is for you to enjoy on a special occasion." If you want to make the gift more personal, find out your boss or co-worker's interests and hobbies. Steer clear of expensive gifts, gag gifts, perfume, or clothing, as they can give the wrong impression. Always follow up with a handwritten thank-you note or phone call after the event to thank the host for his/her hospitality.

Throwing a Cocktail Party (Not a Kegger) Without Breaking the Bank

You aren't in college anymore. Kegs are no longer the main (if not only) ingredient when it comes to throwing a party. In fact, remove the keg from the picture altogether. You've been there, done that. Move on.

Socializing Outside of School: Different/Same, Better/Worse?

Molly, 22, Program Coordinator for an Animal-Rights-Awareness Nonprofit: "You have to try really hard to make social situations happen. You are no longer going to class every day or constantly in a bubble of people your age. On college campuses, especially small to midsize ones, you can usually assume that you have some things in common with your fellow students, since you are at the same school. You probably even know the same people. In the outside world, with all different types and ages of people, this is not the case. You are starting from scratch in a way you never did when you were in college. It helps to do things outside of work (especially if you aren't meeting many people at work)."

How to Get Out There and Be Social. "Most cities have community activities, and not all of them are "for singles" type events that make you feel awkward and desperate. Good examples are signing up for a night class with a local university's extension program (though these can be expensive), taking an art class, joining a sports team . . . anything, depending on your interests. Meetup.com is also a good option for meeting people who like to do the same things you do."

The new postgrad party: a cocktail party. To clarify, Jes Gordon—celebrity event planner and expert on Bravo's *Rocco's Dinner Party* and author of *Party Like a Rock Star*—gave her two cents on how to save yours. But first, you've got to know the difference between a kegger and a cocktail shindig. "When I think of a kegger, I think of young kids rolling the keg unbeknownst to their parents through the garage and worrying about the deposit they just left at the liquor store," says Jes. Sound familiar? Are you cringing right now? I am. Standing in line, a big red plastic cup in hand, waiting to reach the tap of just-better-than-skunky beer that serves one purpose and one purpose only—getting drunk.

Just because you're throwing a party where real drinks are served doesn't mean it has to be pretentious, expensive, and void of fun. Jes suggests:

Beer cocktails. Create an old-school shandy that is simply beer and lemon/lime soda, or even take an old favorite cocktail, such as a Tom Collins, and turn it into a Cerveza Collins just by adding light beer!

Mimosas. You don't have to offer a full bar just because it's a cocktail party. Your friends are coming to your place to hang out and, sure, drink. That doesn't mean you have to have their favorite drinks at the ready, just like you wouldn't throw a dinner party and then make each guest's favorite dish. No, everyone eats the same thing. You want something else, go somewhere else. A cocktail party can consist of one specialty/theme drink. An idea: different flavored mimosas. Ingredients: champagne paired with ten different kinds of juices that your guests can mix with the champagne. If it's a small event and you have enough champagne glasses to go around—great. You can also buy inexpensive glasses at discount stores, and afterward put them away in your "party" cabinet. If not, opt for skinny clear-plastic cups. Part of the fun is being able to see all of the different color juices mixed with the champagne: They can be conversation starters.

FLAIR, FLASH, & FLOWERS

Just because you like beer or you're serving champagne in a plastic cup doesn't mean the decor and the ambience need to go to the junkyard. Ambience can transform a below-average evening into a night to remember. A few ideas:

87

- **Lights.** Add creative lighting, like lots of candles or twinkly lights (yes even hung inside)

- **Fun things.** Hang fun things from the ceiling, like flowers hung upside down by the stems (daisies are perfect), stars made from aluminum foil, or paper lanterns.

- **Flair.** Cover your furniture with festive fabrics or sarongs, and add colorful throw pillows—both on the furniture and on the floor to add comfortable seating.

- **Fresh.** Pick fresh flowers and herbs from your backyard and arrange them simply in vases, teapots, or just Mason jars.

The point is to try. Yes, *put in some effort,* but without being intimidating, which leads to making guests feel uptight. Create an atmosphere that's comfortable, fun, and that promotes conversation and laughter. Don't try to show off in a way that is not true to you. Make sure the ambience reflects your attitude, and the people around you will feel safe enough to have an awesome time.

7 TIPS TO THROWING A "ROCK STAR" PARTY ON A *SERIOUS* BUDGET

You would love to throw *the* party of the year. The one that everybody talks about for weeks and is intimidated by when attempting to throw their own soiree. Problem is: You can't afford it. That's why I asked my (and now your) event planner extraordinaire, Jes Gordon. Here are some of her ideas:

1. **Go disposable.** Use good-quality disposable products rather than renting or buying high-end dinnerware.

2. **Find the one.** For decorating your event, choose one thing that you adore, and just go with that, so if it's candles, just do masses of candles, which is even better because you can buy those in bulk.

3. **Look beneath the top shelf.** For alcohol, you don't always need to buy the top of the line, e.g., get prosecco instead of champagne, or potato vodka instead of a sexier more-famous brand.

4. **Buy in bulk.** Go to a place like Costco or Sam's and embrace those Hormel Party Trays or jars of peanuts that are taller than you. Just display them with your own serving plates, trays, and bowls so it will be your own little secret!

5. **Choose venues that are party-ready.** Don't go to some worn-down castle that needs you to build walls and bathrooms and a kitchen in order to throw a party there.

6. **Go indoors.** The cost of outdoor parties can get out of hand, especially if the weather goes awry. All of a sudden you may need tenting, flooring, heating or air, and bathrooms.

7. **Use in-house items when renting a venue.** If they already have in-house linens or furniture, use theirs and don't rent from other companies; this will drive up your budget considerably.

How to Be a Fabulous, Fun Hostess—Minus the Stress

From the "no one is going to show up to my party" fear, to "are things going to be stolen?" anxiety, and—ugh—postparty clean up . . . throwing a party can sometimes be more stressful than it's worth. So how do you throw a party without the stress and mess? It's easy. As long as you follow Jes's awesome-yet-simple party-throwing tips!

Give yourself a budget, but be sure to not only put your cash into decor and food but possibly into hiring some supportive event staff, such as a bartender or someone to help you clean up in the kitchen! This will make your life über-easy and free you up to be a phenomenal hostess!

Do what you know and what you do well! Don't try to cook Indian food if you never have before, for your first time being a hostess!

Dress comfortably but show yourself off as the hostess. If you're going to try to pull off those seven-inch heels while hosting an event, you are either stupid or a gladiator from Roman times. Dress so you feel like a rock star, but be comfortable and who you are normally; just raise the bar a bit. If you're into the all-black look, go ahead and rock out a hot-pink shoe or an awesome feather in your hair to let your guests know that you are running the show!

Make things simple on yourself. Pre-prepare any food or drinks. You can freeze food items and defrost them when it's party time, and premix some cocktails, too. Do as much as you can beforehand so you can relax and be with your friends once the party starts.

Check out your surroundings and make sure your environment is party-ready. If you've had a running toilet, fix it, because you know that puppy will choose to break during your event. If you have major valuables that you don't want anyone to steal or mess up, by all means hide them!

Create "no enter zones" in your home. Just because you invited folks over doesn't mean that they are welcome to look in your underwear drawer!

89

If you are having an outdoor event, be sure to *turn off your sprinkler* system a few days before your event! Your ground will be a mud bath if you don't. Make sure you have proper bug repellents and outdoor lighting.

Make the invitation process easy! Go electronic, or if you go with paper, make sure you keep track of your RSVPs with an Excel spreadsheet, constantly updating it. It's very important to know who is coming to your party, because it will affect your supply level. And, yes, it's OK to do an electronic invite for a cocktail gathering.

When pouring the libations, do small pours. If your guests are going to be there for a while, make sure the alcohol flows but doesn't flood! A bottle of wine should serve at least four to six guests, and cocktails should be mixed with quick shots of alcohol, not a lingering, long-lasting shot! Trust me, you will be happy you did this!

Don't let guests leave your party drunk! Whether you believe this or not, you are legally liable for anyone who leaves your event wasted and winds up in a car crash. Be sure to have a trustworthy taxicab service on hand.

And last, but most essential: Have fun! Why go through all this s★★t if you aren't going to have a good time?

CONVERSATION STARTERS

Your "Specialty Drink"

A specialty drink is always a convo starter, especially if you name it something fun that everyone will understand. This is where you need to get clever while still being group appropriate. Something that will make people laugh, not stir up anger. Maybe it's letters representing a saying or phrase, challenging guests to try to guess the acronym.

Introductions with Purpose

Of the many jobs you have as host, one of them is to make introductions. But don't just say, "Julia, this is Sarah . . . " then walk away. The result? Julia and Sarah might stand there and stare at each other for a minute, then walk away with only a "Nice to meet you." Make introductions with purpose. For example: "Julia, this is Sarah. I know you've always wanted to skydive, and Sarah has actually done it over ten times!" Again, think positive! Your conversation starter *shouldn't* be, "Julia, this is Sarah. She is also a struggling writer but still living with her parents." Another bad one: "Julia, this is Sarah. She actually used to date your boyfriend Chris—small world!" and then you walk away. Maybe there is a real, concrete reason why Julia and Sarah should know each other, but you need to reveal it!

Introductions with Purpose-Potential:

Common interests, raised in the same state/city, similar or complementary careers, close friends in common.

Stay Awhile

Once you make the intro, you've got to stay for at least a minute to try to get the conversation going. Remember, you are the one thing that they for sure have in common. Pose questions or lead in with a "remember when" story. As soon as you see that they are starting to engage, you can then say, "Excuse me . . . " and walk away. If there is clearly just no connection, zero click, let them exit the conversation without pushing the issue.

PARTY THEMES

Spring/Summer Theme

Spring and summer are all about fresh scents, bright colors, and a kicked-back attitude! Fill Mason jars, cups, even mugs with sprigs of herbs and spices (like rosemary, thyme, mint, parsley, and cilantro). They make a great way to add natural fragrance and decor without spending a ton on flowers. PLUS you can send your guests home with a few sprigs so they can cook with them (or keep them for yourself). Fill bowls with lemons, oranges, and tangerines. Stuff vodka bottles with several sprigs of herbs—each bottle with a different type—to infuse the spirit with fresh flavor and add to the decor. Prepare fresh, light, herb-driven dishes, each highlighting a certain herb. Create herbaceous basil and macerated boysenberry or white peach martinis, muddled jalapeño (a natural fat-burner) and mint mojitos, cilantro and spicy asparagus (a natural hangover preventer) Bloody Marys, and even mint- and lavender-infused Jell-O shots!

Drive-In-Movie Theme

A drive-in-movie party is great for kids *and* adults. Rent a movie screen and projector to place in your front yard or other open space. Use a combo of large picnic blankets, ultrasuede floor cushions, lawn chairs, and even a couch or two for seating. Make this event more grown-up by serving gourmet versions of your favorite movie treats: homemade ice cream sandwiches, spiced popcorn, and rum-infused milkshakes.

Board-Game Theme

Throw a board-game party at the park. Bring a plethora of retro games, like Connect Four, Battleship, and Scrabble, or any of your favorites. Hand out lunch boxes (if you want to go all out, buy some retro ones from eBay that befit your generation) containing school-yard favorites, like peanut butter and Marshmallow Fluff sandwiches, homemade fruit roll-ups, and, in lieu of a juice box, spice up the afternoon with thermoses filled with spiked fruit juice. Pin several picnic blankets together to create a Technicolor dream blanket that tons of friends can relax on together. Bring trays from Target or IKEA to support the board-game playing of your more serious gamers.

Fiesta Theme

A fiesta theme is always popular in the summer. Raise the bar on yours by forgoing the typical elements and focus on what really makes Mexican and Spanish cultures unique. You can have a tequila bar that serves tequila with different infusions and spins on the typical margaritas and mojitos. Be sure to have plenty of fresh ingredients on hand to keep everything authentic. If you can, hire a mixologist to make the bar a real experience. With the menu, embrace the family culture: Have people seated at tables with lazy Susans full of toppings and ingredients for tacos and fajitas. Hire Flamenco dancers to put on a show, and then teach guests to dance as well.

Biggest Mistakes Party Throwers Make

Spending too much money! Enough already! Jes Gordon suggests, "Don't constantly second-guess yourself and continually throw money at your insecurities. Set your budget and stick to it so you don't resent the party later."

It may be your party, but it's not all about YOU! Let your fete reflect who you are, but don't alienate others in doing so. Allow your theme, drinks, food, music, and activities to please your guests, too.

Stressing! Yes. Parties can be stressful on many levels. They are great at extracting insecurities; causing thoughts like *What if no one shows up*? or *I don't have enough friends*; self-pitying; spending too much time, energy, and, as mentioned above, money; and micromanaging once the party has started. To avoid stress: Plan, reasonably execute, then have fun with it.

Too-high expectations. People flake, show up late, bring uninvited guests, break glasses, spill wine, say and do inappropriate things. It

Dress Up Your Party

Lindsay, 28, Works for a Nonprofit: "Tell people to dress up. It's a great way to make your party classy without any work."

happens. You can't control it and you shouldn't try to. Regardless of the little things that go wrong, activities that guests don't want to do, timing that's off, even if only a pathetic few show . . . have fun.

The Cheapest Way to Decorate Even the Most Upscale Party

Decor can define your party as plain and—ugh—more like an eighth-grade get-together than an upscale (on the cheap) shindig intended for adults to mingle, socialize, and maybe even seal a deal. So how can you elevate your event without deleting a nausea-inducing amount of dollars from your bank account? It's all in the details.

LIGHTING

Totally transform a space without heavy lifting. How? Jes suggests creative lighting. Using different lightbulbs can change the color of a room—no paint required. Another tactic—buying gels that you simply apply on recessed lights. Make sure you buy heat-resistant gels made specifically for use on lightbulbs. It's a movie trick that has been used for decades and creates an amazing effect, from a soft hazy glow to a seductive blue or red hue.

MIRRORS

It's true, adding mirrors adds bling, space, sex appeal, blips of brightness, and dimension. A mirror can make it look like your room is much larger than it actually is by creating the illusion of endlessness. You look at a mirrored wall and you might think that the reflection you're seeing is actually an additional room. The sex appeal comes from our innate inability to refrain from adoringly gazing at ourselves as we pass by, or happening to catch eyes with the hottie across the room, staring for longer than usual, liberated within the perceived safety of the mirror. But don't just hang full-size mirrors haphazardly around the room. Picture-size mirrors, floor mirrors, mirrored vases filled with flowers, smaller mirrors used in lieu of coasters, even stick-on minis in the shape of birds or words are perfect to create the effect.

VOLUPTUOUS FLOWERS

Little flowers are fine. But big, statement-making, voluptuous flower arrangements, or even individual blossoms, are even better! They instantly elevate an environment with a splash of color and often a seductive scent, making a room feel more luscious. So what flowers are considered "voluptuous"? Peonies, hydrangeas, sunflowers, stargazer lilies, and dahlias have a presence that allows you to use fewer stems and still fake a bountiful arrangement. Even just a single hydrangea in a small vase is more impressive than ten smaller flowers like freesia or even mini roses displayed in the same small vase.

ODDS & ENDS

Sometimes it's the smallest details that make the largest impact. Place a single flower, a couple of sprigs of your favorite fresh herbs, or a square piece of paper with a short but pointed note or your favorite quote on each napkin, like "QuickieChick Tip: Greet people like you would your dog." Create cool seating cards for your guests, such as writing the guest's name on a rock, a seashell, or, if it's fall, on a big colorful leaf from your backyard.

PLUSH MAKES PERFECT

Sagging, droopy anything—not so sexy. The last detail to tend to: making your pillows, sofas, and chairs look plush and soft. Puff up pillows, toss soft throws on the sofa, add texture that makes you want to touch it—like faux furs, velvet, cashmere materials. Remember, you want people to feel and be comfortable. Stained upholstery or surfaces that guests will be touching, sitting on, or eating off of are nasty. Notice the details.

QuickieChick's Cheat Sheet

1. Be prepared with conversation starters. Do your research before inserting yourself into an after-work social situation. Go in with at least an idea of who's going to be there and what their backgrounds are.

2. When going out to a business event, **be goal-oriented, then show up on time** (not "fashionably late"). Everybody fears that "no one" will show up to their party. If you're one of the first to arrive, you will get the most attention from the host.

3. Get a business card. Giving out business cards looks much more professional than punching contact info into your phone, and it makes you think about how you present yourself professionally.

4. At interviews and work events, **maintain a good balance of listening and talking.** People like to talk about themselves, so let them. But remember, you have something to bring to the table, too.

5. Surround yourself with like-minded people. Reach out to friends, colleagues, acquaintances with similar ideas and form a club or set a monthly get-together to share thoughts, ideas, and resources. Use this time with like-minded, supportive people for brainstorming, conceptualizing, designing, and sharing over coffee or on a Saturday night over wine and cheese.

6. Clean up your Facebook page. Your current or potential employer does not need to know how often you go to Margarita Mondays, Taco Tuesdays, Bottomless Mimosa Brunches, and Happy Hours.

7. Focus on the positive. Bring attention (without being annoying) to what you have done, your brilliant ideas, what you can/will/plan to do, and your positive attributes. Don't *ever* minimize your accomplishments or apologize for what you don't know or I haven't done or achieved . . . yet. Instead, concentrate on what you can contribute.

8. No more keggers. Update your parties with drinks like mimosas and beer cocktails and thoughtful decor like giant flowers or twinkle lights.

9. Intermix your guests. If serving a sit-down dinner, mix up your crowd and seat a friend next to a co-worker. Consider what your guests have in common and introduce them to each other.

10. Be prepared with icebreakers. Plan a few icebreaker conversations and activities to bring strangers together and help make connections.

95

5

Dating & Dumping

FACT: Dating in the real world isn't the same as dating in college. Forget about kiddie games and sweet make-out sessions; this is the big leagues. Learn how to hold your ground and stick to your morals now (which you might need to define), so that you don't wake up feeling like a slut tomorrow.

QuickieChick Quiz

QUIZ

1. **You get home from work, you're stressed from your boss yelling at you. You start telling your boyfriend about it. He . . .**

   A. Shuts you up with a kiss, and pops in your favorite season of *Sex and the City.*

   B. Let's you vent until you are out of breath. He suggests ways you can fix the situation, points out ways you could improve, even to the point that you're annoyed with him now!

2. **You and your boyfriend had date night planned, but you're still hammering away at a project for work that took far longer than you thought it would. He . . .**

   A. Is noticeably frustrated because, he says, you could have skipped your yoga class that day and worked on this then, so you could be ready for date night.

   B. Says it's OK and he goes out with his friends for the night.

   I know these are tricky, but if answer A sounded pretty true to your relationship in both of those scenarios, your guy is not very supportive of your career. Yes, he is trying to be sweet by putting on the TV and taking your mind *off* of work, but being able to vent about the stresses of the day and knowing that your boyfriend is willing to listen might actually improve your quality of work. And, yes, you could have skipped yoga, but you *need* your time, too. He should understand that.

Your Dating Pool Just Shrunk Down to a Puddle

Dating was easy in college . . . the easiest it will ever be. You were constantly surrounded by like-minded people of a similar age and intelligence. It was like a buffet table of eligible options—from lectures, where you were pretty much guaranteed that the guy you chose to sit beside for an hour had similar interests (since you both chose to enroll in the same class); to passing periods, when throngs of students flooded the halls, increasing the options tenfold; to parties, where it was easy to strike up a conversation with some random guy, then another and another if need be until you found that right guy (at least for right then). In college, all day every day your dating pool consisted of hundreds, if not thousands of possibilities, mostly within a four-year age range (with the exception of those who dragged the college years endlessly on). And because someone always knew someone who knew your subject of momentary interest, you were able to get the dirt before investing any more of your valuable time: Is he single? Is he a player? Has he screwed or screwed over any of my friends?

The real world is not the same. You are no longer immersed in a contrived social scene stocked with potential suitors, but instead you are trying to find a smattering of potential dates who add up to a few basic essential criteria:

- Single

- Within the age range you deem appropriate

- Attractive to you and attracted to you

- Adequately motivated, driven, and intelligent

- Not complete players, assholes, or idiots

Once you narrow the options down based on the above, you have maybe a handful of prospects at any given time . . . *maybe*. Yes, your average daily dating pool has now been cut down from thousands to about five—if you're lucky. Not to worry: It's not that you have suddenly become less attractive; it's that you are no longer surrounded by students. Instead, you are sitting at a desk in an office (or wherever your work may be), and the amount of dating prospects has dramatically decreased.

Dating coach and *New York Times* best-selling author Rachel Greenwald, whose book *Have Him at Hello: Confessions from 1,000 Guys About What Makes Them Fall in Love . . . or Never Call Back* was named by *Cosmopolitan* magazine as one of the "Top 4 Best Books of Summer," explains that, beyond the dating puddle, stress has a lot to do with the difference between college and real-life dating. "College is an artificial environment where you don't have the pressures of the real world to see how people react in real life—like paying rent, unforgiving bosses, or even more so the stresses of

trying to start your own company." Those stresses can affect how you treat someone and therefore how you are treated. "In college it's easy to be sweet and funny and giving when chances are your parents are paying your tuition or you have loans that you aren't even thinking about paying back yet." The most realistic, real-world simulation of college-experienced stress is finals week or recruiting season. That's when the pressure is on, when personalities flare up, when people's true selves emerge.

Should You Stick It Out with Your College Boyfriend?

I know . . . he's your first love. But it's time to start thinking about your relationship with your college boyfriend practically. The reality is that you are no longer living the college life, you have different priorities now, and your life is about to shift dramatically.

The fact is that the likelihood that you will eventually break up with your college guy is high. Why? Because:

1. You no longer have as much in common.

2. It's no longer as convenient.

3. Your goals, interests, and daily routines are about to evolve more than you can even imagine.

Those three reasons will be even more amplified if:

A. He is younger than you and has another year or two before he graduates.

B. Postcollege he returns to his hometown, which is different from your hometown.

C. He goes on to a graduate program, and you go on to brave the world.

College life is like living in a gigantic bubble. Once you leave that bubble, a whole world of opportunities opens up to you. You are fascinated by the new people you meet, each of whom has had completely different experiences from you. You get to find out who you really are, on your own, completely independent terms. While your college relationship can be a source of comfort, it can also hold you back.

Saying all of that, I'm not necessarily saying that you should break up with him just because it could eventually happen anyway. What I'm saying is that you should take a good look at your relationship. Start noting both your similarities and differences. Are your goals and lifestyles still aligned? Dating coach Rachel Greenwald reminds us that "You don't always meet someone better just because you wait." However, you might be missing an opportunity to meet someone better for you if you stick it out with your college stud muffin simply for the sake of fulfilling that first-love, happily-ever-after notion of romance. Keep in mind that upon graduating from college, you are also graduating from one phase of life to the next. And this "next" phase that you have entered is one with huge and endless possibilities and learning potential. Beyond the career-based education that you will get by joining the workforce, you will learn and grow through your life experiences and by meeting people with different beliefs, interests, and ambitions. As strange as it might sound, a good chunk of your postgrad growth could very well come from being in relationships with people who fascinate you. Forget "tall, dark, and handsome" and instead pursue people with passion and perspective!

Apparently that whole "timing is everything" thinking is not necessarily so. According to Rachel, college might not be the best time to meet the love

Couldn't Stick It Out for Long

Shana, 23, Assistant Realtor: "I stuck it out for a year. Distance got the best of us. College can be a pressure cooker for relationships, as in, you have so much free time, similar schedules, and friends and are in close proximity, so you're bound to spend a lot more quality time with your friends and significant others. My college boyfriend was a year younger than I was, so I graduated before him. My priorities shifted. My schedule changed. My interests evolved. I would be stressed about finding a job or getting up early for an interview, and he would call me drunk from a keg party. At first we were just out of step, and then after a while it felt like we were doing completely different dances. He was still in college mode, and I was trying to climb the career ladder, and I really needed a boyfriend who understood where I was, where I wanted to go, and even help me get there."

of your life. In an ideal world, that right time doesn't clock in until you're twenty-five or twenty-seven years old, after you've gotten comfortable in your career path, experienced a handful of relationships, learned how to navigate multiple personalities (hopefully not all within the same person), and explored yourself a little more. That "right time" age also has something to do with your fertility, as it's the perfect time to shack up and settle down if you want to have the average two to three kids. But, really? How often is timing truly "ideal"? Rachel has seen way too many women look back at their college boyfriends and wish they could go back to them. Her sage words of advice? "If you're in a relationship with someone amazing, don't dump him if there really isn't anything wrong with him except the timing."

But . . . take it from someone who has been known as a "leaver," always looking for the "perfect" guy who can be more, better . . . everything. I've experienced a lot of really great guys in so many different ways, yet always found a flaw detrimental enough to the relationship that it warranted leaving. Take it from someone who has years, sometimes mere months later regretted some of those brush-offs and breakups upon realizing that he really wasn't so bad after all and I made a decision to dump him too fast. In fact, he was pretty damn close to perfect. As my dad said to me after one breakup with one of those pretty-damn-close-to-perfect guys, "Laurel, what does a guy have to do and be in order for you to realize how great he is for you? When will enough be enough? Or are you just a believer that the grass is *always* greener?" I know, the grass *could* be greener, there *might* be someone better, and really the only way to find out is to go look. You don't want to be selling yourself short. *However,* you also can't expect one guy to provide everything you need. Honestly, guys like that (if they exist) are few . . . I mean *few* and far between.

In order to figure out what you are looking for in someone else, you need to examine what you have found in yourself. Who are you? What are your core values—the values that you will not budge on? Once you figure those out (see the Note to Self on page 101), then you can look at his and see if they align.

Once you have figured you out, when it comes to him, do your core values align? Beyond the core values, ask yourself these questions:

- Is he kind?

- Is he ambitious?

- Does he make me happy?

- Does he have a lot of great qualities that I'm looking for?

- Are his faults *really* that bad?

- If I left him, would I miss him, and why?

Note to Self

What Are Your Core Values?

Tools

Think about who you really are and what you believe are the most important things in life. These are your "core values," the beliefs that define who you are. Imagine a house: These values make up the foundation on which everything else is built. To help you think about what your core values are, here are mine: family, understanding and forgiving, hard work, deep love, love and appreciation of dogs, compassion, passion, nurturing others and self-love, commitment and loyalty, balance, strength yet fragility, learning and experiencing, communication, and trust. What about you?

_____

_____

_____

_____

_____

_____

_____

_____

_____

_____

Now explain what each of those values mean to you, how they appear in your life, and how you embody them.

_____

_____

_____

_____

_____

_____

_____

_____

_____

_____

_____

_____

(You might need more room than this. Mine takes up eight pages.)

Compare him to other guys. But compare *all* of his qualities to *all* of the qualities of other guys—the good *and* the bad. The key is to find the balance that works better for you. Rachel reminds us that if the only thing you're missing is that "maybe" you're missing out on something "better," or that you still have so many goals that you want to achieve and you fear that having a boyfriend *could* hold you back from attaining them . . . keep him and figure out how you can achieve your goals within the relationship.

I'm not saying settle. I'm saying be smart.

Facing His Flaws

Tools

What are some of the sweet things your boyfriend (or ex) does (or did) for you?

_____

_____

What bothers you about your boyfriend?

_____

_____

Starter Sentences

I can't stand it when my boyfriend

_____ ,

because it makes me feel

_____ .

I love it when my boyfriend

_____ ,

because it makes me feel

_____ .

Overall, my boyfriend is a

_____

(positive, negative, supportive, draining) presence in my life (sorry, but you're going to have to get real here), because he

_____ .

Learning About You Through Him

Dating is great for many reasons. One of which, and honestly what I believe to be the best reason (aside from one day finding your perfect match), is to learn more about you, to explore, develop, blossom . . . through them. Personally, I wouldn't even resemble who I am today had I not dated the amazing, conflicted, successful, interesting, colorful, traveled, wealthy, vacant, introspective, generous, fascinating, opinionated, creative, business-minded, loving assholes and gems that I've dated (obviously that is a description of many, as opposed to one person). It's not that I have become those people, but those people helped to shine a light on certain areas of me that might previously have been dull. And because I am a journalist and tend to be fascinated by others' passions, I wanted to learn who they are, what they are impassioned by, and why. After all, passion can be infectious if you're open to it. I also love to learn about things that I don't know enough about. If it wasn't for the various men in my life, I wouldn't know or even much care about food, fashion, beer, champagne, or—gasp—shoes! I also learned about camping, art, owning a company, bike riding, architecture, and the stock market. Not all of which I became impassioned by, but I can appreciate them and can have an intellectual conversation about each of those topics and not sound like an idiot. It was also a way for me to become aware of the areas that I wasn't as in touch with, like world issues and current events. So I began to read specific newspapers—like the *Financial Times* (they also have an amazing weekend style section), *USA TODAY* (for lifestyle and general current issues), The Huffington Post, and Reuters online.

My parents used to say that my boyfriends were grooming me to be more interesting, to be more of a catch, really. I don't know if that was necessarily the intention, but I think that because I was open-minded, and, what's more, enthusiastic about life and learning, my boyfriends wanted to teach me. When it comes to finding someone from whom you can learn more about yourself, it's always been two things: interesting and interested. Why?

INTERESTING & INTERESTED

Interesting

He is interesting. He does interesting things. He goes to interesting places. He has a career that you find interesting and that you actually want to talk and inquire about. He enjoys activities (that you can take part in) that challenge and excite you. He has personal interests and passions that you also find interesting and would enjoy exploring. You are able to have interesting conversations with him that open your eyes and your mind.

Interested

He is interested in you, what you have to say, what you do, and who you are as a human. Why does this matter? Because he makes you feel important, which helps to boost your self-esteem and makes you want to continue to do interesting things and be an interesting person. It also makes you feel like you aren't in a one-sided relationship with an egomaniac who loves to be interesting but isn't so interested in you.

This is not about being fake, disconnected, or trying to be someone you're not. It doesn't mean you are a copycat, imposter, a fraud, or hiding from yourself. It's actually the exact opposite. You are finding thrill, fascination, and joy as you explore the different sides of who you are—many sides that you didn't know existed. It's like a college class but much more fun!

WAYS TO LEARN ABOUT YOU THROUGH THEM
- Be open-minded.

- Try new things. Venture out of your comfort zone without going too far over the line.

- Learn about his favorite subjects and his career. If you are at his place and notice magazine or newspaper articles or even books at his place, read them, collect information, educate yourself.

- Have conversations and engage, don't just listen, nod your head, and move on. If you want to get as much as you can out of the process, make this a back-and-forth conversation. After all, it's boring if he's just talking and you're just listening—boring for both of you, no matter how much he likes to hear himself talk.

Note to Self

How to Listen in a Conversation

Just because you also have a thought in the midst of one of his sentences, doesn't mean that you have to blurt it out immediately or even sit in silence as you go over and over your point or comment to make sure you don't forget it, all the while not listening to a word that he is saying. Instead, take note of your thought, but keep listening. Once it makes sense to express your thought, by all means, say it!

Is Your Guy Holding You Back?

Relationships are complicated enough. Just look at the basics: Two people are trying to cohabitate (or at least coexist) through ups, downs, drama, and joy. In an attempt to avoid conflict, not rock the boat, maintain the sense of security that relationships imbue, or just make it work, it's easy to avert your attention from obvious deal-breaking flaws. So how do you know if your relationship is holding you back from achieving such greatness (or at least honest happiness)?

7 SIGNS YOUR RELATIONSHIP IS UNSTABLE

1. He is possessive of you in an unhealthy way.

2. He questions you whenever you talk to or mention another guy.

3. He has certain values that you don't, for example: He wants a 1950s wife who stays home and doesn't work, and you feel that that's not you.

4. He doesn't want you to take business meetings with men because, as he says, "All men want to get in your pants—business or not."

5. He gets annoyed by the fact that you are "working too much," despite the fact that he works "too much," too.

6. He doesn't celebrate your accomplishments, but would rather one-up you instead. If you tell him that you had a great meeting with a potential new client, instead of saying, "Oh that's great, babe; I knew

you would do a great job!" he says, "Huh, well, I actually signed this amazing new client today!"

7. It's not a two-way street. When he needs your help with a project for work, you dedicate your entire weekend to it. But when you need his advice on a contract you are writing, he acts annoyed and tells you to figure it out on your own.

SO WHAT'S A GIRL TO DO?

A. You could "settle," going through the motions with someone you know isn't right but with whom you're making the best of it. . . . After all, no one is perfect, and no one person can provide you with all that you need.

B. You could continue to strive to find someone and something closer to perfection—even if it takes time and a path littered with heartbreaks and breakups to get there.

When it comes to "settling," Rachel Greenwald says that a lot of women think that settling is the same as compromising. But here's the difference:

Settling: The belief that you don't think you can do any better.

Compromising: Having the maturity to understand that no one is perfect, that you're not perfect, and that a healthy relationship is about give and take.

Sometimes those compromises are substantial, and that's when you have to really sit and analyze the situation and do your best to figure out what the right move is for you, irrespective of what your family or friends think.

Example: If you and your guy (who is the "love of your life") are job-searching at the same time and he has a job offer in one city and you have one

---

Are You "Settling" for the Sake of Being "Attached"?

Charlotte, 23, Magazine Writer: "Ha! My boyfriend of two and a half years and I split a month after graduation. He missed his opportunity to move with me on my terms, and when he actually decided to move to New York to be with me, I realized I wasn't excited, I was pissed. It was a great way to realize I didn't love him anymore. Oh, man, was I settling when I was with him! In retrospect, I wish my friends had said something, but if that was the case, I probably would have been pissed at them. Turns out, it's way better to be single than in a ho-hum, boring relationship just for the sake of being attached."

Note to Self

What's Your Best Relationship?

Tools

Whose relationship do you admire? Why?

_____

_____

Whose relationship do you find unhealthy/unhappy? Why?

_____

_____

What's the *worst* thing a guy ever did to you? Why did it upset you?

_____

_____

Starter Sentences

I have to have these qualities in a boyfriend/relationship:

_____

_____ .

My relationship needs to enhance my life in these ways:

_____

_____ .

I will end a relationship if it ever interferes with these parts of my life:

_____

_____ .

in another, you have to decide: In my ideal marriage, who is going to be the breadwinner—both of us or one of us? If you know, for example, that you don't want to work once you get married and have a family, maybe it's not the best idea to decide to lose the love of your life to pursue a high-powered job that you eventually don't want, instead of moving to your guy's city and finding a job that is fine for now. If it doesn't work out, you can always go back and pursue that high-powered job. But what is love worth to you?

Here's the problem: Rachel explains that chicks in their early twenties are torn between the women in their lives who have influenced them, many of whom didn't have the choice to go out and work, so they became ardent feminists, like Gloria Steinem; all they wanted for their daughters was to have a career first. Now those daughters grew up and realized that they couldn't find love. Rachel calls them the "Cinderella Generation." They broke their glass ceiling with their powerhouse careers, but they also broke their glass slippers. "I work with women who say that they would trade their big job for the love of their life in a heartbeat, but they are too embarrassed to admit those feelings to anyone but me." Her advice? Keep love at the forefront of your priorities as opposed to playing second fiddle to your career.

Expert Insight

Jacqueline Whitmore

Should women offer to pick up or split the check at dinner?

First date: I may be a little old-fashioned, but I believe that a man should pay for a woman's meal on the first date. This is a good reflection of his manners. Once a relationship has been established, then the woman can offer to pay for dessert, kick in for the tip, or split the check.

Dinner meeting: In a business situation where a woman is meeting a man for a *business* dinner, remember that the business arena is gender-neutral. This means that whoever does the inviting should pay the bill.

*"Don't S**t Where You Eat": Why You Can't Use Work as a Dating Pool*

I hate that saying, but it makes sense. "Don't s★★t where you eat" translates to "Don't date where you work." Sure, long hours doing the daily grind leave little opportunity to meet people. Well, that is, meet people whom you don't work with. Because, as people have warned time and time again, it *really* is a bad idea to let your personal and career worlds comingle. Sure, you see him every day, you've experienced ups and downs together, have similarly lofty goals, and let's just face the fact: He's convenient. But think for a second about the day after. . . . The day after you sleep together. The day after you realize that you're no longer into him. The day after you tell him it's over. The day after you start seeing someone else but can't go effusively telling your work friends how excited you are about the new guy. That's when your personal and career worlds don't just comingle, they collide.

I get it, though. Your circle of friends is based, primarily, on your office environment. Those are the people you see every day, lunch with, bitch to, drink and dine with. Those are the people who know you the best if for no other reason than the fact that you see each other the most. They are like your extended family. In fact, you hate to admit it, but you actually do miss them sometimes on weekends, which is why Mondays can seem more like a full-on gab session than a productive workday. Because your office mates—whether above, below, or on the same level as you—know you best, they also tend to be the ones you fall for or the ones who "have such a great guy for you." Dating isn't like it used to be in the stocked pond of college. You can't just throw out a line and know pretty much for certain that a fish will come flopping out directly into your lap. Your office is really the closest place to any real college dating environment. But that doesn't mean it's OK to date colleagues. I know, I know: Many, many office romances turn into real, healthy, long-term, even everlasting relationships. But just think about how many fish you threw back into the water, and were thrilled that you didn't have to ever see them again. And now think about if one of those thrown-back fish actually worked with you and you *had* to see them again and again and again. Unless of course: (A) one of you quits, or (B) one of you is fired for the mere fact that you dated. Yes, it happens. I've seen it personally.

Dating someone you work with may seem fun at first, but it can turn into a disaster or, if anything, an uncomfortable situation. Oh, and not to mention the fact that it's often not permitted, particularly if the guy also happens to be your boss or even just a higher-up. Because here's the thing that sucks: You're disposable. And I don't just mean because you're the girl. I mean because everyone is disposable. It gets even trickier if the person you have your eyes (and hands) on is your boss. Probably taboo. Companies don't like to have liabilities on their hands. By dating a colleague or boss, you are creating a potential drama, and that, no one wants to put up with. So instead of dealing with it down the line, the company just might find it easier to fire you now. And, believe me, he's likely not "the one" you're going to marry, and therefore he's not worth jeopardizing your career for.

However . . . sometimes there is a connection so strong you just can't ignore it. In that case . . . a word to the wise: *Be careful.* Remember that this isn't just a hookup. You have to continue to work with this person, day in and day out . . . even if your relationship doesn't work out. Be discriminating. If the potential love of your life works with you, don't forsake the aura of professionalism in order to sacrifice the thing in life that could make you happy ever after—love. If you start dating a co-worker or a client and that relationship ends, be mature about it. Exit it gracefully so it doesn't become awkward; that's the most important component when it comes to dating a co-worker—yes, how to end it. Don't be a bitch. Don't lie. Don't cheat. Don't be sketchy. Be an adult; have an adult conversation, realizing that this isn't just about love, it's also about business.

Fishing in a New (Non-Work-Related) Pond

Tools

Where have your friends met their boyfriends?

_____

_____

Do you have friends who could set you up?

_____

_____

Where do you spend time other than home, bars, and work?

_____

_____

What are your thoughts on online dating?

_____

_____

Starter Sentences

Instead of using the workplace as a dating scene, I should consider meeting guys at

_____

_____ .

I could also probably meet someone through these friends, family members, or acquaintances:

_____

_____ .

The worst thing that could happen if I ask someone to set me up _or_ if I ask someone out is

_____

_____ ,

but it doesn't actually matter, because

_____

_____ .

Why You Shouldn't Play the "I'm So Successful" Card All the Time

Why is it that so many successful chicks have a hard time landing a date? According to dating coach Rachel Greenwald, it's your "boss lady" attitude. So, below are two scenarios. Who do you think will get the guy?

1. A chick walks into Starbucks, sees a hot guy, and strategically stands close to him. He strikes up a conversation that eventually leads to the inevitable question: "So what do you do?" Her response: "Well, I'm a vice president at (insert a very powerful company name here), and I'm responsible for (x, y, z, and every other important letter in the alphabet), but before that I graduated at the top of my class from Yale/Harvard/Princeton/UCLA/etc. . . ."

2. A chick walks into Starbucks, sees a hot guy, and strategically stands close to him. He strikes up a conversation that eventually leads to the inevitable question: "So what do you do?" Her response: "Well, when I'm not in the office, I'm at a yoga studio. When not at a yoga studio, I'm at Starbucks drinking my latte and planning my next trip to Peru."

So which strategy scores the date?

Answer: Number 2. Why? Let's break them both down:

1. The "boss lady." This chick gave off the vibe that she's so professionally successful that she's practically untouchable, not to mention totally self involved, likely too busy to date, and has standards that are unrealistically high. Sure, she has a great job that she worked hard to get and wants people to know it. But that hot guy . . . chances are he is instantly unattracted to her. In fact, he would rather hire (or work for) her than date her.

Dating a Co-Worker—the Reality

Tiffany, 24, Clerk at a Law Firm: "His work personality and his outside-of-work personality were completely different. He was very professional and confident at work but a complete ass outside of the workplace."

Lesson Learned: "It was weird after the breakup. It was not worth dating a co-worker—and I won't do it again!"

111

2. The free spirit who is interesting, deep, and adventurous. This is a total turn-on. She's likely successful, considering that she has the means to take yoga classes, drink lattes (as opposed to coffee), and plan trips to Peru, but she isn't defined by her career and she doesn't feel the need to shove it up his nose.

Saying all of that, I myself often define myself by my career. I am a lifestyle writer, which means that my life and career often intertwine. So what would I say in that situation? "Well, I'm a lifestyle writer and I absolutely love it! I get to work for myself, from my home or anywhere else that I happen to be—like here at Starbucks drinking a latte. Because I write about lifestyle, my work and life tend to intertwine, and that's a great thing! I take regular yoga classes, hike with my pup several days a week, and tonight I'm going to plan my next trip to Peru."

Life and career are all about balance. Find the balance that suits you.

The Dos & Don'ts of Online Dating

High school through college, dating is pretty much all the same (except for the bases you round, the types of dates you have, your conversations, your depth of interest, and your proclamation of "love"—which tends to be thrown around more in the younger years). Ok, so maybe it's not "pretty much the same." But it IS the same when it comes to accessibility, availability, and the sheer number of fish in the sea waiting, mouths open at the surface of the water, to be caught. And then there's dating postcollege.

Dating postcollege can be—I'm not going to lie—tough. And the older you get, the tougher it gets. Why? For starters, you're no longer surrounded by eligibles within a classroom, dorm, or study hall. Your social circle has shrunk, as have your socially available hours. Of the people in your social circle, many are already shacking up and in serious relationships, if not already engaged or married.

So what's a single, overworked, underpaid, rarely available girl to do? Date online.

The thinking that online dating is for geeks, losers, perverts, or otherwise unmatchables is SO passé. The fact is, Net Geners (that would be you—the Internet generation) almost *need* online dating in order to meet interesting, driven, yes, like-minded peers. Why?

- Because the few off-hours you have to peruse the bar scene with your girlfriends is usually more about gabbing and catching up than actively attempting to attract a date.

- You don't really want to pick someone up (or be picked up) at a bar, anyway.

- There are lots, I mean *lots,* of not just *normal,* but highly successful, intellectual, interesting, age-appropriate, and, yes, *hot* people online looking for dates.

- The number of self-employed, work-from-home, entrepreneurs is huge. And those people aren't surrounded by an at-work social circle, rarely go out with friends, and, honestly, tend to be a bit hermitish. That's not to say they *are* hermits, but they are working for themselves! Translation: They are building something to generate money and to follow a passion (hopefully) . . . and they are online.

According to Rachel Greenwald, online dating is a "fantastic stock to have in your portfolio. Single women need a diversified portfolio of dating activities." When it comes to finding the "one," you want to keep as many avenues open as possible. What do I mean? You should be online dating, socializing, joining groups, going to events, even being open to setups from unlikely sources like Grandma. Just because someone (like your grandma) seems out of touch with you, doesn't mean she doesn't know someone fantastic. While, yes, throwing yourself into online dating is less important in your twenties, the older you get, the more heavy emphasis you should place on it, because you aren't meeting as many men in your daily life. Same goes if you work from home by yourself. You likely don't go out and meet new people often. So strike while the iron is hot! Go at dating from all angles! Online dating is not perfect, and you will have to sift through lots of men—you'll probably have lots of bad dates, too—but you are looking for that one right person, and, as they say, you have to kiss a lot of frogs!

Rachel reminds us that, when it comes to online dating, your expectations need to be adjusted. Two out of ten dates will be good. That may seem low, but the reality is that you will be meeting *lots* of people, many more than you would if you didn't try online dating. One strategy to remember: Whatever time and energy you put into your résumé, put double into your online profile. If you agree that love is more important than a job, then walk the walk. It's OK if you hate the process. Do it anyway. It's a means to an end. Another tip: Be *honest.* Honestly post who you are, with current photos and weight, and who and what you are looking for. If smoking is a no-go, then don't put in your profile that it's OK to date a "sometimes" smoker.

Why is online dating the new stocked pond? Because none of us really have the time anymore to go out and find people to date. I mean really, we hardly have the time to date in the first place, let alone the time to find some-one worthy of spending that time on a date with! That's why you should do the legwork in the comfort of your home, even in your sweats, no makeup, and your hair's a mess . . . on the Internet. But don't just upload your profile to any (of the many) dating sites out there. Follow these Dos and Don'ts guidelines to get the most and best out of online dating.

DOS

- Research the different sites to find one that is not only stocked with great people but also is reputable and aligns with your goals. Some sites are known to be more for one-night stands than long-lasting romance; others are religiously slanted; and then there are those that are common-interest driven.

- Spend time on your profile in order to create an honest depiction of who you are and what you are looking for. So what if it takes you three hours to do it right. Crafting a good profile can save you hours of poorly targeted dates. If it helps, sit with a girlfriend over a bottle of wine and create your profiles together.

- When it comes to your photos, make sure they are current—not you four years or ten pounds earlier. Showing photos of you with your pet, laughing, or doing something fun is a great way to present yourself *and* stand out from the rest.

- Create a list of standard questions before giving out your phone number or e-mail, ones that will help reveal certain aspects of the prospective date. Why ask such insight-extracting questions? Because you haven't met this person in the flesh, so first-impression intuitive insight is much more difficult to use as a gauge. Instead, dig in! A few questions to ask:

  — **"Where do you see yourself in one, five, ten years?"**
  Why ask? It shows what this person's goals are—career, family, lifestyle. . . .

  — **"Tell me five things that most people don't know about you."**
  Why ask? This shows if he is emotionally available and open to being vulnerable. It also lets you know what he finds interesting about himself.

  — **"What is your average day, week, month like?"**
  Why ask? You will know what you are getting yourself into if you end up with this person. Is he a partier, athletic, workaholic, traveler, adventurer, etc. . . .

- Be open and honest in your responses. Be yourself, be funny, sarcastic, whatever it is. Just be you. But remember that typing doesn't carry a tone or facial expressions. Sometimes sarcasm can get lost in translation, and your attempt at being funny can be taken as being bitchy, rude, or crass. If your sarcasm doesn't translate over the Internet, maybe save that part of your personality for your pre-date phone call.

- Talk on the phone before going on a date. Chemistry is important. You can tell a lot from a phone call.

- Tell someone where you're going before you go . . . just in case. Tell your mom, your sister, a friend. Just let someone know what his name is and where you plan on meeting.

- Meet him there; don't have him pick you up. Sure, chivalry is great and, yes, should be a component to your relationship. But you don't know this person. Meet him out. He can pick you up next time if it goes well.

- Let him pick up the tab. Because chivalry is important and you deserve to be treated.

- Call, text, or e-mail the next day to say thank you. If you are completely uninterested, e-mail a brief thank you. It's rude not to.

DON'TS

- Upload a profile photo that shows you drinking, doing drugs, or being too provocative. You never know who's on the site—it could be a boss, your ex, or a family member.

- Reveal personal details, including where you work, live, your license plate number (which can be seen in photos of you by your car), or anything else that might make it possible for someone to find you on Facebook.

- Lie about your age, weight, interests, name, etc. You are who you are. If he doesn't like it, he doesn't deserve you.

- Don't use a photo of you with other people. It's confusing and shows that your focus might be friends, not lovers.

- Have your first date at his house. If he wants to cook for you, that's nice. Not tonight. Maybe next time, if it goes well.

- Bring your friends or be OK with him bringing his friends. This is about you two. Get to know friends (and let friends give you their opinions and two cents) later.

How Far Do You Go on a First Date?

Melissa Berry, 26, Coordinator for FEMA: "It depends on your comfort level. If you've known him a long time and a date was inevitable, you will be more comfortable to kiss/make out. If he's a stranger, a hug might be the most appropriate thing to do."

- Talk about exes or other dates on your date. It's a turnoff. There are *plenty* of other things to talk about.

- Offer to pay. I know, I already said it above, but I have to say it again. Don't offer to pay, don't pay, don't put your credit card down, don't even reach for your purse. Just say thank you when he places his form of payment down. If you want to pay at some point, offer on a later date. Even better, let him know ahead of time by saying, "I would really love to take you to dinner tomorrow night" in order to take away the stress and a possible uncomfortable situation when the check arrives. But again . . . don't pay on the first date.

- Go home with him at the end of the night. Kiss, make out, even cuddle if you can outside, in the car, or wherever. Just don't go home with him, don't get a hotel room together, don't sneak into the bathroom together, don't invite him home. *Don't* have sex. Save *some*thing for *next* time.

- Obsess after the date if you don't hear from him for a couple of days. Translation: Don't hound, harass, call/text/e-mail more than once, stalk (either through Facebook or in real life), or let it consume you. If he doesn't call within five days, forget about him. Even if he does eventually get around to calling. No one is *that* busy that he can't take one minute to send an e-mail or a text.

Remember, when it comes to the Internet, there are plenty of fish in the pond. If this one ends up not being a prized catch . . . next!

Quickies—Yes, "That" Kind

It's tough to be the QuickieChick without at least addressing "the quickie"—yes, that kind of quickie. When it comes to sex, quickies can be great! In fact, I think they are a healthy part of a relationship. Sure, a romantic, candlelit all-night rendezvous can be fab! But sometimes I like the spontaneity, the thrill, the quick and passionate *wham, bam!* No . . . I'm not saying to pick up some random dude in a bar and head into the bathroom. I'm talking about quickies with your guy, your boyfriend! The fact is that time, energy, and sleep are limited right about now with your new, busy lifestyle. As much as I hate to say it, sometimes that extra hour of shut-eye is more valuable than another drawn-out sesh in the sack. And that's OK—make it a quickie instead. You don't have to have the build-up or the postcoital cuddle. There is something exciting in the fast and feverish! So don't let the "I'm too busy" excuse get in the way of your relationship. Sprinkle in a few quickies and you will be good to go!

When to End a FriENDship

Do you have that friend who refuses to support you? Someone who seems to push fatty food on you, encourages you to skip your workout, or simply makes fun of your new healthy lifestyle—even though she knows you're on a diet? Someone who talks you into staying out later than you should and drinking too heavily on work nights, lying to your boss so you can take the day off, and slacking off when you know a potential promotion is in sight? Sad but true, many of us do. Why do we have and *keep* these friends? Well, because:

- By you making changes to better your life, you are inadvertently illuminating the areas in their lives that need improvement, too.

- They like to hang out with you because you are in the same sinking boat, which means that they have someone to commiserate, complain, and pity-party with, someone who "gets" them, who they can relate to.

- Some people like to be the prettiest, most successful, thinnest, healthiest in their group, unknowingly yet specifically singling out less-attractive, chubby-pants friends who highlight just how pretty/fit/perfect they are. By you bettering your image, you are, in some screwed-up way, degrading theirs. I know; it's twisted.

Forget the twenty-one-day "Master Cleanse" and its bizarre water, lemon, cayenne, maple syrup mind/body detox, and the whole spring cleaning of your house to clear the clutter. Sure, absolutely those are great ways to start fresh, but what's the area of your life most likely in need of serious pollutant purging? Your personal life. Yes, people can be toxic, too! It's time to take a good, hard look at the people you surround yourself with—both old and new—and figure out who is good for you and who, well, has got to go. Sometimes it's time to break up with a friend.

HOW TO DECIDE WHO STAYS & WHO GOES?

Having DNA in common or sharing a long history shouldn't dictate whether or not you allow someone to stay in your inner circle. Nor does being the two newbies together at a job or sharing a wall (yes, the neighbor in the next apartment). Look at the people whom you *choose* to surround yourself with, and the people you feel you *have* to surround yourself with—for whatever the reason. Now think about, or even make a list if it helps, how each person "serves" you. What do they provide for you? Is it a two-way, mutually beneficial, uplifting, encouraging, enlightening, or comforting relationship? Or do you feel drained, exhausted, angry, sad, insecure, unimportant, uninteresting, or annoyed after hanging out with them? It's those people—the energy suckers, the Debbie Downers, the ego deflators, the demotivators, the people who pull you back, hold you down, or serve no healthy purpose in your life—that you simply don't need anymore.

I'm not saying that you need to completely shut them out, lose their number, or tell them you never want to see their faces again. What I am saying is that those people don't need to be in your inner circle. You don't need to check in with them, hang out with them, open yourself up and share with them anymore. Those are the personal-life pollutants whom you need to distance yourself from.

WHO SHOULDN'T MAKE THE CUT & NEEDS TO BE CUT

- They discourage you from doing the things that uplift you—be it working out, sticking to a healthy diet, seeing your family, working, or whatever.

- Each time you hang out with them, you leave feeling sad, angry, unmotivated, insecure, uninteresting, or exhausted.

- You realize that after you see them you consistently get into a fight with your boyfriend, mom, other friends, boss, etc.

- They bring out "the worst" in you or encourage your bad habits.

- You feel like you are constantly walking on eggshells when you are with them.

- They expect you to behave in a certain way that is unnatural and uncomfortable to you when you are with them.

- They are constantly judging and criticizing you.

- It's all about them all the time. Your interests, opinions, feelings are not important, considered, or respected.

118

NOW WHAT?

Like the mold in the corners of your shower, ignoring the problem and allowing it to persist unchanged is not going to make it go away. In fact, it will only allow it to fester, get worse, and possibly even make you sick. As nerve-racking as it may be, it's time to make the necessary shift in your relationship.

- **Have a heart-to-heart.** If you think that the relationship has the potential of being fixed, or at least improved enough so that it makes sense for you, it's time to have a heart-to-heart. This is not an opportunity to place blame, point fingers, or get nasty. That's why it's called a "heart-to-heart." Be honest. Express how the relationship is hard for you. Instead of saying "You do this to me," say "It is hard for me when I feel . . ." The heart-to-heart approach is for relationships that you believe are either salvageable or are with people who you simply cannot cut ties with. In that case, now is the time to not only express your concerns, but talk about new ways to interact, setting boundaries, expectations, and coming to an understanding of where you each stand and how you would like to be treated and feel.

- **Back off.** It may seem like sort of a cop-out way to go, but simply backing off of the relationship, without addressing it, could be your best, nonconfrontational way out. Stop returning calls as swiftly, stop being so available for plans, stop making the time for elongated chats. Not everyone will so easily let you simply fall away, and it's not always all that appropriate either. In that case . . .

- **Break up.** Some relationships, like romantic relationships, longtime friendships, and sometimes those with family members require you to actually have the dreaded "breakup" conversation. The reason is that you have invested a lot of time into the relationship. And it's likely you did that for a reason. Maybe the relationship has shifted and "things just aren't the same anymore." Maybe you have moved on, up, or elsewhere in your life, in a direction that the other person hasn't—which isn't his/her fault. If you have to break up, it's best to do it in a loving, nonthreatening way, explaining why you don't think maintaining such close ties makes sense for either of you anymore. Don't be mean. Just be honest and fair.

You've allowed yourself to take a breather from your toxic friend's presence, now see how you feel. Do you feel like a weight has lifted? Do you feel like you can finally exhale? Are you no longer stressing whenever your phone rings or hiding in your apartment with the blinds closed in case your neighbor decides to drop by? Are you more positive, productive, and enlivened? Are you nurturing relationships with people you may have disposed of but really like? That's when you know that letting those polluters go was the exact right decision to make, even if acting on the decision was at first hard.

QuickieChick's Cheat Sheet

1. In college you date for fun, so you get "serious" faster, and sooner than later it fizzles out. Post-grad you're looking for something more substantial, so you **take your time and "date,"** then, when you find someone with real "right" potential, you settle into a relationship that tends to be more emotionally involved and time-enduring.

2. Except on rare occasions, **college boyfriends just don't cut it in the end.** Whether the excuse is physical or emotional distance, time, energy, or a difference in interests, it seems cutting the cord (the sooner the better) is the best way to move forward in the real world.

3. Your boyfriend should never be holding you back from being the best you can be as an individual. It's fine if he wants to spend more time with you because he loves you. It's not fine if he doesn't want you going to networking events because he is jealous. Learn to recognize these differences.

4. You can always get something out of a date. Even if the guy isn't the love of your life (in fact, maybe he's an intolerable jerk), ask him questions. Try to learn as much as you can about each "type" of guy. It will help you know what to expect as you continue on your dating adventures.

5. Dating a colleague has consequences that, generally, aren't worth the short-lived fun to be had.

6. Be realistic about your guy's flaws. No one is perfect, and that includes you. Don't get rid of the guy just because he obsesses over video games. If he misses your anniversary dinner in favor of a new video game, that's a different story. . . .

7. A great way to communicate with your guy, even if you are clueless as to what he's talking about? **Ask questions and respond to his comments.** Try to understand his perspective and point of view. Why does he think that way? Why does he feel that way? Why does he have an interest in that topic? It's not just about communication, it's about learning about him . . . and therefore learning whether he's right for you.

8. On the first date, never pay, go home with him, or talk about exes. You want to seem available but not easy.

9. Be wary of what you post on Facebook. I know the camera always seems to be around when you're dancing on a table, but if you want a guy to take you seriously (and to take you out more than once), then you need to update your privacy settings.

10. Friends can be caustic. Just because someone has been in your life since you were five, held your hand during your lowest lows, and is the keeper of all of your darkest secrets doesn't mean you have to keep that person around if he/she is now bringing you down.

121

6

How to Eat, Drink & Drop Weight (Without Breaking the Bank)

FACT: When there's no cafeteria preparing your buffet-style meals, suddenly you realize just how time, energy, and bank-account draining eating can be! But it doesn't have to be.

Now that you are out of school, you no longer have a cafeteria serving up hot and fresh(-ish) food whenever your stomach rumbles. The endless options (the same options that helped you pack on the pounds) are no longer at your disposal (which might actually be a good thing). And now that you're über-conscious about money, even going out for happy hour leads you to calculating how much you're spending and how many hours you had to work to make the money to pay for that meal. Yes, one big kick-in-the-pants reality of being on your own is that you now have to prepare your own food. Oh, and pay for it . . . which can be quite pricey for first-timers. Food is one of those expenditures that you might not factor into the mix when figuring out your daily/weekly/monthly budget, but it can bite you in the butt when, after months of draining your bank account, you realize that you are spending more on food (and booze) than on any other expense (including rent, if you really let it get out of hand).

 *QuickieChick Quiz*

1. Yes or no:

N Y   After eating a few too many Milanos (you know, those fab chocolate-filled cookies), you cancel on girls' night out. You feel too bloated to even be seen. You'd rather just sleep it off.

N Y You ate *way* too big of a lunch and you know it. But when dinnertime rolls around, you do feel a legitimate hunger rumble in your tummy. Even though you broke the calorie bank *big time* today, you eat a normal-size dinner.

N Y One of your friends is *so* skinny. Like model skinny. You make sure to *never* be photographed next to her.

If most of your answers were in column 2, you may have a less-than-healthy relationship with food. Don't stress; many of us go through it. This chapter should help.

2. **Your friend has been acting sad and not going out much the past few days. She finally reveals to you that she thinks she has gained weight (and she has . . . noticeably). You respond with:**

   A. No you haven't!
   B. Why don't we try going for a little walk together before work in the mornings? Or how about instead of drinks before dinner tonight, we take a yoga class?

   The correct answer (if you're honest and supportive) **is B.** You didn't laugh at her or show a face of disgust at the recently flabbed-up arm she's showing. But you didn't deny the weight gain, either! Rather, you looked immediately for a solution that can help her achieve the weight loss that she obviously wants. And the best thing is that you can do it together!

3. **Which is more fattening?**

   A. A mai tai
   B. A beer

   A mai tai, big time! Averaging 620 calories (for a 9-ounce serving). I know we associate beer (averaging about 150 calories per 12-ounce serving) with beer-bellied frat boys, but just imagine what those guys would look like if they'd been filling their kegs with mai tais!

Is Freedom Fattening?

The good thing about being responsible to dish out the dough to cover your food costs? You have the opportunity to lose the weight you likely gained during those four (or more) university years, where your meals weren't monitored by anyone—including you. But before we get down to the fat-dropping phase of this book, let's figure out why you packed them on in the first place. After all, the best way to change unhealthy habits is to first understand the root of the behavior that started it. Daphne Oz, cohost of ABC's *The Chew*, a 2008 graduate of Princeton University, and author of the national best-selling book *The Dorm Room Diet*, assures us that you're not alone. In fact, it's common to pack on the pounds while away at school. Why? First, two surprising biggies:

- Homesickness

- Academic and social pressures

Confused? Daphne reminds us that the college experience is a total life shift. You make a whole new group of friends as you immerse yourself into a life and environment that can be drastically different from where you grew up. "The transition period can force even the most well-prepared eater to turn to food for comfort if she doesn't recognize and stop emotional eating in its tracks, and find constructive ways to cope. The most important thing to remember is that you are in charge of where, when, what, and with whom you eat—you have all the power! And you also have all the responsibility." And that can be the downfall right there. You're not used to having such amazing and total control of the food you buy, make, and eat. The freedom can be fattening. A postcollege fact you are now facing in the mirror.

From home-cooked meals in high school, to cafeteria concoctions in college, to finally being on your own—how do you switch gears and relearn how to eat? Daphne says that "figuring out a healthy lifestyle is all about moderation. That is to say, never let yourself feel deprived." To clarify, this is not about "dieting." You shouldn't, as Daphne says, "go" on a diet, because that represents a departure from our typical way of eating. This new way of eating is focused on food as fuel, fuel that you also thoroughly enjoy, savoring every tasty morsel that hits your tongue. Yes, you can relish food's glory without getting fat and, yes, even lose weight. Daphne's advice? "Your diet— your everyday eating plan—should include a whole lot of healthy fruits and veggies, complex carbohydrates, and some good fats and proteins, of course. But I also want you to make room for occasional indulgences for those special treats that help you feel like you participated, had a great experience, and

Note to Self

Splurge *Don't* Gorge

The two are very different!

Take Note

Splurge = a piece of cake, a couple of slices of pizza

Gorge = a cake, an entire pizza

Splurges are fine sometimes, but don't derail your entire, fit week with a gorge. It's not worth it!

Learning to Love Celery

Julia, 23, Environmental Educator: "I gained a college 20."

How did you lose it?

1. "Leaving pint nights and pitchers of beer behind me in college. Social drinking is definitely part of my postgraduate life, and savoring a whiskey over keeping pace with the beer guzzlers is infinitely kinder to my wallet and waistline.

2. "Making exercise a nonnegotiable (and enjoyable) part of every day. Regarding it as my de-stressing routine instead of a chore.

3. "Cooking *small* portions/always halving or quartering recipes. I just don't have the self-control against the siren call of a full dish of leftovers lurking in my fridge.

4. "I've learned to love celery."

are even more resolved to keep yourself on the healthy bandwagon the other 99 percent of the time."

Of course, moderation is key, but if you want that chocolate chip cookie, red velvet cupcake, or brownie on occasion, by all means, *splurge*—on *one*, not all of them. And enjoy every sumptuous, rich, taste-bud–coating bite. So how is the occasional unhealthy indulgence going to keep you on the healthy bandwagon? Because if you deprive yourself, you will find yourself fixating on those things that you don't allow yourself to indulge in. Then, during a moment of unfortunate weakness, you are more likely to not just splurge, but gorge—big-time!

I've got to say, I *love* Daphne's personal food motto: "Substitution where you can, moderation where you can't."

What's that mean?

Crisp, crunchy apple . . . or . . . nasty, dry, processed, store-bought brownie? If you're happy to have an apple instead of a stale, plastic-wrap–flavored, dry, wholly unsatisfying, and honestly totally disappointing store-bought brownie, that's a great way to limit unnecessary, processed fats and sugars. You can also keep in mind that the beautifully crisp, perfectly sweet apple is also 0 grams of fat, 120 calories. Whereas the brownie averages 17 grams of fat and 350 calories.

Thin slice of rich, creamy, decadent cake . . . or . . . nothing, but feeling left out? Sometimes it's better to have a small slice or bite of your friend's birthday cake instead of declining and then drooling and feeling emotionally deprived just so you can say you didn't have any.

We all, yes all, struggle with weight. But that doesn't mean you have to allow it to consume you. In fact, that's a surefire way to keep on gaining, instead of keeping it off. Many of us have such a hard time finding that healthy and oh-so-delicate balance between when to indulge and when to refrain. A friend of mine once told me (when I was having some serious body-image issues and not treating it as well as I should have been), "This is the only

Sound the Alarm! Policing Bad Eating Habits

Tools

What food can you just not put down once you start eating it?

_____

_____

What do you like about that food (texture/taste)?

_____

_____

What triggers you to overeat (boredom, loneliness, anger, seeing an ex)?

_____

_____

What foods are your emotional go-tos?

_____

_____

What time of day do you tend to overeat?

_____

_____

Starter Sentence

I am going to keep less

_____

_____

in my kitchen, because I know me, and I know that I can't stop eating it if it's there, so instead I will replace it with this healthier alternative:

_____

_____.

body you've got to run around in on this planet! Be nice to it!" That really stuck with me. Even if you have that perfect, runway body you've worked so hard for, if you're starving, tired, and moody, it essentially detracts from everything else you want or have to do. You may have the perfect body, but are you having *any* fun in it?

It's all about paying attention to *your* habits, *your* feelings, *your* body. That's the only way to be a healthy, happy eater.

Stocking Your Fridge & Pantry: The Basics

Stocking your fridge is the first step to defining your new fit mentality. Of course, we all have different taste preferences and fave foods, but there are some basics that you should have to get started.

BEST-BET BASICS

Cold Cereals

Focus on: fiber. Choose cereals with 6 grams or more of fiber.
Examples: Fiber One, All-Bran, Kashi cereals (Heart to Heart, Go Lean), Bran Flakes, Shredded Wheat, Puffins Cinnamon

Hot Cereals

Focus on: plain, unsweetened, not flavored. You can add your own flavors with dried or fresh berries, if you'd like.
Examples: plain oatmeal, oat bran, quick-cooking steel-cut oats, Kashi Heart to Heart Oatmeal, Quaker Oatmeal Express (not the flavored or sweetened options)

Bread

Focus on: fiber. Choose bread with 3 grams or more of fiber per slice.
Examples: rye, whole wheat sourdough, whole wheat bagels, whole wheat English muffins, La Tortilla Factory Fiber & Flax tortillas, corn tortillas, whole wheat tortillas, whole wheat pita bread. I'm also obsessed with GG Scandinavian Bran Crispbread—super high fiber, super low calories/carbs. I always, always have at least a few packs of it on hand.

Pastas

Focus on: avoiding white flour pasta.
Examples: low-carb, whole wheat, high protein, rice pasta, soba pasta, spelt pasta, corn pasta, kamut pasta (10 grams protein in 2 ounces!). Or try pasta alternatives like spaghetti squash or Tofu Shirataki (pasta)—both of which have little to no carbs, are seriously low in calories, and are majorly tasty. Treat them just like you would pasta.

Grains

Focus on: whole grains (not white rice), which have more flavor, fiber, and nutrients.

Examples: brown rice, whole-grain couscous, lentil pilaf, wild rice, quinoa

Snacks

Focus on: filling, not fattening, craving-satisfying snacks. And watch out for snacks that are heavy in fat, salt, sugar, or calories.

Examples: reduced-fat Triscuits, Ak-Mak crackers, RyKrisp, Kashi TLC crackers, Wasa Crispbread, reduced-fat Wheat Thins, rice cakes, fat-free graham crackers, soy chips, popchips, mini popcorn bags, baked tortilla chips, frozen juice bars, unsalted peanuts, almonds, pistachios, pecans, pumpkin seeds, nimble™ by Balance Bar®.

Salad Dressings

Keep in mind that some salad dressings can turn your "light lunch" into a meal that's more fat-loaded than a cheeseburger. Yes. Most creamy or oily dressings are just that—heavy cream or oil. Translation: fat. If you're out at a restaurant and you order a salad, always ask for dressing on the side, then dip your fork in the dressing, then into each bite. That's enough dressing to provide the flavor without the insane amount of fat. Or be sure to ask for light dressing.

Examples: Newman's Own Lighten Up, Girard's Light, Follow Your Heart Lowfat Ranch, balsamic vinegar, Bragg Liquid Aminos, champagne vinegar, or substitute these for dressing: salsa (my fave), low-fat hummus, low-fat cottage cheese, lemon juice

Mayonnaise

What I just said about salad dressing . . . same goes for mayo. Lighten up. Even if you just use a spoon-size smear that you slather on your sandwich and barely even notice is there . . . even that has loads of fat. Go for the lighter, healthier version instead if you must.

Examples: light mayonnaise, olive oil mayonnaise

Margarine, Spreads & Oil

I do love butter. And butter loves my butt. There is a time and a place for real butter, and that's when you are having just a little little bit of high-quality salted butter on a beautiful piece of homemade bread. Aside from that, lighten up.

Examples: Brummel & Brown, Earth Balance, Promise Light, Smart Balance Omega-3, Smart Balance Light, I Can't Believe It's Not Butter Light, extra virgin olive oil, Pam Organic Canola Oil spray (if you're cooking with it).

Another way to lighten up butter: egg-butter! Hard boil an egg until cooked through, remove and dump the yolk, chop up the white, add it to two tablespoons room-temperature light butter, add a little salt and pepper to taste, and you have just extended your butter, cut the fat almost in half, and transformed it into something so delicious you won't even be able to handle yourself.

Nut or Seed Butter

Focus on: avoiding additives. The ingredients list should consist of one thing—nuts or seeds.

Examples: natural peanut butter, natural soy butter, natural almond butter, natural sunflower seed butter

Dairy

Focus on: nonfat or low-fat options. They still have the creaminess without the weight.

Examples: nonfat or 1 percent milk, nonfat light yogurt (less than 22 grams sugar), nonfat cottage cheese, nonfat plain Greek yogurt (I'm kind of obsessed, less than 20 grams of sugar per serving, plus even more protein), Alpine Lace cheese, low-fat provolone cheese, low-fat mozzarella cheese, low-fat parmesan cheese, Laughing Cow Light or Mini Babybel Light cheeses, light string cheese, Land O'Lakes Fat-Free Half & Half (great to use on pasta when you want to make a fat-free Alfredo sauce!)

Dairy Alternatives

Focus on: light options. Just because it's organic or natural doesn't mean it's low fat.

Examples: White Wave Silk Soymilk, EdenSoy, Hain WestSoy milk, 8th Continent Original Soymilk, Rice Dream nondairy milk, Follow Your Heart Vegan Gourmet Cheddar, Tofutti Mozzarella, Soyco Mozzarella, Galaxy Foods Veggie Slices

Top-5 Diet Secrets

There is a reason that the majority of chicks consider themselves to be "on a diet." Because we ALL (yes, all, including me) make mistakes when it comes to healthy eating, and sometimes we have to edit our food. Daphne Oz shares her top five diet secrets.

1. **People don't plan to fail; they fail to plan.** Set yourself up for success by crowding out the less-healthy alternatives with tons of delicious, healthy snacks and meals on hand.

2. **Moderation is key.** Don't jump in cold turkey, thinking you'll never be able to enjoy your favorite cake again. The whole idea behind a healthy lifestyle is that nothing is off-limits! You are in complete control, and you can have anything you like. Take the time to count to your age before indulging, to make sure you've really thought through the choice to eat something and are sure it's something you really want to savor and enjoy (as opposed to just eating because . . . well, because there is nothing else to do, you're bored, lonely, sad, or just addicted to the action of hand to mouth).

3. **Always eat breakfast.** Studies show that eating a donut for breakfast is better than eating nothing at all. That's not to say you should eat a donut; it's saying that you have to break your fast in the morning in order to get your metabolism moving, naturally burning calories. By eating something first thing in the morning, even if it's just a banana or yogurt on the run, you are starting your system.

4. **Quit yer whinin'.** Talking about your dieting woes to every ear that will listen gets tiresome, for you and your unfortunate listener. Even worse, it centers your thinking around what you can't have. The more you fixate on trying to stay away from the bag of chips or candy bar calling your name, the more power it has over you. Food should never be the number-one focus of your life. Make being healthy a priority, but don't let what you're eating—or not eating—be the only thing you can think about. Here's the interesting thing: Make a point of not thinking about it—I mean really try not to think about it—and pretty soon several days will have passed and you will suddenly realize that you haven't fixated on food or your weight. And that feels good.

5. **Balance and reward.** If this is truly going to be a permanent healthy lifestyle, you need to take care of all of you, not just the physical. Caring for your mental and emotional health are equally important, so find supportive-friend groups and fun activities that let you feel like part of a community. Getting the endorphins flowing with a

Comforting and Calorie-Free

Tools

Which places make you feel relaxed (e.g., beach, backyard, bedroom)?

_____

_____

What activities make you feel invigorated?

_____

_____

Note It

Make a list of ten healthier alternatives to eating in response to different food triggers:

1. _____
2. _____
3. _____
4. _____
5. _____
6. _____
7. _____
8. _____
9. _____
10. _____

When weakness hits, you won't even have to think about what to do instead of eat. Just glance at the list (which you can post on your fridge) and find a guilt-free substitute.

Starter Sentences

In order to reduce stress (which can lead to overeating) I will spend more time here

_____

_____

doing

_____

_____ .

In order to find happiness in my life *other* than food, I'll do more of this

_____

_____ .

131

great group workout, or bonding with new friends over a shared love of backgammon gives you a much-needed outlet, a great way to bond with others, and an opportunity to de-stress and decompress, which we all need! And when you've been doing a great job keeping yourself on track, show some self-love: Buy yourself the flat iron you've been pining over, or treat yourself to a manicure. Let yourself relax and rejuvenate, and the going will be that much easier.

"Freshman 15" to 20-Something Sexy: The Best Diet to Get Your Prom-Queen Body Back

The best diet is not a diet at all, but a permanent healthy lifestyle. That's the only surefire way to lose weight that won't come creeping back. Finding an eating plan that works for you is about figuring out the foods you can live without and the ones you need to always make room for. For Daphne Oz, it's Swedish pancakes, a family specialty. "Rather than limiting myself to once a year or some other Draconian measure, I let myself have a little bit whenever someone is making them. If I have a bite or half of one whenever they're around, I'm able to indulge whenever I like, but I'm also able to stop myself from eating a whole batch, because I know I won't have to wait another year to enjoy them. For some, eating any at all opens the floodgates, so you need to be aware of what works for you and what doesn't."

Now . . . when it comes to that prom dress; let me be honest: You might never fit back into it again. Why? Your body has changed. Your hormones have transformed you into, yes, a woman. And that's very good news, actually. Look at how puerile and immature and oddly shaped high school bodies are. Seriously. They are often unproportional, inconsistent, and awkward. Why? Because they are in the midst of developing, growing, forming into their shapes. This new shape of yours has evolved for a reason—to house a baby. That might be the furthest thing from your mind right now, but when it comes down to it, a woman's body is, among many things, a vessel to grow another human. That's why when chicks are too thin they tend to lose their periods. Their bodies are no longer capable of nourishing infants from tadpole to toddler (well, not exactly, but you get the picture, and that's the point). Another hard fact about aging: Your metabolism (your body's natural calorie-burning mechanism) starts to slow down, making it more difficult to drop weight, requiring more exercise and less food. That doesn't mean that you can't look smoking hot again. Because you can, and you will if you adopt a healthy, balanced lifestyle. In fact, you'll look even hotter. Why? With age you come to understand how to work with your looks, how to dress them up, flaunt them, and even how and when to tone certain areas down. You will also have more confidence, which translates into instant beauty.

How does Daphne deal with the reality of an aging body? "I'd be lying if I told you I was looking forward to the sagging and drooping that is sure to occur as I age. But I am ecstatic thinking about what a full and fulfilling life I will hopefully have had by the time those lines and saddlebags begin to set. Thinking about the changes your body goes through as it ages as badges of honor for all the life experience you've had is one way to replace negative association with positive. Keeping up a regular fitness routine that keeps you limber, toned, and flexible is a way to stave off the dramatic changes to begin with. And loving every minute you have on earth, making the most of the best body you could ever have because it is your own, is a must."

Is Your Boyfriend Making You Fat?

Whenever you're single, you're in the best shape of your life, right? Yeah, me, too. When you're single you *have* to "try." You eat right, work out diligently, and watch your waist. And then you find "Mr. Right" (or "Mr. Right Now"), and suddenly you shift your focus from you to you two. It's not abnormal to gain a few "happy pounds" when in a settled, committed relationship. But the question is: Are you happy about those pounds?

If the answer is "not so much," there are things you can do about it, like—ahem—incorporate a fitness lifestyle into your life! Sure, your fitness lifestyle used to be all about you, but it's easy to get him in on the action, too. In fact, being healthy together can help improve the health of your relationship, even better, your sex life; yes, couples who work out together tend to have better sex together.

7 WAYS YOUR RELATIONSHIP IS MAKING YOU FAT

1. Eating dinners out
2. Taking excessive couch time

133

3. Always splitting a bottle of wine (as opposed to opting for just a glass or none at all)

4. Eating foods you wouldn't normally eat (like dessert after every dinner or chips while watching TV)

5. Eating when your partner is munching

6. Not needing to impress anyone anymore because you're in love

7. Not making time for yourself

Now it's up to you to figure out how to curb at least a few of the issues above . . . unless of course you are happy with the growing bulge between the two of you. If you're not, then thankfully that's what this chapter is for.

7 Reasons _Not_ to Drink Diet Soda

Frightening fact: Some people may eat a healthy amount of calories, then drink as many as 2,000 calories worth of soda! Considering that 3,500 un-burned calories equals one pound of fat, that is a recipe for major weight gain. Juice isn't the answer either! Why? First of all, lots of juice drinks are really mostly sugar, plus a little juice. Even if they are pure juice, the calorie content can still exceed that of soda. A calorie is a calorie is a calorie. Yes, you're getting more nutrients, but if you're drinking 2,000 calories, that's still 2,000 extra condensed calories. And then there is diet soda.

While diet soda may have zero calories, it doesn't mean it's good for you. Here are seven reasons why you should skip diet sodas, too:

1. **Unexpected cravings:** Just like subliminal messages in advertisements, artificial sweeteners have you wanting something that you didn't even know you wanted! Just a few sips of something sweet makes your body expect more sweets. While you were trying to cut calories with a diet soda, you may find yourself with unexpected cravings for real sugar later.

2. **Bloat:** The gases in the soda become gases in your body. Carbonated drinks, diet or not, can make you feel and appear bloated. Not quite what you were going for when you reached for the diet?

3. **Dehydration:** Diet soda is a dehydration demon. Soda drains your body of water. Add to that the fact that caffeine is a diuretic, and you're losing essential water in more ways than one.

4. **Weight gain:** Diet soda may be the last thing you want when on a diet. Researchers have found that those who drink diet soda have more difficulty losing weight than those who drink regular soda. This

could be the result of the mind games diet soda plays on you. Many dieters reason that the swap of regular soda for diet entitles them to those few extra bites of food.

5. **Expense:** The average American family spends five hundred dollars per year on soda. Think of anything you want that costs that much. Would you still rather have the soda? How about water from the tap with a squeeze of lemon? It's practically free.

6. **Enamel destruction:** Too much soda can cost you more than just money in the long run. Many of the ingredients in diet soda are known to destroy the enamel on your teeth. Since diet soda drinkers tend to reach for a few extra zero-calorie cans, they are even more at risk for this side effect.

7. **Tampering with taste buds:** Pick your sweets. You may not notice it, but artificial sweeteners are much sweeter than real sugar, making other sweet foods taste less flavorful. Want to enjoy an apple or even your favorite movie snack? Skip the diet soda.

8 SODA ALTERNATIVES

I get it, you don't like just plain water. Fine. That doesn't mean that you now have a right to dehydrate yourself by not drinking *anything*. Water isn't just about hydration, it's also about flushing out toxins, keeping you fuller longer (so you have fewer cravings for food, when you're really not hungry), and basic functioning in life. Not to worry, I wasn't just going to leave you hanging there, stripping you of the one "diet-friendly" drink that you actually like and not offering a replacement to fill the void. That would be just cruel. Below are eight alternatives to soda that are healthier and even crave-worthy. You won't love them all. Which is why there are eight to choose from.

1. **Cranberry spritzer:** Combine three parts water (sparkling or flat is fine) to one part 100 percent cranberry juice for a refreshing, de-puffing, detoxifying, low-cal, vitamin-rich drink that you can sip all day long! Note: I said "100 percent cranberry juice"; I *didn't* say "cranberry juice drink" or "cranberry juice cocktail." Those "drinks" and "cocktails" are generally made with more sugar or filler juices, like "white grape juice," than cranberry juice. Why? Fillers are cheaper than pure juice. They are also loaded with empty calories. 100 percent cranberry juice will pucker your lips. It's bitter. That's why you should dilute it. Then drink up!

2. **Pomegranate green tea:** Brew a big batch of green tea. Let it cool. Combine three parts green tea with one part pomegranate juice

for an antioxidant-loaded all-day-guzzling drink with fab natural sweetness. Or even just green tea. I go through at least three tea bags of green tea each day. No need for the hot water, simply drop a bag in your cold water, let it slowly soak through, and enjoy the flavored, antioxidant-rich, calorie-busting water. Then refill the water and use the same bag. Use each bag twice, then swap out for a new one.

3. **Lemon water:** It might sound like a chore, but add a squeeze (or lots of squeezes, even half a lemon worth) to water and you have instantly transformed plain, tasteless water into something that not only tastes good but is also a natural antibacterial, and a detoxifying fat burner. Add a slice of cucumber and, voilà, spa water!

4. **Kombucha:** Most people don't believe that bacteria and food mix particularly well together. I would tend to agree, except in a few instances—like blue cheese and yogurt—veiled by the words *active enzymes* or *contains acidophilus*. Now there is a new bacterially enhanced beverage that delivers a healthy dose of healing microorganisms. It's called kombucha (kom-BOO-cha) and I am obsessed, especially to GT's Enlightened Synergy organic Raw Kombucha. Kombucha is a raw, fermented, handmade tea, originally from China, that is filled with naturally occurring active enzymes (like those you might find in yogurt), probiotics, amino acids, antioxidants, and polyphenols. Some say it has helped with digestion, metabolism regulation, immune-system bolstering, appetite and weight control, liver function, and preserving the health of skin, hair, and cells. Is this not gold? Could it be the antiaging elixir that scientists have been attempting to re-create? Why are we not shouting kombucha's praises from the rooftops?! Yes, it tastes a little like vinegar. But I love it and I don't care. Kombucha is a must in my fridge and a daily diet-soda alternative (even a wine and coffee alternative at times) for me.

5. **Emergen-C:** Packed with one thousand milligrams of vitamin C plus other vitamins and minerals, this nutrient-dense packet is bursting with flavor and ups your energy. Considering that high doses of vitamin C have been shown to help support the immune system and even help burn fat, umm . . . why wouldn't it be your go-to drink too? I drink one daily.

6. **Crystal Light:** OK, yes, there are artificial sweeteners in Crystal Light, which is not a good thing (if you read my diet-soda rant above), however, the amount of sweetener is low (comparatively). The packets, which you can easily slip into your purse for those of

you (like me) who need immediate gratification, come in lots of fab flavors. Should you drink it all day? No. But it's OK as a tasty, hydrating drink. I *love* the pink lemonade and fruit punch flavors.

7. A newer, updated on-the-go low-cal drink mix that I am becoming obsessed with? **Hansen's Natural Fruit Stix sweetened with Truvia.** I love the strawberry lemonade flavor! Same concept as the Crystal Light, just with different ingredients.

8. **"Special tea":** This is a tea that I made up, and now I drink it at least once a day. Why? Because it is simultaneously a natural fat burner, detoxifier, hydrator, and craving-killing body warmer. I usually drink it after dinner as an alternative to dessert, because somehow it kills my craving for sugar and even wine. Here's how to make it:

> mug of hot water
> 1 whole squeezed lemon (use a knife to scrape out fibrous innards)
> 3 shakes cinnamon powder
> 3 shakes cayenne powder

Skinny Jeans in the Kitchen

Skinny jeans aren't supposed to make you feel bad about your weight, size, or shape. You're not supposed to hold your breath, lie down, suck in, and honestly pray that the zipper actually goes all the way up today. The point of skinny jeans is to make you look and feel *sexy*. Not feeling it? Happens to me all the time. Instead of throwing your once-favorite jeans into the back corner of your closet, your best line of defense may be to give them a new temporary home—your kitchen.

Yes, hang your skinny jeans on your pantry door—unless, of course, you have a date or friends are coming over and you don't want to share your body issues with the world.

The point? No, not new decor. Nor is it the intention to rub your nose in the fact that you simply don't fit into them anymore. It's actually to stop your tendency to eat *too much*, even when you're not hungry, not paying attention, and sometimes honestly full, which is likely the biggest reason *why* those damn jeans don't fit. Just seeing those skinny jeans hanging there on your pantry door is a pretty powerful deterrent that forces you to think twice before stuffing that heaping spoonful of peanut butter into your mouth right out of the jar.

And here's the thing: In a few weeks (or months based on how far off the wagon you've fallen) you'll be able to slip (instead of squeeze) into those skinny jeans again. You just need to work on it and not let short-term splurges get in the way of long-term success. Really, what the skinny jeans do is force

you to think twice, question your cravings: Is that mound of peanut butter, chocolate truffle, bag of chips, container of pasta, etc., really worth it? Because, honestly, in thirty minutes, you won't have that decadent taste of chocolate in your mouth anymore. But if you keep avoiding those short-lived moments of taste-bud bliss, in a few weeks you will feel amazing about yourself all day long. And you will be thanking your skinny jeans for the reminder!

"It's Not Worth It": Post-it Notes in the Pantry

Warning: Now that you are living on your own, when you are all alone, you may very well have the inclination to stop whatever you're doing, stand in front of the fridge or pantry, and splurge on whatever happens to strike your fancy at that moment. A "fancy" that can translate into hundreds, sometimes even thousands of mindless, unnecessary, soon-to-be-regretted calories.

You might be the most vigilantly healthy person all day long, limiting your fat and sugar, keeping portions at their correct serving size, and staying true to your fit-lifestyle philosophy. Then, after you've had your healthy dinner and you're settling into your favorite decompressing TV show or finishing up some work before bed, you get hit by the weakness stick, head into the kitchen, and "snack." It's called "vampire eating."

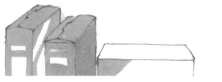

Suddenly you find yourself opening the refrigerator door and eyeballing everything (as if you don't already know what it's stocked with), perusing the pantry, and rifling through the freezer. You may be great at late-night self-convincing that enjoying a few (or a heaping handful) of M&Ms is OK and that, no, you won't regret it in the morning. That is, until the next morning, when you wake up with the disappointing realization that you not only let your diet down and negated your day's workout, but you let yourself down.

SOLUTION: POST-IT NOTES

Here's a cure that generally does the trick: Post-it Notes. Just place Post-it Notes with little reminders in your kitchen, pantry, fridge, freezer, even on the container of ice cream, if you have to:

- Don't eat that cookie.
- It's not worth it!
- Do 100 jumping jacks instead.
- Go for a walk.
- Try on your skinny jeans.
- Can you fit into your bikini?
- It's not worth it.
- You're better than that.
- Seriously?

And worst case—the result of eating that cookie:

- Sugar = fat ass

It works. There's also the more extreme cure: At 8 P.M. each night you tape your refrigerator and pantry shut. Not that you can't simply untape them, but at least it will be a very strong reminder that you must . . . not . . . give . . . in. Of course, if you have company coming over, you might want to remove the Post-it Notes. You don't want to seem crazy or anything. Hey, whatever works!

Expert Insight

Daphne Oz

Daphne's Weight Loss "Trick"

The only "trick" I've found is to think positively. Whenever I feel positive about myself—knowing that my workouts are working, that I'm getting fuel and pleasure from my food, that food is not ruling my life, etc.—I miraculously start to really look better and even fit in my clothes better. I don't know what happens, or if it is even possible, but there you have it. At the very least, the extra boost of confidence feels great!

Aside from that? Eat less and exercise. Sorry, but that's the only real way to do it healthily!

Face the Facts: You're Overweight & This Is Why

For years I was totally opposed to the concept of a "food journal." And then I went to school for nutrition and one of my required assignments was to keep a food journal. I thought it was the lamest project. It conjured the notion of my pained prepubescent "Dear Diary" moments when I would feverishly scribble my thoughts, love sagas, and breakup dramas for pages on end in a locked little book. The food journal wasn't that at all. What I almost immediately discovered was that writing down my depression-/anxiety-/celebration-/whatever-induced food foibles and feats forced me to fess up to myself, facing the facts of my food issues and illuminating what drove me to inhale a dozen chocolate chip cookies last night, when the night before I felt fulfilled after just one.

A food journal isn't a quick fix. It's actually seriously enlightening and can have long-term effects, pinpointing unhealthy trends and patterns that you may unknowingly partake in, the actual reason why you are overweight (which can also tell you what you can do to lose it: change the pattern). You

Food Therapy (the Bad Kind)

Tools

Write a list of the situations that make you feel sad/angry/stressed/depressed:

_____

_____

Write a list your comfort foods:

_____

_____

Starter Sentences

If I'm eating

_____

_____

I should ask myself *why?* What's the reason I am eating at this moment? Was I triggered to eat by stress, a disappointment, a sad circumstance, or something else?

_____

_____

If I'm eating for reasons other than hunger (like emotions), what can I do *instead* of eating that will *really* make me feel better, something I won't regret doing once the emotion passes?

_____

_____

can create your notes in a chart format in order to make the whole process as painless as possible. Example: Create a weekly calendar. Each day you write what you ate. Or, if one food item in particular is your issue, focus the chart on that food, making a "Cookie Chart" or a "Chips Chart," and every day you have to fess up to whether you succumbed or survived the day without indulging in your food vice. Personalize it. That's the point. No one is judging you or grading you. No need to take notes every day, but *definitely* after each guilt-provoking binge fest, you should be keeping track!

FACE-THE-FACTS JOURNAL OR CHART COMPONENTS

1. So . . . what happened? (Ran into my ex with his new fling at a bar.)

2. Your post-incident response (Balled my eyes out over a box of ready-bake cookies . . . before even baking them!)

3. Post-response response (Felt fat and out of control. Balled my eyes out again.)

4. Rewrite a better post-response response for the next time the diet-derailing incident occurs. (Went for a run to make my ass look better than that bitch's.)

Diets Worth Doing & Food Fads Not to Follow

The Master Cleanse, Baby Food Diet, Cabbage Soup Diet, Grapefruit Diet, Ice Cream Diet, Cookie Diet, etc. The fact is that fad diets are often just gimmicks. So maybe they work for the time being, but, really, can you live on only baby food, cookies, cabbage soup, or, um, air (yeah, that's a crazy diet trend, too)? The real reason why fad diets tend to turn you from pudgy to trim faster than a normal diet-and-exercise routine is because the food is so limited you pretty much starve. Even when it comes to the cookie diet, there is only so much of the same thing you can eat before you just choose not to. And behold—weight loss!

DIET DETECTIVE: I TRIED, I LOST, I GAINED

As a fitness writer (and once body-obsessed chick), I have tried my share of diets, many of which definitely worked . . . for a short, and I mean *short,* period of time. I slurped bowls of cabbage soup, went raw, created perfectly portioned macrobiotic meals, tried the Every Other Day Diet idea, and of course gorged on just burger patties with Atkins. Sure, I did try most of those diets for the sake of magazine articles in which I was the guinea pig. And while they were all different, there was one consistent theme: With each diet, after a while, I wasn't able to maintain the weight loss. In fact, I ended up gaining all the weight back and more—no joke.

The Pros?

- Yes, to be honest, I did love "banana day" on the Cabbage Soup Diet. (I made myself probably ten banana smoothies that day.)

- The unbaked pizza on the raw diet was shockingly crave-worthy. I mean, I've actually eaten it several times since, just as a healthy component to my current diet, which is not a diet at all but a healthy way of eating.

- I really enjoyed the holistic approach to macrobiotic eating, and in fact I liked the food a lot, too.

- The Every Other Day Diet was great because I never felt like I was restricting myself.

- And Atkins, well, let's just say I ate about a dozen McDonald's cheeseburger patties topped with those oddly tasty pickles and ketchup—no bun or fries—and loved every diet-abiding bite!

But that was the positive side.

The Cons

- Cabbage soup got really old really fast.

- Raw left me with an allergy to walnuts (walnuts are a primary source of protein in the diet), and for the first three days I had such an intense headache I felt like my brain was in a vice.

- Macrobiotic was too incredibly labor-intensive to prepare.

- The Every Other Day Diet really sucked when I had a dinner party or an event to go to on one of the "other" days of less food.

- On Atkins I became seriously obsessed with chocolate croissants. I mean, I literally would have dreams about them, kind of like when you wake up in the middle of the night after an evening of drinking and you realize that you have been dreaming about drinking water!

In the end, the problem with each and every one of the above diets was that they didn't teach me how to eat in normal, daily-life situations. I didn't learn about portion control, carb/protein/fat ratios, calories, or nutrition. Translation: The diets weren't sustainable. But I did eventually learn a lesson: Once I went off the diets, I gained weight, then lost that excess weight by going back to my healthy, balanced food and fitness mentality. The lesson learned was *moderation*. That's it. Obviously I didn't learn moderation

Sustainable Slimming

Tools

What's a dieting technique you use that you *know* isn't good for you? (Skipping dinner? Fasting every other day?)

_____

_____

Where is your problem area with eating? (Too-big dinners? Ice cream every night?)

_____

_____

List your favorite foods

_____

_____

Grab some snack-size Baggies and portion away!

Starter Sentence

I wouldn't have to use my dieting technique that I *know* isn't good for me if I made these adjustments:

_____

_____ .

from the diets themselves, but rather from the aftermath and recovery from the diets.

If you want to lose weight, don't diet. I mean, don't diet in the conventional "I'm on a diet" sense—the kind that makes it so that you can't enjoy a cookie here and there, and on which you deprive yourself of certain foods, or even food groups. If you want to lose weight and stay fit long-term, you should:

- Eat a healthy balanced diet consisting of lots of vegetables, lean proteins, and healthy carbs.

- Eat the foods you like.

- Substitute lower-fat alternatives where possible.

- Exercise every day.

Remember: Sometimes a splurge is OK. Just try to squeeze in an extra thirty-minute workout if you can. Food is a pleasure in life. Just balance it out by also including exercise as another pleasure, and you'll be just fine.

4 Reasons the Real World Is Making You Gain Weight

It's easy to "decide" to lose weight, get healthy, and make a long-term permanent change. And then there's the reality of it. Many of you have a lifestyle that feeds into unhealthy habits—like your weekly dedication to Margarita Monday, Taco Tuesday, Thursday Happy Hour, and Sunday Funday. If you don't show up, your friends think there's either something wrong or you're simply "no fun anymore." Besides, your friends and family "love you the way you are" and really, truly "don't want you to change," and that "not changing" could include not losing weight, not getting serious about your job, or not skipping the weekly Margarita Monday drinking fest.

Daphne Oz broke down the top-four ways that the real world can ruin our weight-loss success:

1. **Time.** Sometimes, there isn't time to pull something healthy together, and grabbing food on the run can leave you with very few options.

   Solution: Plan ahead. Keep healthy snacks on hand (like little Baggies of dried fruit and almonds, a squeeze-pack of hummus and baby carrots, a protein bar with less than 2 grams saturated fat and less than 180 calories). If you know you'll be short on time, bring food with you (if you're out), like you did in grade school. If you're home, set up your meals twice a week—*all* of your meals. I like to do it on Sunday and Wednesday. I poach, grill, or bake five chicken breasts, prep veggies (so I can easily cook them), and sometimes put side dishes or even healthy sauces in Tupperware containers so that everything is ready to go in an instant. The point is that when you're hungry you don't want to have to think about it. That's the secret downfall with unhealthy snack and fast foods. You don't have to think about them. You just grab and go. If you do the prep work ahead of time, your healthy foods will be just as easy, convenient, and quick!

2. **Money.** Healthy food can cost more money. But we have the power to change that by voting for healthier options with our money every time we choose what to eat.

   Solution: Even fast-food chains have healthier menu options. Ask for the "Nutrition Facts" before ordering to ensure you make informed choices. Beyond fast food, you aren't exactly breaking the bank by buying a banana, a head of broccoli, or frozen chicken breasts. Cut the price tag even more by clipping coupons (yes, couponing is back in) and using "club cards" at your local grocery store. Even stores like 99¢ Only Store, Sam's Club, Smart & Final, Costco, and other discount stores often carry produce and lean proteins for budget shoppers. And of course your local farmers' markets or produce stands are great sources of fresh, often less expensive produce.

3. **Storage.** Given many people's tiny refrigerators and cupboards, keeping healthy food items on hand that won't perish can be a challenge.

   Solution: Make weekly trips to the grocery store to stock up on fresh fruits and veggies.

4. **Friends/boyfriends/family.** Cohorts who are not on the health kick that you're trying to follow can steer you in the wrong direction simply by being around.

   Solution: They just need to be bossed around a little bit so they get on the health train, too—peer pressure! Get a group together to set get fit goals. Walk, hike, or bike with them on weekends; check in on weekdays with "How is your food today?" or "What did you do to work out today?" texts, IMs, or e-mails. Creating a support system, having others to lean on, and sharing a common goal and an outlet are often essential components to staying on the fit bandwagon long-term.

Skinny Chicks' Food Tricks

These aren't just tricks of skinny chicks; they are tricks of smart and skinny chicks. They might be little things, but it's the little things that add up, the daily Quickies that can make all the difference. Think about it this way: You might do your one-hour workout that burns 350 calories, but then you eat a few bites here (150 calories), slurp a soda there (another 150 calories), and have one extra slice of pizza during your dinner. Why not? that slice is about 400 calories—that's why not. Yes, it's the little things that count.

Healthy "Little Things" That Fight Off Fat

Stop 3 Bites Short

By leaving three bites on your plate during every meal, you are saving yourself an average of 100 calories. Subtracting 100 unnecessary calories per day per meal from your daily count will keep those pounds from creeping up.

Eat 8 Bites of Protein

Portion control is one of the key components to weight loss and weight management. But it's so hard to remember what one portion size of protein, carbs, veggies, etc. is. Here's the general rule: one serving size of protein equals eight bites. While there are those diets that lean on protein as the main component to a dish, if you want to drop pounds and keep them off, your key ingredient needs to be veggies—especially greens. That doesn't mean they have to be boring! Low-fat sauces, some prep work, and a little salt plus an acid (like lemon or vinegar) to punch up the flavor can go a long way when it comes to green veggies. And you can eat *lots* of them (an average cup of veggies is 40 calories)!

Love to Bake?
Chew Gum While You're Doing It

When I bake, I chew gum. Why? Because I happen to be a huge fan of cookie dough, and, more often than not, the formed raw cookies don't make it into the oven. The problem is, just a "little" hunk of cookie dough actually has a lot more fat and calories than you give it credit for. Think about that little hunk and its ability to expand into a gigantic cookie in the oven. Yes, a hunk here and a hunk there and suddenly you have devoured five cookies before the baking has even begun! Chew a piece of fresh flavor-bursting gum while baking to help you resist the urge to lick the spoon.

Not Every Day Is a "Special Occasion"

Whether you eat a bit too many bites of cake on your birthday, your boyfriend's birthday, or your best friend's birthday; whether you indulge in an extra serving of turkey, pie, mashed potatoes, or tamales on one of the many annual holidays; or even if you just can't help but dig into the ice cream carton on a rainy day—it's okay . . . on occasion. Just remember that not every day is a holiday. That type of justification is how you get yourself into trouble. Oh, and remember that you don't *need* to splurge just because it's a "special occasion." Do you really think you will miss that slice of cake or that the chick two cubicles over will be pissed off (or even notice) if you don't eat any at her office birthday celebration? No.

Drink 8 Glasses of Cold Water Daily

Here's a trick: When you're "hungry," drink a glass of water first. Oftentimes we mistake hunger for thirst. It happens all the time. You guzzle a glass of water and suddenly realize that those hunger pangs are gone. Lots

146

of us simply "forget" to drink enough water to stay adequately hydrated. In fact, the rule of thumb tends to be that "if you're thirsty, you're already dehydrated." Beyond hydration, water aids weight loss, makes you feel full, and the cold temperature causes your body to burn a few more calories to warm it up. Can't stand the cold or the lack of flavor? Add a green-tea bag to room-temperature water. The bag will infuse the water and give you a pleasantly flavored, antioxidant-enhanced, energizing boost of hydration. Bottoms up!

Splurge, Don't Gorge

If you splurge, don't let that one setback end your healthy attitude. I know how easy it is to go into "Well, I have already screwed up this healthy day; I may as well go all the way and really ruin it" mentality. *No!* You have not ruined the day . . . yet. And that attitude definitely won't help your cause! Everyone caves in every so often. One carton of ice cream is better than one carton of ice cream plus a bag of chips plus a pizza and a cheeseburger added while you're at it. That's called a binge. Think rationally and get back on track. If it makes you feel better, eat a little healthier the next day or work out for an extra hour that week. You have not completely sabotaged your program; you've just thrown a very easily remedied wrench into it. Get back on that healthy wagon and keep pushing forward.

Consider the Cause

If you find that you are in the above self-sabotaging situation often, maybe it's time to start thinking about the cause. What is propelling you to overeat in the first place? If it was a holiday or a legitimate special occasion, fine. But if it was because you were depressed, happy, bored, or anxious, it's time to address the issue. Think about it:

- What was the cause of the splurge?
- How did you feel after?
- What can you do differently next time?

If you come up with a list of healthy alternatives now, you won't have to rack your brain for one when in a moment of desperation later. Believe me.

Eat Off of a Smaller Plate

Instead of a big "dinner" plate, serve up your meal on a smaller "salad" plate. It's probably the easiest way to trick your brain into thinking that you are consuming lots of food while really eating only a little—or at least less. But here are two essential secrets to remember:

- Don't make up for a lack of circumference by adding inches to the top and piling on the food like a pyramid!
- Don't go back for seconds to make up for the decrease in size.

147

Go to Bed (Just Slightly) Hungry

Now, I'm not saying to go to bed starving! Just a little hungry, that's all. You see, if you are a tad overweight, your body is used to consuming a specific amount of calories to support your current state of weight. If you cut your calorie count, you will likely feel it in the form of hunger at first. It takes a few days for your body to readjust to the new, slightly less calorie norm. Again, I'm not saying not to eat, that you should skip dinner, that you should go to bed starving, that you should be on the verge of passing-out-hungry or be awoken from your sleep because your stomach is rumbling. Just be smart, chickadees.

Graze

That whole "five small meals" thing actually works. If you eat several small meals instead of three big meals, you are keeping your metabolism stoked and continuously burning a higher rate of calories throughout the day. Therefore you will likely burn more fat and lose more weight even if you are eating slightly more food. The idea is to never feel full, but also never feel famished. Try to stay pretty even throughout the day. Yes, graze! Just make sure you are grazing on healthy food and not junk.

Start Your Meal with an Orange, a Grapefruit, or Soup

Why? Peel the orange or grapefruit before eating it and you stimulate your senses, making you more aware of what you're eating. Then you're more likely to eat mindfully. You are also eating a lot of liquid: Citrus fruits are filled with liquid, which makes you feel fuller faster so that you eat less food during the rest of your meal. It has also been shown that eating half a grapefruit before meals helps with weight loss. Same goes for soup—not cream soups, but broth-based veggie soups. You might also find that after the citrus or soup you're not very hungry at all. Why? Dehydration may have caused you to think that you were hungry when really you were just thirsty.

Keep a Scooper in Your Cereal Box

Trying to guess if you're eating the correct serving-size amount of cereal is generally a recipe for overeating. Stop eyeballing and get real by scooping out the correct serving size (ranging from one-half cup to one cup depending on the cereal) every time. At least then you'll know exactly how many calories and grams of fat you're consuming.

Note to Self

Talk Yourself Out of Gaining Weight

First of all, let me say that this is probably best done when not in the presence of anyone else . . . or at least only in the presence of people who know and "get" you.

Think Out Loud

One of the reasons we overeat on sweets, fried, fatty, and salty faves is because we aren't thinking. We're not thinking rationally about what we're doing as we stuff those chocolates/chips/fried calamari into our mouths. If, instead, you narrate your indulgences, you are less likely to turn a simple splurge (which is fine) into a total gorge (not so fine). Example?

Say out loud—yes, loud enough to be heard:

"I am about to eat this entire bag of chocolate chip cookies because I'm pissed off at my boyfriend because he didn't call me when he promised he would."

Then with each additional bite, you repeat the sentence or alter it based on the reason of the moment.

"I am going to eat another chocolate chip cookie because I feel bad for myself and I'm now angry at myself for eating five already, so I may as well eat the entire bag."

Chances are you will look at yourself and think *Really? Come on now, it is so not worth it.*

149

How Not to Destroy Your Diet on Weekends

Just because you are going out with the girls or fine dining on a date doesn't mean you should completely sabotage the healthy diet that you have been working on all week. But here's the thing: It's not necessarily that calorie-laden steak frites or fat-loaded lava cake that you have to watch out for (you already know how bad those are for you); it's the two pieces of bread with butter before dinner, the couple of glasses of wine or margaritas during your meal, and the request for extra salad dressing that are actually weighing you down.

So how do you prep for a night out? Go into it with a healthy mentality by taking a power walk first! Yes, I am a big believer in a quick fifteen-to-thirty-minute power walk before an evening on the town in order to not only burn off a few extra calories, but also to set the mood—reminding myself about how hard I have been working all week to be healthy. No reason to ruin it in one meal. Another trick? Have a small cup of fat-free yogurt to keep the hunger pains away, averting your desire to immediately dive into the bread basket the second it's presented at your table.

In case you aren't sure about just how bad some of those girls-night-out splurges are, here are some average calorie counts:

Bread (not including butter)

Housemade white bread: 250 calories for 2 slices

French bread: 515 calories for 2 large slices

Sourdough bread bowl (minus the soup): 580 calories

Housemade dinner roll: 275 calories for 2 rolls

Dressing

Ranch dressing: 73 calories/8 grams fat per tablespoon

Caesar dressing: 78 calories/8 grams fat per tablespoon

Vinaigrette: 75 calories/8 grams fat per tablespoon

Alcohol (just another reminder of the potential damage your fave drinks can do)

Beer (12 oz.): about 150 calories per glass

Mai Tai (9 oz.): 620 calories per glass

Margarita (10 oz.): 550 calories per glass

Wine (4 oz.): 100 calories per glass

Dessert wine (4 oz.): 189 calories per glass

(more of your faves are listed in the next section)

Like a credit card bill that is insanely huge thanks to lots of little charges, the little "insignificant" things add up—fast!

Tricks to Keep the Bills and Weight Down

Lindsay, 28, Works for a Nonprofit: "I had to stop dining out and make a budget. When going to the grocery store I try to have a list, but that usually doesn't happen. I go to the produce first and fill up on cheap greens for the bulk of my meal, then figure out what complements them. Fresh veggies are a must. It's not a meal without something green."

"Skinny" Sipping

Like hard candy, alcohol is an incredibly condensed form of calories. But just because you're watching your weight doesn't mean that once in a while (if not a bit more frequently than that) you might want to imbibe when out with your guy or girlfriends. And while a margarita, piña colada, full-bodied beer, or dessert wine may seem appealing, ask yourself this: Is "just one" measly drink really worth your entire workout? Yes, the frustrating-but-true fact is that you could be downing more calories in one drink than in your entire meal. But if you choose wisely, you won't.

WHAT DOES ALCOHOL HAVE TO DO WITH FAT?

Empty calories. Why empty? Because they offer few nutrients with lots of calories (remember: 3,500 unburned calories transforms into one pound of fat). That's an empty calorie—like candy. Those calories fast-track into your bloodstream, and since they can add up faster than you are able to burn them off, you start to pack those calories on as pounds. Other issues with alcohol when it comes to fat? Willpower. Or a lack thereof. When you're drunk, or even just tipsy, you might find it easier to forget about your healthy diet as you convince yourself that you really do "need" that entire pizza dipped in ranch dressing (an extra 8 grams of fat per tablespoon), bag of chips dipped in nacho cheese, and carton of ice cream. And then you wake up full the next morning as the reality of what you did the night before takes over. . . .

151

CALORIES IN YOUR FAVE ADULT BEVERAGES

Thankfully, cocktails don't have to be such diet destroyers. There are bad and better options. Here's the breakdown:

Daiquiri (8 oz.): 449 calories

Piña colada (12 oz.): 586 calories + 57 carbs, 5 grams fat

Mai tai (9 oz.): 620 calories

Mud slide (6 oz.): 556 calories

Mojito (12 oz.): 235 calories (substitute Splenda or Truvia for the sugar and it's only 140 calories)

Apple martini (3 oz.): 148 calories

Cosmopolitan (5 oz.): 200 calories

Margarita (10 oz.): 550 calories

Long Island iced tea (10 oz.): 543 calories

Vodka Red Bull (9 oz.): 177 calories

Whisky sour (4 oz.): 193 calories

Sweet dessert wine (4 oz.): 189 calories

Cabernet (4 oz.): 97 calories (not bad, but consider the small size of a 4 oz. pour)

Pinot grigio (4 oz.): 96 calories (not bad, but again, consider the small size of a 4 oz. pour)

Sierra Nevada Pale Ale (12 oz.): 200 calories

"SKINNIER" MIXED-DRINK OPTIONS

The following drinks contain less than 100 calories:

Citrus Fizz

Orange-flavored vodka
Crystal Light lemonade
A little soda water (or champagne)
Squeeze of lemon

Mexican Summer

Blanco tequila
Watermelon juice

Skinny Margarita

Reposado tequila
Lots of fresh-squeezed lime juice
1 packet low-calorie sweetener (like Splenda or Truvia)
A little soda water to cut the bite

Ginger Goodness

Sake or Blanco tequila
Diet ginger ale

Greyhound (my personal fave and go-to)

Gin
Grapefruit juice

Vodka Soda

Vodka
Soda water or diet tonic water (*not* regular tonic water, which has about 90 calories per serving)

Spank It . . . & 3 Other Ways to Make Your Own Fat-Burning Skinny Cocktails

Forget about sticky, fruity, sugary, hangover-waiting-to-happen, uninspired cocktails. The newest thing in cocktails is herbs—yes, fresh from the garden (or grocery store). And the great thing is that herbs are bursting with benefits (fat burner: jalapeño; stomachache aid: ginger; detoxifier: mint), and they add a ton of flavor without the calories. There are four ways to add herbs to cocktails, each creating a slightly different effect:

1. **Muddle it:** If you have a cocktail shaker, great! If not, just use a glass. Place the herbs at the bottom of the glass and muddle them—smash them with a spoon or cocktail stick to break up, bruise, and release the oils, which is where the flavor is. Once muddled, add the alcohol and ice. Shake it violently to marry the flavors. Dump the whole thing in a serving glass. The herbs almost become textural in addition to the flavor (think: mojitos, where the mint is in the drink).

2. **Shake it:** You don't need to muddle in order to release the flavors. Place the herbs, alcohol, and ice in a cocktail shaker and shake like mad. The herbs are broken up in the violent act of shaking. Strain the cocktail into a serving glass. The ice cuts the herbs into little pieces, then the larger pieces of herbs are strained out, leaving the flavorful oils and aromatics.

3. **Spank it:** Create your cocktail using any method you want and pour it into the glass. Now take an herb leaf and spank it in your hand to bruise it and release the oils. Then drop the whole leaf on top of the drink. Don't eat the herb. Just use it as an aromatic garnish. Remember, much of flavor actually comes from scent, so even though you aren't actually chewing the leaf, the oils released from the spanking coupled with the scent will be enough.

4. **Infuse it:** If you don't want to mess around with herbs while making your cocktails, infuse the alcohol beforehand instead. This is the original way of adding herbs to alcohol. Take a bottle of alcohol and add herbs or spices directly into the bottle, then let it sit for several hours or even a couple of days, allowing the herbs to release their oils into the alcohol. Then, you use the infused alcohol in any cocktail you want! A few tasty combos?

   Tequila with jalapeño

   Tequila with rosemary

   Vodka with garlic, jalapeño, and basil for a tasty Bloody Mary base

Vodka with whole berries

Rum with ginger and pineapple

Gin with cilantro and jalapeño

TWO FAB SKINNY HERBACEOUS COCKTAILS

Skinny Jalapeñito

Beyond the mojito, it's the jalapeño that ups the ante in this fab cocktail. How? Hot peppers are known natural fat burners. Fat-burning foods tend to literally be "burning"—mouth burning that is. They also naturally heat up the body while helping to increase digestion, circulation, and metabolism. If you can find a hot-spiced cocktail at your fave local bar, great! Or you can just make your own at home. Here's how:

Ingredients

12 mint leaves (fights gas, antiseptic, digestive aid)

Juice of 1 lime (fat burning, immune boosting)

4 jalapeño slices, no seeds (fat burning, metabolism boosting)

3 packets Truvia (or other sweetener)

1½ ounces white rum

Ice

Splash of soda water

Directions

1. Muddle mint, lime, jalapeño, and sweetener. Muddle again.
2. Add rum. Muddle.
3. Add ice. Shake in a cocktail shaker.
4. Pour into a glass.
5. Add soda.
6. Drink!

Garden Refresher

Play with your herbs! Have fun with what you have growing in your garden. Choose different flavors. Mix them together. Find your fave combo. Here's one of mine:

Ingredients

4 cucumber slices (fights plaque buildup)

Juice of 1 lime (fat burning, immune boosting)

1½ ounces vodka

1 packet Truvia

Ice

1 basil leaf (blood-sugar stabilizer, antioxidant)

Directions

1. Muddle cucumber and sweetener.
2. Add lime. Muddle
3. Add vodka. Muddle
4. Add Ice. Shake in a cocktail shaker.
5. Strain into glass.
6. Spank basil. Float on top.

How to Avoid a Hangover

Unlike in college where it's totally OK(ish) to go out late, drink entirely too much, pass out on your friend's couch, and roll out of bed just in time to make it to class (still smelling like booze) . . . or not quite make it to class at all and instead just get a friend's lecture notes, allowing you to sleep it off—that's not going to fly in the working world. Regardless of the way you feel the next morning, you still have to get your shit together, shower off the stench of the night before, appear rested, put together, and professional. How? Follow my advice below and you will be less likely to wake up *that* way:

DRINK ORGANIC ALCOHOL

News flash: The grapes and grains used to produce many of your favorite alcoholic beverages are doused in chemicals during the growing process. Those chemicals then seep into the ground, polluting the soil and water, and become ingrained in the makeup of the grape and grain themselves. (Think about a daisy that you put into a vase filled with blue food-coloring-infused water: The once-white daisy turns blue.)

Translation: If you knock back a couple of conventional spirits, just know that you're actually sipping on chemical cocktails. Beyond the disgusting concept of guzzling chemicals, according to some naturopathic doctors, drinking organic spirits is less taxing on the liver and, because the function of the liver is basically detoxification, that means that drinking organic spirits can help your liver pump out the alcohol faster. The easier it is for the liver to digest, the less likely it is that you will be bedded the next day by a hangover.

ENDURE THE PEE SMELL & EAT ASPARAGUS ANYWAY

Yes, for many of us, asparagus turns the scent of pee into something wholly ungodly, thanks to a sulfuric compound called mercaptan (also found in onions, garlic, rotten eggs, and skunk spray). However, it's been studied (poor scientists) and proven that the pungent fibrous plant can also curb hangover symptoms.

Translation: Eating a healthy serving of asparagus before going out will not only stink up the bathroom within fifteen to thirty minutes of consumption (yes, it's that fast), but the high concentration of amino acids produces enzymes that help to accelerate the breakdown of ethanol (the active ingredient in alcohol, which creates the hangover as well as the toxic effects on the liver). Eat asparagus before, during (as in, with dinner), or after drinking (but before the hangover sets in), and the next day shouldn't be so painful.

DOWN COPIOUS AMOUNTS OF WATER BEFORE BED

Downing water before, during, and after drinking helps dilute the alcohol, making the toxins move through the liver in a less concentrated form, allowing more time for the ethanol to be broken down, resulting in a less-torturous hangover. A few great tricks to guzzling water:

- Drink an entire glass of water between every alcoholic beverage.
- Order your drinks "on the rocks," then make sure to crunch and swallow all the ice before moving on to the next.
- Before falling asleep, drink as many glasses of water as you consumed alcoholic drinks throughout the evening (no matter how sober you "think" you are).

FINISH YOUR NIGHT WITH A SHOT . . . OF WHEATGRASS

Wheatgrass is a natural detoxifier. It is said to cleanse the body's blood and water, hydrating and energizing the cells. Considered a "life-sustaining food," the chlorophyll in wheatgrass helps clear your insides out, naturally deodorizing, maintaining pH balance, healing the intestines, and delivering powerful antioxidants and enzymes to support the body both inside and out. So what does this mean when it comes to minimizing a nasty next-morning headache? Enzymes help break down and clear out toxins from the liver, which nips hangover symptoms in the bud! Drink a glass at the end of the night for instant detoxifying and hydration, then again the morning after to further detox and energize.

MIX UP A TOMATO/CAYENNE CHASER

Water is great, but tomato juice with cayenne pepper, sugar, and lime should also be added to the hydration options. The kooky concoction helps replenish electrolytes and get blood sugar back on track. No tomato juice in the house? Try a glass of water with a dash of salt, sugar, cayenne, and a squeeze of lime both before bed and immediately upon waking up.

DRINK ORANGE JUICE BEFORE BED

Love a midnight breakfast when the drunk munchies set in? How about just the juice part? After a night of drinking, before getting in bed, gulp down a glass of orange juice. The vitamin C helps your liver break down alcohol and flush it out of your body faster. Plus you're hydrating yourself even more, and every drop of a nonalcoholic beverage before bed helps!

DOWN AN EMERGEN-C

No OJ? Well, if it really is the vitamin C that helps avoid the hangover, Emergen-C is also packed with the powerful vitamin. Plus Emercen-C has zinc, quercetin, and antioxidants to support your immune system, seven B vitamins to enhance energy naturally, and electrolytes to nourish the body. I like to mix the stuff into cocktails to make my signature QuickieChick's Emergen-C Cocktail (you can find the recipe on Emergen-C's Facebook page).

IF YOU'RE SOBER "ENOUGH,"
BLEND A HONEY & YOGURT SMOOTHIE

If you're sober enough to work household appliances . . . make this smoothie before bed:

3 tablespoons honey (the fructose speeds up the breakdown of alcohol in your liver)

1 cup Greek yogurt (the enzymes break down alcohol without the high sugar content of other yogurts)

1 cup orange juice (the vitamin C helps to break down alcohol)

Don't think you're going to remember all of the above when in a drunken, alcohol-induced delirium? Write it down and post it in your pantry or wherever else you tend to look after a late night of overdoing it.

"I'm Never Drinking Again"—Hangover Remedies to Help You Get Over It Faster

When suffering "the day after," it's pretty common to question "the night before." Was it really worth feeling *this* awful? And then there's the "I'm never drinking again" that you utter, feeling sick to your stomach just imagining the taste of alcohol ever touching your tongue again. Worse than feeling awful, hangovers can actually wreak havoc on your immune system, digestive track, and organ function.

WHY DO HANGOVERS HAPPEN?

Hangovers happen when our already overburdened livers struggle to clear out the excessive amount of toxins and chemicals ingested from too much alcohol. Our blood sugar dips. Our bodies are dehydrated, and overall fatigue takes over. Basically, you are creating a toxic internal environment,

157

and your body is letting you know. Here's how you can help your liver and ease the pain faster:

CARDIO

While the last thing in the world you may feel like doing is working out, the fact is that getting your heart and blood pumping delivers fresh oxygen to your brain while helping to push out stuck toxins—yes, the same toxins that are making your head feel like it's in a vice. Can't get out of bed? I hear you. Try the Hangover Helper Quickie Workout in Bed below to help quell the pain and allow you to finally start your day!

HANGOVER HELPER QUICKIE WORKOUT IN BED

This workout starts with a good stretch to ease you into moving, then you get right into the cardio—pumping your arms, kicking your legs, and getting fresh oxygenated blood pulsing through your body (and your liver) while helping to get the stuck toxins and residual alcohol out! You might sweat sooner than usual, a side effect of the alcohol, but that's a good thing! Your body is doing everything it can to rid itself of the booze. Just remember to hydrate. It will not only push those toxins out faster, but it will help ease the headache, too. Here's your workout (do each move for 3 minutes):

Caterpillar

Sit with your legs straight out in front of you. Elongate your spine straight and tall and fold your torso over your legs as far as you can without straining your hamstrings. Once you have lengthened out as far as you can, release your neck, dropping your head down, letting gravity take over as you slowly release your body even more, little by little, onto your thighs if you can.

Snow Angel

Like when you make a snow angel in the snow, lie on your back and quickly open and close your arms and legs in unison.

Backstroke

Like when doing a backstroke in the pool, lie on your back, kick your feet, paddle your arms up and back, starting at your sides, then extending up into the air and back over your head, and open out to the side, swishing back down to your sides. Repeat.

Foot Warmers

Lie on your back, bend your knees, bottoms of your feet on the bed. As if you're on skis, swish your feet forward and back fast, fast, fast!

Lazy Arm Circles—Small

Lie on your back, lift your arms straight up to the ceiling. Keeping your arms straight, circle your hands as if trying to draw small circles on the ceiling. First circle both hands in. After 1½ minutes, reverse the direction of the circle, circling both hands out. This move is fast. You are engaging your core, pressing your shoulders and your shoulder blades down into the bed.

Lazy Arm Circles—Big

Like above, but these circles are big—between one to two feet in diameter. After 1½ minutes, reverse the direction of the circle, circling both hands out.

Repeat entire circuit three times.

Photocopy and tape it to your bathroom mirror!

6 NATURAL WAYS TO HELP "THE DAY AFTER" NOT HURT SO MUCH

1. **Try Tiger Balm to help the headache.** Blended from camphor, menthol, cajuput oil, and clove oil, Tiger Balm is a popular topical used traditionally in Asia as a multipurpose remedy. Smear the potent salve on your temples, neck, and forehead and let its analgesic and blood flow–promoting properties ease your ache. Tiger Balm may not be made to mitigate hangovers, but I find it to be one of the best topical headache cures around. You can buy it online or at your local natural-foods market, such as Whole Foods Market.

2. **Soak in wasabi to stimulate detoxification.** Your skin breathes. It also helps clear toxins from your system (um . . . pimples are a great example). In fact, as much as a third of toxic body waste is cleared through the skin. So doesn't it suddenly make complete sense to soak in a tub of toxin-purging wasabi? Don't dismiss the hot stuff as a mere smear on your sushi! It turns out that wasabi root (which is actually a member of the cabbage family) has the ability to increase blood circulation through the organs and promote oxygenation of the cellular tissue, helping to clear cells of metabolic waste. Infuse your bath with two tablespoons of wasabi paste or ¼ cup wasabi bath powder (you can find it online or at some natural-foods markets), and its stimulating nature can help ease a hangover (and might leave you craving raw fish).

3. **Take a mustard bath to flush out alcohol.** More than merely a condiment to slather on a hot dog for added oomph, mustard is noted

for its ability to increase circulation and draw toxins out from the organs. Once the organs are flushed, they are naturally replenished with clean and vital blood. Translation: Mustard has become a little-known hangover-healing health secret. Now, I'm not suggesting you take the squeeze bottle of yellow mustard and make like a hot dog. There are actually mustard bath powders with added mineral salts, such as eucalyptus and camphor, which even further amp up the detox ability; you can find them at some natural-foods markets and online. You can also make your own mustard bath by pouring two tablespoons of pure mustard powder into warm running bathwater. Steep for twenty minutes. Dry off. Take a nap and let the mustard take effect.

4. **Rub your hangover out of your feet.** I know, when you're lying there in bed, head throbbing and on the verge of praying to the porcelain god, only a few things sound pleasurable. But the one thing that I never refuse is a massage. Reflexology, often in the form of a foot massage, is a known remedy for a slew of ailments, including hangovers. Rub your aches and pains away (while assisting speeding up liver detoxification) by stimulating the outer-edge area of the right foot, about halfway between the middle of the foot and the little toe. This is the reflex to the liver. A "crunchy" texture is a sign that there is some congestion in the area associated with that spot, which is obvious considering how awful you feel. No one to rub your hangover away? Rub it out yourself. Just a few minutes on each foot will help get the circulation going, flushing out the toxins and the pain.

5. **Bad headache? Get up anyway and drink your coffee.** Alcohol causes blood vessels to expand. This is what you experience as a headache. Luckily, everyone's favorite morning pick-me-up, coffee, is a vasoconstrictor. This means it helps contract those pulsing blood vessels. Just stick to one cup, though, as coffee is a diuretic, and if you're hungover, you are already dehydrated as it is.

6. **Do yoga.** Purge your liver of excess alcohol by ringing it out—kind of like a dishtowel—with the Seated Twist. Here's how:

   • Sit up on your bed or on the floor with your legs extended straight in front of you.

   • Bend your left knee and cross your left leg over your right, placing your left foot down beside the outside of your right knee.

   • Keeping your butt firmly in place, twist from your waist and rotate your torso to the left.

- Bring your right arm across your body and place your right hand on the bed or floor beside your left butt cheek. Use this arm to help you twist even more.

- Inhale big belly breaths. Hold the pose for thirty seconds.

- Switch sides.

QuickieChick's Healthy Food & Drink Obsessions

These "obsessions" are some of my absolute musts! They are my personal go-tos, the things that are always stocked in my pantry or fridge. They are often sitting on the kitchen counter as easy-access reminders of healthy snacking options when that late-night noshing vampire shows its fangs and threatens a pantry raid! They are versatile, healthy, and they make me happy—and that's why I am sharing them with you.

GG SCANDINAVIAN BRAN CRISPBREAD

161

Mini Babybel Light cheese, sunflower seed butter, hummus—these are all things that I love and that need to be spread on something. But I don't want to consume 150 extra calories in a piece of bread just to enjoy my other favorite snacks. When I discovered GG Bran Crispbread, everything changed (well, in the snacking department). One slice contains just 12 calories and 5 grams of dietary fiber. If you make a sandwich with it, you're looking at 10 grams—that's already one-third of your daily fiber. Why do I want more fiber? Because I want just about anything that will kill my cravings for junk food, especially my vampiric eating habit, and fiber keeps you full longer. *Plus,* it helps to, um, clear things out of your system. Another fab find? GG Fiber Sprinkles. I add them to just about everything—soup, yogurt, oatmeal, for crunch without the fat and calories of granola. Love!

POPCHIPS

Why is the action of snacking so satisfying? Putting my hand repeatedly in a little plastic bag of whatever it may be that day and hearing that crunchy sound of each bite can keep me happy for hours (which can also be very dangerous when it comes to my waistline). Yup, I like to snack. I try not to, for obvious reasons, but there are certain times when I just feel left out if I don't partake in a little between-meal munching. Like at the movies. Or girls' night in with cocktails and cookies. I had to find some way to not feel like I was totally missing out but also not to feel ten pounds heavier after the snack session was over. And then I discovered popchips, which are not only the perfect healthy snack that satisfies my hand-in-bag/hand-to-mouth craving, but they are *delicious* . . . even crave-worthy. The flavor-packed, super-crunchy, all-natural potato chips are popped (not baked or fried), then seasoned. That's it. And that's how they taste so insanely good without all the fat. It seems there is a chip flavor for every situation. Here are a few of my faves:

- **Movies—cheddar.** It's much tastier, crunchier, and less fatty than buttery popcorn caked in artificial cheese.

- **Mexican food night—jalapeño.** Accompany your burrito or tacos with these instead of fatty tortilla chips. Not only do you still get that satisfying crunch, but they are perfectly salsa/guacamole dipable, and they also have a little fat-burning spice, which is always nice!

- **Dateless/heartbroken—sweet potato.** You probably need a night in, and the pantry is calling you. Go ahead. Snack a little on the original-flavored popchip, just as comforting as the Lays potato chips you chomped on after a high school heartbreak. If you want, spray a little butter-flavored spray directly into the bag, then sprinkle in a packet of Truvia or other sweetener and cinnamon, and shake. The salty, sweet, spice, crunch is like a churro!

- **Cocktail party—sour cream & onion.** If you're anything like me, you're the one who eats up most of the snacks laid out at your own party. Instead of fatty chips and even fattier sour cream dip, get all those flavors with way fewer calories in this flavor.

- **My popchips specialty—cold nachos.** It's made up of a few of my favorite things: Knudsen Lowfat Cottage Cheese, Pace Picante Sauce, and Jalapeño popchips. More than a filling (not fattening) snack, the calcium in the cottage cheese, and the hot peppers in the salsa are known natural fat burners.

LA TORTILLA FACTORY FIBER & FLAX

I'm a Southern California girl, so half the food found in my kitchen growing up was Mexican food. After a while, eating a lot of the carb-heavy (and often lard-enhanced) ingredients quickly made me grow in the wrong ways. La Tortilla Factory tortillas saved the day (and my love of quesadillas, burritos, and wraps). They are low in fat (less than 1 gram) and calories (45 calories), and taste great! But unlike other tortilla brands that only remove things (e.g., fat and calories, even cutting back on carbs), this one actually *adds* things— nutrients and flavor, and they are still able to keep these bad boys low fat and low cal. Seriously . . . they are a true kitchen must! Their Fiber & Flax

Corn and Multigrain tortillas are big on nutrition and beyond tasty. I think I have tested them in every way I can! I like to whip together a tortilla pizza or quesadilla with low-fat cheese when I'm on the go. If I have the time, I'll cut them into triangles, add a touch of salt, and bake them for healthy tortilla chips. That's Mexican food the QuickieChick way!

NIMBLE™ BY BALANCE BAR®

OK . . . so I must, at all times, have at least one, generally two, protein bars in my purse. Because I tend to switch out purses, and I like to have each one appropriately stocked for quick-outfit-change ease. That means that each of my main purses has two bars. Now, the purpose for the bars isn't necessarily for meal replacement (though that has happened on occasion), but instead for meal supplement. If I am out running errands all day, in a meeting that runs over into lunchtime, on a plane that—oops—doesn't serve dinner, or if I end up taking the eight-mile loop instead of the three-mile loop on my morning hike, or just need a little something to tide me over before dinner—there's a bar for that. And that bar is usually a nimble™ by Balance Bar®. Not only does nimble™ come in some seriously awesome flavors (like Peanut Butter and Yogurt Orange Swirl), it's only 120 calories with 4 grams of fat, has 10 grams of protein, *and* is souped up with necessary chick goodness like folate, calcium, fiber (always need more of that), antioxidants, and lutein (a miracle skin nutrient). nimble™ is also sweetened with Truvia® sweetener from the stevia plant—which helps keep the calories down and the flavor up! Because I'm all about feeding my moods (in a healthy way), I like the Yogurt Orange before a workout when I am on the go and have no time for a full breakfast. Peanut Butter is my purse "must" because it's so tasty yet somehow tame enough to satisfy any craving, sweet or salty. It's also pretty fab after a bad date or a breakup instead of doing a full-on pantry-raid binge! Obsessed is an understatement.

OATMEAL & EGG

First let me say that I am obsessed with this breakfast. I mean, the night before, I literally look forward to eating it. Now, if you believe that "oatmeal should be sweet"—stop. It's time to view the grain as, well, as a grain—just like pasta, rice, and risotto. (You're not putting maple syrup and brown sugar on pasta are you?) This is the perfect complete meal filled with healthy fiber, protein, and nutrients to keep me fuller longer without packing on the fat. Here's how the ingredients break down:

- **Oatmeal**—healthy carb. It helps to control blood sugar, calms the nerves, cuts fat, keeps you fuller longer, raises serotonin levels, making you happier.

- **Egg**—protein. Omega-3 fatty acid, a good fat that helps reduce inflammation and build muscle. With 6 grams of protein and 5 grams of fat. The yolk is filled with lecithin, great for connective tissue to help fight cellulite and wrinkles.

- **Milk**—filled with bone-supporting calcium, helps curb hunger and minimize fat stores.

- **Sriracha**—chili-based hot sauce that heats up your mouth and your insides, making it a natural fat-burning condiment.

How to Make It

Boil 1 cup of water with a pinch of salt. Add ½ cup nonfat milk. Bring to a simmer. Add 1 cup slow-cooking oatmeal. Stir occasionally. Add about ½ teaspoon Sriracha and stir in. Crack egg into center of oatmeal. Let sit for thirty seconds. Using a spoon, gently pull white from yolk. Make sure nothing is sticking to bottom of pot. Add white pepper and Spike seasoning. Break yolk and mix in. Pour in bowl. Add a third of an avocado, if you'd like.

KOMBUCHA

If you haven't tried GT's Organic Raw Kombucha, you may have heard of it. Ancient Chinese health gurus called the stuff the "immortal health elixir," and for good reason. This slightly acidic stuff is said to help detox, reduce anxiety and depression, aid digestion, and is extremely rich in antioxidants. My fridge is never without at least six bottles. I like to mix up my flavors to reap all the different benefits, each of which I enjoy (like most everything else) based on my mood.

- **To recover from a workout**—Synergy Mystic Mango. Vitamin C plays a major role in collagen repair, the production of proteins, scar tissue, tendons, ligaments—yup, pretty much everything affected by a serious session on the elliptical. And mango is loaded with vitamin C. It's also important for the maintenance of cartilage and bones, which you definitely want to take care of if you're pounding down on pavement or even a treadmill on a regular basis.

- **Instead of that glass of wine**—Synergy Trilogy. The same way a fine wine reveals its many flavors slowly, so does Trilogy with its raspberry, lemon, and ginger flavor components. You'll definitely still be getting the antioxidants that were your excuse for guzzling that "grape juice," but along with the countless other benefits of Kombucha. And no hangover.

- **Settle your stomach**—Synergy Gingerberry. Ginger can ease the movements of your intestines, preventing vomiting and nausea.

Blueberries are also packed with antioxidants to ward off any future incidents like the one that may have gotten your stomach churning.

EXTRA DESSERT DELIGHTS

Sometimes I need to take it easy on the snacking for a few days. Gum comes in handy big-time for that. I am never without a pack (or three) of Extra Dessert Delights. Some people keep a bag of chips in the center divider of their cars to chew on in traffic. I keep this gum. It's also a great dessert substitute. You may not realize it, but usually just a little bit of a sweet flavor, rather than a whole piece of cake, will make you feel satisfied. I love the Key Lime Pie flavor. It's like the gum in Willy Wonka's Chocolate Factory with multiple dimensions. First, I can taste the key lime, then the graham-cracker crust reveals itself, and finally the whipped cream. I never feel deprived of dessert this way.

QuickieChick's Cheat Sheet

1. Cocktails can be diet killers! Instead of downing upward of 300 calories per drink, try a skinny version with sweeteners or fresh fruit juices instead of bottled syrups (aka flavored sugar).

2. Hangover prevention: Asparagus, organic spirits, wheatgrass shots, OJ, coffee, tomato/cayenne chaser, midnight smoothie, and lots and lots of water can help you avoid a hangover.

3. Why diets fail: Too much whining, failing to plan, not enough moderation, or you're not eating *breakfast*.

4. No more diet soda. It ruins your teeth, your diet, and your bank account.

5. Forget fad diets. Healthy living is about sustainable choices. Stick with an eating and workout routine that you can learn to enjoy every day.

6. Post Post-its in your pantry, on your bathroom mirror, on the inside of your front door, beside your sneakers, and at the foot of your bed as reminders to work out and eat right. Some people prefer negative reinforcement ("sugar = fat ass"); others prefer positive ("You're beautiful and sexy and that candy bar isn't worth it"). Whatever you prefer, put it on a Post-it.

7. Hanging your skinny jeans in the kitchen may seem extreme, but they are a constant reminder of where you once were and where you want to be again. Each time you see those jeans, you will think to yourself, Nope, this boredom splurge just isn't worth it.

8. Keeping a food journal isn't just some lame way to record your daily intake, it's also a way to track your feelings toward food: *Did I eat that because I was pissed off that I saw my ex with his new girlfriend, but after I ate the entire pizza I felt even worse about myself?*

9. Ditch the college eating habits. Swap out beer pitchers for skinny drinks. Stock your fridge with healthy basics like whole grains, vegetables, and lean proteins. No more midnight eating!

10. Cook an egg in your oatmeal for a savory, filling, satisfying, complete, and completely addictive meal. Remember, oatmeal is a grain, just like rice. Treat it that way.

"Freshman 15?" Not after This Chapter

WEIRD WAYS TO MOTIVATE AND WORK THAT ASS OFF!

IF YOU PACKED ON A FEW during those college years and you have yet to drop them, it's time to transition into a new healthier lifestyle and out of your "Freshman 15" jean size. It's not easy. I'm just being honest. But you can do it. With help, which you will find here.

QuickieChick Quiz QUIZ

1. **When you workout you . . .**

   A. Do the most challenging, calorie-burning exercise that you *hate,* just because you sweat so much and can really feel the burn.

   B. Stick to the machines/equipment/workout that you just have fun doing, even though you don't sweat much.

   C. Alternate between the high-results workout that you hate and the fun, less-intense option.

   D. Test out lots of workouts until you find one you really love that is also effective.

   Obviously, the best answer is D. But when trying to lose weight, many people go for A and try to force themselves to do a workout that they don't like because it's the "in" workout to do, their friends do it, or they think it will deliver the fastest results in the shortest period of time. The problem is, if you don't like it, eventually you will stop doing it. The reason I don't like B is that you might start to feel like you are "wasting" your time, since you make the effort to get yourself ready for your workout then see little to no results. Here's a tip: You change with change—your body will change if you challenge your body by changing up your workout. Unless of course you're fine viewing the gym as solely a social hour. C is great to challenge your muscles and gets the results you want faster. But if you want to up your chances of maintaining and even looking forward to your regular workouts, the best answer is D—actually enjoying what you're doing makes you want to do it more! Keep in mind that working out doesn't have to be your traditional "slave away at the gym" style of exercise. You can also get a workout in by joining a sports team, taking regular dance classes (or even just going to a club and seriously getting your groove on), or pairing up with a girlfriend for regular tennis matches. The point is to sweat, get your heart rate up, and, on occasion, feel your muscles burning the next morning—that's how you know you've had a good workout.

2. **How many times a week do you work out?**
   A. 1–3
   B. 4–7
   C. 0

If you're falling below the 4–7 range (please don't tell me it's 0!), maybe it's time to try a new form of exercise that you actually enjoy. If you force yourself to do the most painful exercise, maybe that's why you dread going to the gym more than once a week. Or maybe it's just that you're not making your workouts—and therefore your body and your health—a priority. *Make* time, don't *find* time to exercise.

3. **Someone tells you that you look like Heidi Klum, Jennifer Aniston, Penélope Cruz, or whichever envy-worthy celeb you might be compared to. You . . .**
   A. Go on a diet, fit in extra workouts. Heidi Klum doesn't have that droopy chin or love handles, and you want to look like her!
   B. Are super grateful for the compliment! And go on about life as usual.
   C. Say thank you, but you really don't believe what the person is saying and actually feel really awkward about it. I mean . . . is he/she just trying to be nice?

For the same reason I don't like scales, I don't like answer A. Holding yourself to a very specific image/body-mass index/number on the scale is only likely to make your weight fluctuate. If you sense for a moment that you gained one pound (or maybe your cheeks are no longer as sculpted as Heidi Klum's), you suddenly drop all carbs and work out twice as hard . . . only to realize this is not sustainable and you bounce back, regain weight (maybe more than before), and it's a whole emotional roller coaster. Feel like you're on track with how you would like to look? Just keep doing what you're doing. Next time someone compares you to a celeb, just say thank you. You know what you're doing—that's how you got to look like you do in the first place. If your answer was C, well, there are lots of chicks out there just like you. You are insecure about your looks and therefore you have a hard time accepting compliments. My advice: *Digest it!* Let it be your comfort food. They are complimenting you because they want to, not because they have to. Then, next time you find yourself attempting to seek comfort in food, think back to that compliment and allow that to comfort you instead. At least it's a comfort that you won't later regret (as you would that cookie).

"Baby, I Think Your Ass Is Getting Bigger"

What do you do when you know, I mean you really know, that you are gaining weight, but not quite ready to address it? Despite the fact that you didn't want to admit it, you have secretly acknowledged the gradual bulge that's been occurring. Your jeans have been fitting just a tad too snuggly, your face is noticeably fuller, and you can just feel it all over your body. But instead of addressing the gain head-on, you choose not to wash your jeans—you know, so that they will maintain that comfortable slightly stretched-out feeling.

So what would you do if one morning you were unable to ignore it anymore? Say, for example, your boyfriend notices (or at least finally decides to speak up) that your body seems to have expanded . . . and he brings it up. Imagine this scenario: As you're getting dressed, in a very sweet and nondemeaning way, he asks:

Boyfriend: "Baby, have you changed your diet at all?"

You: "Not really. I guess I've been snacking a little more late at night when you're working. But other than that, no. Why?"

He: "It looks like you might be gaining some weight on the back of your thighs and your bum. Just a little bit. I'd guess five pounds. Are you still working out?"

You: "Yes, of course I am. But I've just been so busy and haven't had enough time to really do a full workout."

He: "Well, that's the reason then. You have to work out every day, baby, you know that. If you want to keep eating and going out for drinks on the weekends, you have to do it."

You: "But I take walks every day."

He: "Yes, I know. But you're not getting your heart rate up enough, and you're not challenging your muscles. You need to do some upper-body work to keep your metabolism pumping. You know this stuff. . . . Maybe we can work out together? Let's go for a bike ride or take a yoga class! My gut has been getting too big, too."

What do you think of the scenario? Rude? Or helpful? This scenario actually happened with me and an ex. We didn't break up over this. In fact, I appreciated it. He was right. I was just getting lazy. And it was time to make a change. I had to remember how to get back into my routine, remember how good it felt—by just doing it, even when I didn't feel like it. I also had to remind myself NOT to reach for that totally unnecessary bowl (or three) of muesli late at night and to put the Post-its BACK on the fatty foods in the pantry. (I had taken them down for a party.)

The fact is, I know myself and my areas of weakness, and he did, too, and I know that sometimes I simply have zero self-control. And you know what? Every day after that conversation with my now-ex BF, he made sure to tell me just how beautiful and sexy I was, even if I'd gained a few pounds. Anyway . . . now you know some insight into who I am—a chick who struggles like everyone else. I've just come up with some ways to finally take control.

On the flip side, you may just be completely devastated to have your guy point out your pudge. In fact, if he is like most guys (unlike my ex), he probably either won't notice or would never *dare* to say anything and instead he just had the faith that you'd realize the new jiggle yourself. Hopefully, he'd be right. . . .

If you are more on the sensitive side and don't want your man's eye to ever notice your gain, be sure to remember this one thing: DO NOT mention it to your guy or ask him to confirm it. A married friend of mine told me how his wife told him repeatedly for months that she thought her ass was getting fat. He hadn't noticed. But after hearing her say it enough, one morning he woke up, turned over, and thought *Maybe there IS less room in this bed now.* Not only did he notice, but he also began to be less turned on by her and started to notice other bouncing body parts, too—like her larger arms and folding stomach skin. So if you find yourself wanting to ask "Do I look fat in this?" . . . *don't!* Chances are he hasn't even noticed (unless of course he's my ex.). But if you ask, "Honey, is my ass getting fat?" forcing your boyfriend to look at you from your point of view rather than seeing you as the embodiment of perfection, you will force him to notice. And, really, what's the point in that? If your guy is oblivious, consider it a blessing and quietly squeeze in extra workouts without making a big deal about it.

Get Out of Your Head & into Your Bikini

It's exceptionally easy to come up with excuses not to exercise. Well, now you won't have an excuse anymore. Here are some ways you can actually burn calories without even breaking a sweat and motivate yourself to move!

KEEP YOUR NORMAL ROUTINE . . .
& STILL LOSE WEIGHT & SAVE MONEY

This is your permission slip to stay in your comfort zone and stick with your normal, day-to-day routine. We're just going to amp it up a bit so that you can get a few extra benefits without even really trying. If you already do have a dedicated fitness routine, but your scale seems to be stuck, these tweaks can help you overcome that slump and pop out of that plateau, so that you start seeing results again. And then there's the financial part that makes this invigorated exercise mentality alluring. You don't have to spend any more money to get fit. I totally understand the temptation of watching the latest fitness infomercial featuring your favorite celeb assuring you success if you just buy the newest, greatest exercise equipment (it's kind of like those impulse buys in the checkout line at the supermarket, but more expensive). And while it's easy to justify the pocketbook pinch if you truly will lose weight and therefore find happiness, this time around, honestly, what's the likelihood? Instead of throwing money at the idea of getting in shape, take what you already do and just tweak it, transforming your body, no strings (or hefty dangling price tag) attached.

LOSING WEIGHT STARTS IN YOUR HEAD

Even personal trainers, athletes, and celebrities struggle with those "off" days, when motivating to move seems to be a lost cause. But here's where they're different: Somehow they muster that something inside of them that propels them to get out of bed, off the sofa, out of their "I can't" mentality and hit the pavement running. Maybe it's because they're paid in part to look good—and you're not. But regardless . . .

How do they muster the motivation to work out even when it's the last thing in the world they want to do? It's all in their heads (and sometimes on Post-it notes on their bathroom mirror or at the foot of their bed, on their steering wheel, or on their fridge).

If you're having a hard time getting started, it helps to first figure out what motivates you to exercise in the first place. Is the post-workout infusion of energy the reason you slip on your sneakers? Maybe it's to fit into your skinny jeans, get your body bikini-ready, or look your best for your big walk down the aisle on your wedding day. Your longevity might be your incentive, knowing full well that your belly pouch is actually a health risk.

Whatever the reason, keep it in mind, use a Post-it note if you have to and fix it to your bathroom mirror. You already know how to brush your teeth, so that minute and a half that you absently stare into the mirror in the morning is wasted. Instead, focus your attention on your reason for wanting to lose weight.

10 WAYS TO MOTIVATE TO MOVE

1. **Get in with the "Yes You Can" Crowd.** Nothing is more of a Debbie Downer than wanting and trying to better yourself and finding that those closest to you are anything but supportive; in fact, they tend to have a "you can't" attitude about the whole thing. Find the "yes you can" crowd and do what they do!

2. **You Don't Think I Can? Watch Me!** If some people don't think you have it in you to lose weight and be healthy, use that as motivation to prove them wrong!

3. **Don't Leave Home Without Them.** No time to work out? Keep your sneakers in your car or in your desk drawer. You will be shocked when you realize how often you find time to slip a few moments of exercise into your day. Have twenty minutes to kill between meetings? Pull your sneakers out of the car and take a quick walk while you wait.

4. **Mind Your Body.** You can actually get more out of your workout if you view it as a way to relax as opposed to an exhaustive chore. That doesn't mean that you have to have a calm exercise session. Work out to the point of standing in a sweat-soaked shirt if you want! Just rewire your mind to view every single drop of sweat as beads of stress that you successfully pulled out of your body, leaving you more relaxed after. More than just a mind shift, you will also find that you can have a better workout with an increased calorie burn! Why? When you're stressed you are using considerably more energy than when you're calm. If you are relaxed during a workout, with your mind at ease, you will have more energy to dedicate to your exercise session. Which means you will actually be able to work out longer and harder and therefore burn even more calories if you want to. Make it about your mind, and your body will follow.

5. **Make a List.** Do you tend to go through life being stressed, rushed, spending too much money, trying to please others, drinking and eating too much? Sometimes simply tweaking your mind-set can be enough to inspire yourself to work out instead of settling into a bowl of ice cream. Write down your Notes to Self—a list of everything

that makes you upset, sad, or annoyed—those things that trigger you to reach for food or go on online shopping sprees in hopes of finding comfort. Now decide on a healthier response for each. Literally write out a list of Notes to Self and keep it handy.

6. **"No" Is not an option.** Before you go to sleep at night, put your sneakers at the end of your bed (along with your exercise clothes). Set your alarm thirty minutes early. Place the alarm on the other side of the room so you can't "accidentally" hit snooze. Get up, immediately slip on your exercise attire, and force yourself to go outside and start to walk, jog, run, skip, ride a bike . . . I don't care which. The point is that by the time you really wake up, you will already be down the block, and by that time, you may as well just work out!

7. **Look good, feel good; feel good, look good.** Yes, a good mental image often comes from a positive physical image. When you are doing something good for your body, like exercising, you automatically start to feel better about yourself. Sure, it definitely has something to do with the immediate gratification of the happy chemicals pumping through your body post-workout, but long-term, just the fact that you are doing something to improve yourself—physically, mentally, emotionally—will help build your self-esteem.

8. **Have fun again!** Take care of your body. It's the only one you've got. There are a million ways to move your body that will help it feel good. Anything you can do to get your heart rate up releases chemicals in your body that just plain make you feel better. I don't just mean feel better, I mean feel GREAT! Have fun, play, get your heart rate up! Remember what a blast you had when you were a kid and you went to the park or the playground and just ran around, played handball, hung from the monkey bars? Those were all serious workouts—you just didn't think about it back then. It's time to have fun again.

9. **Love yourself.** Sounds lame and cheesy. Fine. But love yourself. Take care of yourself as you might take care of someone else. That includes looking good for yourself, eating well for yourself, exercising for yourself. If you love yourself and take care of yourself, you will want to do things that you know will make you even stronger, healthier, and more energized long-term—like exercise.

10. **Fitness bank.** Every time you really don't want to exercise but you do it anyway, or you so badly want that cookie but you don't eat it, put one dollar in your fitness bank. As soon as you can reward yourself for your weight loss, take that money and buy yourself something fab, like stilettos!

173

HERE'S WHAT MOTIVATES *ME* TO MOVE

We all have our own personal reasons as to what motivates us to move our butts, eat a healthy diet, and live a fitness lifestyle. For me, it comes down to the three Bs:

1. Body

2. Brain (work)

3. Beignet (my pup)

Body

As much as I would love to lie and say that my body has nothing to do with why I exercise, I am a horrible liar, so that's just not going to happen. The fact is that I have struggled with body-image issues my entire life. Working out keeps me thin, and that's important to me (especially because I also *love* to eat—a lot). Here's a little bit about my own personal body-image struggles (just so you can have a little insight as to where I am coming from):

At a very young age I was a competitive ice-skater, with every morsel of chocolate being edited out of my diet by my coach. In college I chose to be a dance major (brilliant for someone with body issues), where the pressure to be skinny was so intense that many dancers resorted to very unhealthy and dangerous tactics. More than motivation to stay thin, dance was my form of expression. That was until my motivation to move was abruptly X'd out when I severed all of the ligaments in my left ankle in ballet class. I couldn't dance. I could hardly walk for six months. No longer able to express myself with my body, I became depressed. And so I ate—a lot. And so I became more depressed. And the cycle began. I gained twenty pounds—a lot on a five-foot-two frame. When I was finally able to exercise, I experienced it completely differently. I was finally exercising just because it felt so good to move again, not because my coach or professor was screaming at me. Soon, my body regained its lean shape and I came back into balance. What was interesting was that I was exercising less for my body and more for the feeling I got from it. Sure, I still struggle with my body and its image. But don't we all?

So that's the body-image saga.

More than staying healthy and fit for my own self-image, I have to admit that it's also because my boyfriend loves my butt. And you know what? I'd like to keep it that way.

Brain (Work)

If I don't get a workout in before work, my brain is sluggish. I need the natural high that comes from a good morning sweat session. And here's the interesting thing: Even if I am exhausted when I first force myself to get out of bed, after I exercise I'm energized.

Beignet (My Pup)

My pup, Beignet, is a black Lab who requires lots of exercise. Honestly, that's part of the reason I rescued her. I knew that on those days when I was just not in the mood to work out, she would motivate me to do it. If I don't, she just stares at me with the most depressed big brown eyes. But the second I grab that leash, she does this jump and spin that, no matter what mood I'm in, instantly puts a smile on my face.

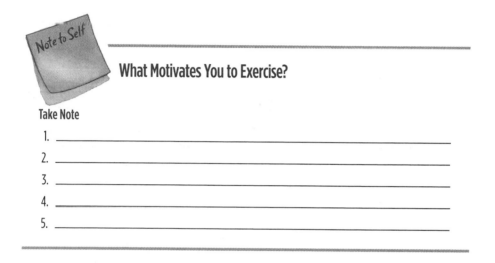

What Motivates You to Exercise?

Take Note

1. _____

2. _____

3. _____

4. _____

5. _____

5 SOLUTIONS TO YOUR BIGGEST WORKOUT EXCUSES

"I'm not in the mood," "I'm tired," "I don't want to have to shower after," "I'm too busy." How many excuses do you have to not work out? We all do it. The funny thing is, oftentimes after you take the time to rationalize not working out, you just sit there and watch TV, stare blankly at the computer screen, or surf on Facebook. Essentially you are wasting time that would have, in the end, been much better spent actually slipping in that workout, burning off the happy-hour drink that you are going to have later that night, or getting some fresh oxygen pumping into your brain. That way you will be infused with a little more energy that will then help make you even more productive.

The thing about excuses is that what may start as a quickly conjured idea as to why you can't become cemented in your brain as you convince yourself of the fact that you definitely cannot work out because of . . . Excuses are instant motivation killers. And, as you know, motivation, or rather lack thereof, is one of the most powerful obstacles to getting in shape.

Need a counterexcuse? Here are five excuses and five solutions to override the excuses:

1. **Excuse:** No time.

   No Excuse: Schedule it. *Make* time, don't *find* time.

2. **Excuse:** I can't afford it.

   No Excuse: Exercise doesn't have to cost much, or anything at all! Get outside and walk/jog/run/bike/hike/play basketball! Follow a workout DVD in your living room. "Play" a fitness video game. Do a Quickie Workout in Bed. Just sweat!

3. **Excuse:** But I want to hang out with my friends.

   No Excuse: Include them! Forget happy hour. Exercise can be your social hour!

4. **Excuse:** I have no idea what I'm doing.

   No Excuse: No one does at first. The point is to move. Even if you're just marching in place, flailing around, skipping, doing jumping jacks. Think back to PE class in school. What did you do to work out back then? Relay races, running around a track, boot-camp-style exercises, whatever. Just *move!*

5. **Excuse:** I don't have the right shoes.

   No Excuse: You don't need shoes to do a Quickie Workout in Bed. You wear stilettos when you go to a club and sweat (yes, that's a workout, too). Beach volleyball doesn't require shoes. Push-ups, sit-ups, seated dips, the plank, etc.—no shoes required for those either.

Even Skinny Chicks Have Cellulite

You might not have it yet, but the fact is that cellulite affects over 85 percent of women—fat and thin. Yes, the unsightly rippled dimples are unbiased, tackling women of all shapes and sizes, even supermodels and celebrities (both Tyra Banks and Kim Kardashian have admitted to having it). And guess what? Some fat people don't have cellulite at all.

One major area of confusion when it comes to cellulite is that it's not fat's fault. It's also not a collection of rogue toxins trapped underneath the skin (another misconception). Cellulite is actually a connective-tissue issue. Cellulite is free-floating fat cells that have penetrated a weakened lattice of connective tissue bands separating the layer of normal fat from the dermis (the middle layer of skin) and have become trapped just below the surface of the skin.

176

So what actually causes cellulite to tack itself all over the average woman's thighs, butt, and sometimes arms and abs?

- **Hormones** (which is why most men don't get it)

- **Genetics** (thanks a lot, Mom!)

- **Lifestyle** (that's all on you)

Despite its prevalence, doctors have yet to find a definitive cure—the one that will reverse the rippled dimples and make them go away forever! Not even plastic surgery.

Thankfully there are some incredibly effective techniques to slow the occurrence, minimize the appearance, and strengthen slackened tissues. Sure, cellulite is a cosmetic problem, but more than that, it's a progressive medical problem that gets worse with age. There may not be a cure, but (similar to diabetes and hypertension) you can manage it. Since it is a connective-tissue issue, really the only thing that can help prevent and slow the spread of cellulite is strengthening the fibers of the connective tissues so that the rogue fat cells can't permeate the dermis even more.

CELLULITE MANAGEMENT

In order to effectively manage cellulite, you need to heal, strengthen, and hydrate the cells and connective tissues. Sure, topicals and medical treatments can help tame the sticky situation . . . for a pretty penny. Because cellulite is not a fat problem, dieting and exercise are not curatives, though they can help minimize cellulite's appearance and help fight off even more from taking over your currently smooth backside and thighs. Thankfully, there are other less-expensive and even free ways that are often the most effective modes to minimize the unsightly stuff. Here's how:

Diet

Certain foods and supplements strengthen connective tissues, repair cell membranes, and increase circulation. A few pointers:

Breakfast. A healthy breakfast of whole grains and fruits to boost antioxidant levels. Antioxidants help fight off the signs of aging (like cellulite), keeping your skin moist and healthy.

Water. Stay hydrated throughout the day with water, juice, fruits, and vegetables. Think about it this way: Imagine healthy skin as cookie dough, formed into a thin cookie before it goes into the oven. You can bend it, press your finger into it, and it still remains intact. Now bake that cookie, cooking out all of the moisture, until it is a crisp cookie. Try to bend it. It snaps in half. The moisture keeps your skin malleable.

Not that your skin will snap in half, but by keeping it hydrated, you are maintaining its malleability.

Eggs. Eat one or two eggs each week (including the yolk, which is filled with lecithin and helps strengthen connective tissues).

Raw fruits and veggies. Regularly consume raw fruits and vegetables. cooking them extracts much of their water and nutrients. Raw produce is filled with two essentials mentioned above: water and antioxidants.

Goji. Snack on goji berries, a fruit that is considered to be as close to a "wonder food" as they come. It is rich with amino acids, trace minerals, anti–inflammatories, and five hundred times the vitamin C of an orange and more beta–carotene than a carrot! Vitamin C is a serious antioxidant that will boost your skin's health and fend off the signs of aging.

Exercise

When you work out you are getting your blood pumping, nourishing your cells with fresh oxygen, and keeping things moving! Exercise encourages better circulation, which can help get things (like fat cells) moving. But more than that, it minimizes the appearance of cellulite because, if you are thin, there is less surface area to display the stuff.

Sun Exposure

Want to destroy your connective tissue? Lie out in the sun. UV rays can actually break down cell walls and connective tissue, causing blood vessels to weaken, making cellulite more visible. Avoiding sun exposure helps maintain skin's integrity. Believe me, I am very much aware that tanned skin has the ability to hide the appearance of cellulite. Spray tan or self-tanning creams create that same "flawless" appearance without screwing up your skin in the long run.

Get Happy!

Laugh, play, have fun! I know, sounds strange, but when you are having a blast you are increasing your circulation, which can, yes, help your anticellulite cause. So go out and do what makes you happy—exercise, yoga, massage, etc., and tackle the sticky issue with a smile on your face.

Cellulite or not, stop stressing and obsessing—that certainly won't help the problem, I assure you. Cellulite is more common than not, so you may as well just take the best care of your body that you can and love it unconditionally. It's the only one you've got, and you know what? It's a beautiful thing.

Forget Cocktail Hour. How About Cardio Hour?

You haven't seen your girlfriends in days, weeks, even, and it's time to catch up and reconnect . . . over a cocktail, right? I know, it's often the go-to. I hear myself saying all too often, "It's been too long; we should grab a drink and catch up." Why the drink? Must you be drinking in order to chat with girlfriends, reminisce about old times, discuss the latest gossip, get the down-low on who you're dating and what drama he is causing in your life? How about instead if you make happy hour a cardio hour instead of a cocktail hour?

Particularly when it comes to spending time with my girlfriends, I have recently come to prefer cardio to cocktails. The thing is, we are all time crunched. We are trying to fit in both our workouts and our girl-time. The perfect solution: Do both! Schedule a weekly walk if that helps, just like you would schedule drinks, a meeting, or a mani/pedi. Even better: Make it a group get-together!

I have a group of girlfriends (but sometimes it's only two or three who can make it) whom I hike with, same time, same place, every Sunday afternoon. Those hikes are our social hour to really talk, be real, get feedback on work and guys, and, of course, get in a good workout. We get so involved in our conversations that we can walk for hours without even realizing that time has passed. The great thing is that it's hard to flake out because I'm "too tired" or "too busy" when I know that my friends are depending on me to be there. They do their best to show up for me, so I show up for them.

The point is this: Just because you're not playing a team sport doesn't mean that exercise can't be social. If you want to create a fitness lifestyle, you have to fit fitness into your lifestyle. Working out with friends and family is the perfect way to do it.

The 1-Song Run That Will Help You Lose Weight

Dress size, weight, minutes—when it comes to fitness, numbers stress me out. What do I mean? Instead of motivating me to keep going and keep it off, numbers feel like pressure to me. In fact, they actually derail me. Example?

HOW TO STOP STRESSING ABOUT THE NUMBER

Dress Size

My clothes were feeling a little snug and I needed new "adult" outfits like slacks and button-up shirts. I went to a department store, and the saleslady sized me up (visually), asked what I needed, pulled a few styles, and placed them in the dressing room, then proceeded to join me. She was one of those personal shoppers who feel the need to tend to your every whim. I grabbed the first pair of pants hanging in the dressing room and saw that they were two sizes bigger than what I normally wore. "No, this is way too big," I snapped, shocked that she would even *think* I was that large. "Actually, I think it will fit," she responded. "Just try it on so I can see if I need to get you another size." I was pissed but aggressively put on the damn pants so I could "show her" how wrong she was. They fit. Perfectly. "Well, this brand obviously runs small," I said as I grabbed the next pair, which was the same larger size. They fit, too. My face turned bright red. I began to sweat. I started to cry, caved in, and bought the big-girl pants. Instead of using that as fuel to get back into my old fitness and healthy food routine, I ate more, exercised less, and gained even more weight.

Lesson: I don't look at size, I look at fit. If I have to see the size, and it's a big-girl size and it fits, I take a Sharpie and black it out. Then I wear it, eventually forgetting what size it is. Really, size *doesn't* matter. Fit does.

Weight

Similar to my aversion to knowing my pants size, I have a hard time tracking my weight by the scale. I prefer using "tester jeans." Tester jeans are jeans that you have tailored to fit your size perfectly. Therefore, the jeans are essentially sizeless and simply a representation of your shape. Tester jeans should not be worn in public (which could stretch them out) or washed (which could shrink them). The sole purpose is to measure your size loss and gain. That's all.

So instead of being a slave to the scale, once a month try on your tester jeans and vary your workout and food programs according to the jeans' fit. Believe me, this might save your sanity.

Minutes

For a short period I had a trainer. He told me that the only way I could improve my cardio ability was to run. I hate running. I am a walker. I can do it for hours. But running—not my thing. I canceled the next session. Eventually I realized that I was being ridiculous. What was my issue with running, anyway? He put me on a treadmill and timed it out, counting down from ten minutes, letting me know the second each minute was completed, as if to minimize my stress and illuminate my progress. Each time he shouted out that another minute had gone by, instead of feeling relief, I felt like my throat was closing. After a few seconds it would wear off and I would get back in the groove of whatever song was pumping on my workout mix. "Five minutes left," he would then belt out, derailing me once again. When he called out the final minute, it was as if, hard and fast, I could not take one more step. I pulled the emergency cord and stopped the treadmill, disappointed in myself for being unable to complete the run.

THIS IS WHERE THE 1-SONG RUN COMES IN

After that first agonizing session, we realized that it was less the run and more the time component that I couldn't handle. The next session he timed with a stopwatch in his hand but didn't shout out the minutes, and I just listened to the song, running along without any "I can't breathe" issues for the entire three-song duration. That was until I saw him look down at the stopwatch out of the corner of my eye, then I was stuck wondering where I was in the timing. Was I almost done? How much longer? Simultaneously, it felt like my throat was closing. I got through it. Barely. That last minute, as he stared at that damn watch the entire time, was torturous, as I did my best to pretend I had blinders on, like a racehorse, forcing myself not to see that he was staring at the clock in a silent countdown.

The following week I told him that we needed to find a new technique. I asked him not to look at his watch even once. Instead I had made a new workout mix that, each third song, totaled ten minutes. I ran the full three songs just fine. I even ran a fourth just because I was feeling fine and totally forgot about the time. No breathing issues, no stressing. In fact, when he said "time," I had lost track of the number of songs that I had passed and could have gone at least one more song.

Now I time myself based on songs. Even if I am just on a walk, I will challenge myself to run for one song. One measly song—how hard can that be? Almost every time, that song turns into two, oftentimes three. The other day, it was seven! And I was just fine. But here's the best thing: If you run your one song and you can't muster the energy or drive to endure a second, that's fine—you've already accomplished your goal! Instead of running another song, walk it! Once your breathing regulates, maybe up your speed and try to run one more song. Suddenly you have turned your average stroll into an interval workout that will help you burn even more calories, build your endurance, and even strengthen your bones!

So, if you're stressed by the idea of running ten minutes, don't! Run one song. As that song is coming to an end, see how you feel and decide if you can run for two more, setting a three-song goal. At the end of song two, gauge how you feel. Maybe you are up for five songs? The key is to create a workout mix filled with music that makes you move, plus make sure that there isn't a lengthy break between each song. Anything that can distract you from the music can derail your cause. Today just might be the day that you are finally able to embrace running . . . and like it!

MY ULTIMATE WORKOUT MIX

"Super Bass"—Nicki Minaj

"Dirty Little Secret"—The All-American Rejects

"Womanizer"—Britney Spears

"Naughty Girl"—Beyoncé

"Push It"—Salt-N-Pepa

"Disturbia"—Rihanna

"The Boys of Summer"—The Ataris

"Don't Stop Believin' "—Journey

"Stronger"—Kanye West

"Rhythm Nation"—Janet Jackson

"Down on Me"—Jeremih and 50 Cent

"Irreplaceable"—Beyoncé

"Just Dance"—Lady GaGa

"We R Who We R"—Ke$ha

"S&M"—Rihanna

"I Like It"—Enrique Iglesias

"Whole Foods Parking Lot"—DJ Dave

"Set Fire to the Rain"—Adele

"Survivor/I Will Survive"—Glee Cast

"Jai Ho!"—A. R. Rahman & the Pussycat Dolls

"Crazy Bitch"—Buckcherry

"Ain't No Other Man"—Christina Aguilera

"Girls Just Want to Have Fun"—Cyndi Lauper

"Listen to Your Heart"—D.H.T.

"Lose Yourself"—Eminem

"Brain Stew"—Green Day

"Hot N Cold"—Katy Perry

"Money Maker"—Ludacris

"Hot in Herre"—Nelly

"Live for This"—Hatebreed

"Addicted"—Saving Abel

"Untouched"—The Veronicas

"LaLa"—Ashlee Simpson

"Footloose"—Kenny Loggins

"Baby Got Back"—Sir Mix-a-Lot

"Party Rock Anthem"—LMFAO

How to Fake a Perfect Body Now!

If you have to drop a few pounds in time for a fancy event or (fingers crossed) life-changing date in ten days (or tonight!), you've got to do a combo of cardio, diet, healthy lifestyle, plus a sprinkling of fast fixes and, honestly—faking it!

FIGHT WATER RETENTION (YOU SWEAR YOU SWELLED UP OVERNIGHT!)

You have been eating light and nutritious meals, like sushi, salads, and Chinese steamed vegetables. You've been working out more and drinking alcohol less. You feel svelte and sexy. And then you wake up the day of your important night and you could swear you gained five pounds! Your clothes just don't fit, your face is swollen, you even have a pouch on your stomach that you definitely didn't have yesterday. What the f★★★?!

Don't worry. It's not fat, it's water! Well, that's all well and good, except for the fact that you have to look good *tonight,* and water or not, you are still bigger!

Yes, water retention can be to blame when it comes to looking like you've gained five pounds overnight. It can also make you appear "full and bloated" for a day, weeks, even months, weighing you down and filling out your jeans. And while it will disappear as soon as you can harness that water and convince it to drain out of your puffy body, coercing it out can feel impossible. But it's not. It's just that the remedies are slightly counterintuitive. How? Drink more water.

Drinking *more* water can actually get rid of water retention. Yes, it in fact flushes out stuck liquids, keeping the system moving and helping to maintain a trim, healthy figure. You see, when the body feels like it is being deprived of enough water to properly function, it holds on to it as a survival mechanism, instead of trusting that it's OK to let it go, since more water will soon be flowing in. Over time, when you are dehydrated your body excretes less water, and bloating can set in. More than flushing out bloat, water clears your kidneys and your entire digestive system, hydrating your body and brain, dissolving and transporting nutrients, such as oxygen and minerals. It also helps with digestion, metabolism, and removing waste from the body. Water helps flush out toxins from fat cells, helping to actually burn more fat. Building up to the big event, drink lots and lots of water.

STOP CARBOHYDRATING

Each gram of carbohydrate you consume holds around 2.5 grams of water. Yes, carbs are water carriers. The more carbs you have in your system, the more water you will be holding on to. By cutting back on carbs, you are actually simultaneously releasing water retention.

FOODS THAT BREAK DOWN FAT

There's a reason for the old-fashioned grapefruit diet. Citrus is great at fat breakdown and digestion. A natural fat fighter, vitamin C helps minimize fats' effectiveness, actually liquefying the sticky stuff and making it less likely to latch on and bulk you up. Most citrus fruits will work, but the two most potent are:

- Tangerine peel
- Grapefruit

FOODS THAT BURN FAT

Fat-burning foods tend to literally be "burning"—mouth burning that is. The naturally "hot herbs" heat up the body while helping to increase digestion, circulation, and the metabolism. A few include:

- Fresh ginger
- Szechuan peppercorn
- Cayenne pepper
- Jalapeño pepper
- Cinnamon bark
- Fennel

FOODS THAT FLUSH OUT FAT

Another way to avert a fat attack? Fruit pectin and lecithin. The naturally occurring chemicals keep fat from being absorbed by your cells, flushing them out before they have a chance to bind to your body. Here are a few to know:

- Soybeans
- Peanuts
- Apples
- Berries

Carbs increase insulin. Insulin, a hormone produced when we eat carbo-hydrates, causes our kidneys to retain sodium, and sodium causes the body to retain water.

Cut carbs and you are cutting calories in general. But don't cut all carbs. Stick with carbs that are natural, highly nutritious, and high in fiber, like brown rice, whole grains, and green vegetables, such as kale and Brussels sprouts.

Keep in mind that carbs are a key component when it comes to energy—both physical and mental. Cutting carbs long-term is a bad idea. But for a pre-event fix, restrict white rice, potatoes, pasta, and—the no-brainer—bread!

EAT FAT-BURNING FOODS

No one told you that that "Freshman 15" would stick with you through senior year—and even up to now! And what's worse is that it only gets worse. As you age your metabolism slows down, your busy schedule makes it tough to slip in exercise, and your body takes the brunt. But that doesn't mean that you are s★★t out of luck. Fight off that fat with food—the right foods. More than mindlessly shoveling foods down the hatch, think about how they can help your cause. Some foods are naturally multitaskers, help-ing to break down, burn, or flush out fat! See the list on the previous page.

DO CARDIO!

If you want to cut the fat, you've got to sweat. Cardio is the best way to burn calories and fat, slimming your body and making way for your muscles to show their gorgeous definition beneath. Ramping up cardio will burn extra calories. It also gets those endorphins flowing, boosts your energy, and helps you feel more confident—all very good things when it comes to strutting your stuff!

The Day of . . . Here's How to Fake It!

If you simply don't have the time to get in slim, trim shape before that all-important must-look-good outing, cut yourself some slack and just fake it—for now. Here's how:

EAT

Break your fast (breakfast) first thing in the morning to get your metabolism pumping and your body burning calories by eating good healthy carbs, fats, and proteins, such as oatmeal and egg, berries and yogurt, almond butter slathered banana, or a green smoothie. For lunch and dinner eat lots of veg-gies and healthy proteins—such as fish, hemp seeds (also a great source of fiber), almonds, or lean high-quality meats—and *veggies* (oh, did I say that

DIURETIC FOODS TO ENCOURAGE DE-PUFFING

Many of these also help in detoxification.

- Celery
- Celery seed
- Cranberry juice
- Dandelion
- Green tea
- Dandelion-leaf tea
- Fennel
- Juniper berries
- Nettle
- Parsley

HIGH-WATER FOODS THAT (YES) HELP ELIMINATE EXCESS WATER

Eating high-water-content foods is another way to increase the elimination of excess fluid retention. I know, it sounds counterintuitive:

- Artichokes
- Asparagus
- Carrots
- Cucumbers
- Lettuce
- Honeydew
- Green beans
- Watermelon
- Watercress

already?). But try to keep away from gas- (and bloat-) causing veggies like Brussels sprouts, broccoli, and cabbage. Yes, even though they were great to eat for the past week, today's not the day. If you have a hankering for something sweet, have a small chunk of dark chocolate (at least 65 percent cocoa).

More than what you *should* eat, there are certain foods that you *shouldn't* eat—which isn't always just the fatty stuff. If you're lactose sensitive, you should stay away from *dairy,* because it can cause bloat and gas, neither of which are attractive on a date or big night. *Salt* is another stay-away-from spice if you don't want to look like an inflated balloon.

DROP WATER WEIGHT

Since it is literally impossible to drop fat on a day's notice, yet you still want to look as if you've "lost weight," your best bet is to, yes, drop some of that excess water weight. After a week of upping your water to help pull more water out of your system (again, I know, counterintuitive), it's time—just today, the day of the big night—to restrict the amount of water you drink, but again, this is just a quick fix. Do this long-term and it will backfire, producing the reverse effects. You need to be careful about not totally dehydrating—that's dangerous! And don't do this for more than three days max! Another water-dropping trick? Eat foods that pull water out of your body—diuretic foods. See the list on the previous page.

Note: If you plan on drinking alcohol on this big night out, and if your body is dehydrated from not drinking enough water, you are risking a terrible hangover tomorrow. . . .

UP YOUR POTASSIUM

If you couldn't help yourself (or just forgot) and splurged on soy sauce–dipped sushi, fish sauce–slathered steamed Chinese veggies, or canned sodium-filled soup, there is a trick to pull out that extra salt. Potassium. Potassium-rich foods actually counterbalance the puffing qualities of salt and alcohol, acting as a mild diuretic. Here's a list of potassium-rich foods that you should slip into your diet right now:

- Avocado
- Beets and beet greens
- Edamame (soybeans)
- Papaya
- Cooked sweet potato
- Medjool dates
- Spinach

- Butternut squash

- Dried apricots

- Banana

- Broccoli

- Orange juice

- Yogurt

- Unsalted almonds

- Pink grapefruit

- Salmon

WORK OUT

Focus on last-minute touch-up toning on any exposed muscles. The rush of blood to the area will temporarily engorge the muscle, making it appear to be more toned and tighter than it actually is. Try tricep dips, calf raises, the plank, push-ups, lunges, and squats to target areas most noticed in dresses.

OTHER SLIMMING/DE-PUFFING TRICKS

Take a Bath

Bath products that contain caffeine or algae actually help reduce puffiness and, over the long run, may minimize the appearance of cellulite! No special de-puffing soaks on hand? How about coffee grinds? You can soak in coffee grinds or simply rub them all over your skin in the shower for an exfoliating, circulation-stimulating, de-puffing rinse!

Self-Tanner

Self-tanner, when sprayed evenly all over the skin, naturally makes you appear smaller. (Come on, you should know this: Dark clothes—and tanners—make the body look slimmer, while whites have the tendency to make even the skinniest chick seem thick.) But more than looking like you just returned from a trip to Maui, strategically applying tanner to certain areas of the skin creates definition that looks totally natural. When applied correctly, self-tanner can accentuate muscle tone on the chest, abs, legs, and arms with strategic spraying that creates the illusion of depth and muscle definition.

Stilettos

Have you ever walked around on your toes and noticed how your calves and thighs instantly appear more toned, lengthened, and sexier? The longer your legs appear, the slimmer they appear. So how do you achieve both sexy attributes: stronger and longer? Wear high, I mean *high*, heels. More than length and tone, they add a dose of sex appeal and confidence. Now, that's slimming *and* sexy!

See page 207 for some of my stiletto workouts.

Skinny Chicks' Fitness Tricks

Losing and keeping off weight isn't just about the big picture (getting fit/ losing ten pounds/fitting into your skinny jeans); it's so much more than that—or rather, so much less than that (the sixty-minute daily sweat sesh helps to get you out of your bad mood, de-puff from last night, or feel like you accomplished something good for yourself today). In fact, if you want to lose weight, take a cue from chicks who are not just skinny but smart about it.

Beyond the full-on sixty-minute workout, you've got to think of the little things—lots of little things. Sure, you might burn 400 calories in the one hour spent on your treadmill, and that's great, but did you know that just standing up, making out, laughing out loud, giving a massage, walking while talking on the phone, and Quickie Workouts in Bed can burn twice as many calories collectively, keep your metabolism stoked all day long, and maintain a fit mentality, which will help you make healthier decisions over- all? I mean, really, why would you eat that gigantic piping-hot cookie and negate the calories that you just walked off while taking the stairs instead of the escalator? You see, smart skinny chicks don't necessarily *think* about fit- ness. They live it. They have infused tricks and little things into their lives, making fitness a lifestyle as opposed to a chore. And that's the best, easiest, and least-invasive way to lose and keep off the weight.

Here are a few skinny chicks' fitness tricks that you should infuse into your life, too.

WORK OUT WHILE WATCHING TV

I am a multitasker, filling my day with as many things at once in order to make the most out of every moment (except for those days when I can hardly motivate myself to change out of my sweats, but that's a different story). Because sometimes I can't seem to find the time to slip my workout into my completely full day, but of course I already penciled in the after-dinner hour to watch my must-see TiVo'd TV, I created a TV-circuit workout to ensure that I get in my exercise, even when I overschedule myself.

Do the math: Your average 1-hour show is actually 44 minutes of show, plus 16 minutes of commercials, each lasting an average of 30 seconds. The key to the circuit is to do cardio during your show, and resistance during the commercials. Here are a few of my go-to TV moves:

March in Place

If you are watching TV, talking on the phone, even brushing your teeth, *walk!* This is not about strolling. I'm talking about marching—fast, and in place—like power-walking in a box! Swing your arms, lift those knees, really exaggerate the move in order to get the most out of it. Get your heart pumping; maybe even sweat a little. Want to change it up? Do side touches: Take big steps out to each side; keep those arms swinging; make this move big!

Plank

Hold this top of the push-up pose for the length of one commercial. If you aren't feeling the burn by the end of the first one, keep it up through a second, or all of them if you like. What's great about the plank is that it's a total-body burner, and you're not even moving! Every muscle—calves to abs to chest—is engaged. You may not feel every area at first, but as one muscle fatigues, another takes over to carry the brunt until it fatigues, then another takes over, etc.

Plank ➡

Side Plank

To add a little more oomph to your average plank and really dig into your obliques (your side abs), add a twist. Get in plank position, then rotate onto one side, balancing on one hand and the side of one foot, and hold this pose for the entire commercial. You can even do this one during the show since you are still facing the TV. Make sure to switch sides for an even workout.

Sit-up Stay

. . . And don't roll back down. This is similar to the boat pose, on pages 200–201 except that you are keeping your knees bent and feet on the floor (as opposed to forming your body into a V as you would in the boat pose). Balance on your butt with knees bent and feet on the floor. Sit up straight, then hinge your upper body back a couple of inches until you feel your ab muscles engage. By holding there, you are challenging your abs even more, forcing other less-used core muscles to come into play and help hold you up. Hold this pose for the entire commercial. It's another seriously effective one-pose, no-movement exercise.

Leg Raise

To target your lower abs, lie on your back with your legs straight together in front of you. Inhale, engage your core, and lift your feet together six inches off the floor. Hold this pose for the entire commercial.

Wall Sit

Sit on the wall as if you are sitting on a chair, with your back firmly pressed against the wall, your thighs parallel to the floor, and your calves parallel to the wall—exactly the position that you would be in if sitting in a chair, but without the seat. As with the plank, hold this pose for as many commercials as you can endure. If the commercials aren't engaging enough for you, take your mind off the burn by opening your mail. Try to sit through three commercials (about 90 seconds). To up the exercise, place a small stack of books on your lap, creating more weight and therefore increasing the resistance.

DAILY 100S

The perfect exercises to do when you have a few minutes to spare are daily 100s. A daily 100 is 100 seconds or 100 reps of an exercise, *any* exercise. It's a great way to jump up your metabolism, burn a few extra calories, tone your muscles, and get in a fit mind-set. Here are a few ideas:

100 seconds of:

Plank (page 190)

X-Plank (page 202)

Boat (page 201)

Sit-up stay (page 191)

Wall sit (above)

Shadow boxing (page 214)

100 reps of:

Jumping jacks

Push-ups against a wall

Crunches

Bicycle sit-ups

Skipping (yes, like when you were a kid)

Lunges

Squats

Jump-rope rotations

TAKE THE STAIRS, CHANGE THE CHANNEL ON THE TV, AND MORE LITTLE THINGS

I know, these are so cliché and totally overused examples of how to add a little exercise to your day. But it's true, they work, and you should do them, too. Forget the escalator and take the stairs instead. Park far away from the grocery store or mall entrance. Walk across the room to pick up the phone instead of toting it with you everywhere you go. Get up and change the channel on the TV instead of using the remote control. Yes, the little things do add up.

6 Ways to Work Out While Getting Ready to Go Out . . . Seriously

Regardless of whether it takes you thirty minutes or three hours to get ready to go out, you can slip in a workout that won't necessarily make you sweat but will burn some calories—all while getting dolled up. Think about it: Much of the time that you are prepping is actually spent standing around. Sure, you have a curling iron, toothbrush, or lipstick in hand, but the fact of the matter is that you are standing there, your legs pretty much worthless, while your hands are doing all the work. It's time to make the most of those moments and burn a few extra calories during that hour-long prep by putting your lower half to work. Believe me, once you arrive at the big event and your mouth starts watering at the sight of those fatty appetizers being passed around, you will be thrilled that you did a little extra "party prep."

1. **Waiting for your face mask to dry.** You already know (or at least you should know if you read the last section of this book) that marching in place is one of my fave ways to pass the time at home, whether I'm talking on the phone or watching TV. It's also the perfect exercise to do while waiting for your skin-tightening/-quenching mask to dry.

2. **Brushing your teeth.** You already know how to brush your teeth. You've been doing it day in and day out for years, decades even. Do you seriously need to stare at yourself in the mirror, watching the toothpaste foam in your mouth . . . just to make sure you're doing it correctly? I doubt it. Instead, take a seat. On the wall. Yes, *sit on the wall* with a wall sit (see page 192). Wall sits activate the abs, butt, and thighs, and they are perfect if you want to get in a quick calorie burner without the bouncing from marching.

3. **Staring at the closet deciding what to wear.** You have been staring at the clothes in your closet for the last 5 minutes, yet you still can't seem to come up with a suitable, flattering, confidence-oozing outfit for tonight. Getting the blood pumping has been proven to help activate the brain. So if you are just completely perplexed when trying to decide what fab outfit to wear, peer into your open closet while doing 10 to 100 jumping jacks. Remember to keep your abs engaged

and your lower back straight to maximize the benefits. Oh, and make sure you haven't yet put your heels on. You wouldn't want to twist your ankle or, worse, snap the heel.

4. **Blow-drying your hair.** Wearing a short skirt? Don't you want toned calves to show off? Heel raises are great for toning your legs and butt without causing too much of a sweat, plus the slow and controlled move keeps your curling iron from accidentally burning your scalp and your eyeliner from accidentally puncturing your eye. Place your feet hip-width apart and slowly press your body up onto the balls of your feet, then lower back down slowly and with control. To get the most out of this move, tighten your tush with each heel raise and focus on engaging your core. (Imagine that you are about to be hit in the stomach; what do you do? That's what I mean by "engaging the core.")

5. **Curling/straightening your hair.** After you've done enough heel raises to feel the burn, slightly change your position to a V heel raise to work your inner calves and saddlebags. Form your feet into the shape of a V, with your heels glued together. Repeat the above exercise while keeping your heels pressed together the entire time.

6. **Putting on your makeup.** For some of you, putting on makeup can be an art form. You carefully paint on your face, accentuating your eyes, narrowing your nose, making your cheeks look apple plucked. It takes precision. And then there are those of you who just slather on the basics—a little concealor, a little color, and voilà! Regardless of your makeup methodology, you can still add a little slow and controlled exercise to the equation. The plié is another perfect calorie burner/leg toner that gives you the freedom to still properly put on your makeup,

Working Out . . . for Free

Summer, 24, Art-Gallery Assistant

- Running is free (minus the shoes; but investing in good shoes is critical; don't skimp!).
- Walk whenever you can.
- Take advantage of free gym memberships. There are a gazillion gyms within a fifteen-minute radius of my apartment, so last winter when the weather was too miserable to work out outdoors, I just rotated through the different trial memberships and had a lot of fun exploring. It's definitely not what everyone wants to be doing, but if you feel your budget is tight for a month, it's a great way to get your exercise!

194

curl your hair, brush your teeth, and bake cookies. Stand up straight with your feet 2 feet apart toes pointing slightly out. Engage your core and your butt. Bend your knees, allowing your torso to slowly and with control push down. Imagine that your shoulder blades are being pinched together without arching your back. As you bend your knees down into the plié, focus on lengthening and elongating your torso. And of course, go slow and steady to avoid sticking your mascara wand in your eye.

Now you have a reason to spend extra time "getting ready". You're working out!

Behind Every Great Woman Is a Great . . . Behind

Skinny jeans might be sexy. But if the process of putting them on includes lying on the floor, holding your breath as you suck in your stomach to zip them up, then once you're wearing them you're hardly able to sit or even walk, then it sounds utterly awful to me! Instead of enduring the torture, try to trim your tush, thighs, and saddlebags so those jeans slip on more easily.

No matter what size your rear end is, the last thing you want is flab. To tighten up the jiggle and minimize the overstuffed sausage appearance, it is important to both tone (resistance) and burn (cardio, cardio, cardio). If you need a little extra help defining your derriere, these five "do it 'til it hurts" toners should do the trick!

TUSH TONER

Open, Close (see photo below)

This is a total saddlebag, thigh, and butt toner. And it's so simple to do you will be shocked you haven't been doing it all along!

← Open, Close

1. Lie on your side, with your top leg stacked on your bottom leg, knees to feet.

2. Bend your knees so that your body is in the shape of a Z, with your quads (your thighs) perpendicular to your torso and your calves.

3. Engage your core and raise your entire top leg up like a Pac-Man mouth, maintaining the bend in your knee.

4. Slowly and with control release down.

5. Repeat until it hurts. Then do 5 more. Switch sides.

Clam (see photo on page 197)

Tackle the sides of your butt and thighs (ahem . . . saddlebags) by engaging and exhausting the muscles that wrap around your backside.

1. Lie on your side, with your top leg stacked on your bottom leg, knees to feet.

2. Bend your knees so that your body is in the shape of a Z, with your quads (your thighs) perpendicular to your torso and your calves, like *Open, Close.*

3. Glue your feet together, engage your core, and pull your top knee up into the air, keeping your feet glued together (like a clam opening its shell).

4. Slowly and with control release down.

5. Repeat until it hurts. Then do 5 more. Switch sides.

Elevated Clam (see photo on page 197)

1. Do the exact same movement as in the clam, but elevate your feet in the air, keeping your lower knee pressed against the floor, then do the clam in the air.

2. Repeat until it hurts. Then do 5 more. Switch sides.

Reverse Clam (see photo on page 197)

If you really want to feel the burn and lift your butt, do this exercise. Whew! You'll definitely feel it in the morning.

1. Start in the same starting position as in the clam.

2. Now, instead of gluing your feet together, glue your knees together and lift your top foot up into the air. Be sure to keep your hips stacked and square. No rolling forward onto your pelvis.

3. Your foot will remain elevated for the entire exercise.

Clam

Elevated
Clam

197

Reverse
Clam

4. Raise your top knee up and away from your bottom knee. (You will feel this all over your butt but particularly right beneath it.)

5. Return your top knee to your bottom knee, keeping your foot in the air the entire time.

6. Repeat until it hurts. Then do 5 more. Switch sides.

Butt Lift

Target the area where your butt and top of your thigh connect to help lift, tone, and lighten.

1. Lie on your back with your knees bent, feet flat on the ground, your heels a few inches from your butt.

2. Engage your abs and press your butt straight up toward the ceiling until you have created a straight line from your kneecaps to your neck.

3. Slowly and with control release back down until just before touching the ground.

4. Repeat until it hurts. Then do 5 more.

BEYOND FITNESS, IT'S ABOUT FIT!

A Bra for Your Butt

Avoid sausage butt and create the appearance of your own set of perfectly plucked cherries by selecting a style of jeans that lifts and separates (kind of like a butt bra). Look for five-pocket, tight-fitting, stretch-material jeans, with a specifically contoured waist and back rise. Every butt is different, so go to a store that has lots of designer options, then stand patiently in the mirror and try them all on until you find the one that lifts and separates! Just like no one wants a "uni-boob," no one wants a "uni-butt."

Perfect Pocket Placement

Half the battle of having a great butt is paying attention to the type of pants that you wear. Back-pocket placement and size can dramatically change the appearance of your behind. For best placement, the pocket should end right above the crease between your butt and thigh. When pockets are too far apart they tend to make your butt appear wider. Pockets that drop below the butt and down onto the back of the thigh make the butt look saggy.

Quell the Swell

To flush out your system and minimize fluid retention and bloat, drink lots of water with lemon (lemon acts as a mild diuretic). Believe it or not, after a night of sushi and soy sauce (loaded with salt), your butt will bloat!

The goal is perky cherries, not swollen cherries! De-puff post salty meal to help quell the swell.

Sexy Abs—Stat!

Sexy abs aren't just about endless mindless sit-ups. In fact, if you find that you are doing hundreds of crunches, feeling nothing the next morning, and not noticing any change . . . you're not alone. Sure, you might feel like you can't do another sit-up because your stomach is sooo exhausted, but that's *not* necessarily because your muscles were working to tone and tighten. If you want sexy abs stat, you've got to go about it in a whole new way. Here's how to achieve gutsy greatness:

- **Cardio** (to burn off the flab that sits on top of the muscle)
- **Ab exercises that actually work** (to tone the muscles effectively and efficiently)
- **Diet** (because sexy abs start in the kitchen)

CARDIO

If your stomach is covered by fat, no one's going to see those fab abs that you've been sculpting beneath. Cut the fat first. How? Cardio. Don't worry, those sit-ups weren't for naught. Once you get rid of the flab, you will still have some pretty fab abs hiding out beneath and ready for their long-awaited big reveal!

Not sure if you have flab covering your underlying abs? Do a quick gut check. Engage your abs then pinch as much fat on your stomach as you can. That's how much fat you've got floating on top. I'm not saying that you want all of that soft stuff to be burned off. Personally, I like a little bit there (it looks feminine to me), but if your hands are overflowing and you want to trim it up, focus on cardio first.

Do a minimum of forty-five minutes of heart-pumping cardio at least three to five days a week. To really engage your abs, choose activities that require abdominal rotation, such as racquetball, surfing, and cross-country skiing, or try belly dancing, kickboxing, or power-yoga routines. Each of these can burn up to 600 calories per hour.

Creative Cardio

Your body changes with change. If you want to reduce belly fat, change up your cardio routine every week in order to work different muscle groups so you burn more fat. If your body expects a certain movement, or series of movements, it gets accustomed to the moves and doesn't have to work as hard. I'm not saying do a completely new routine, just do *something* different. Even if it's simply changing the order.

Effective Cardio

Want to see results faster? Step it up!

Don't walk on a treadmill for hours on end at a speed low enough for you to simultaneously read a novel or the small print of your fave magazine.

Don't ride a stationary bike on level 2 wearing flip-flops. That's hardly considered cardio. I mean really, if you were working to a level that warrants being called a workout, while wearing flip-flops, those sandals would fly through the air within a few pedal rotations.

To be the most effective when it comes to cardio, you've got to get your heart rate up, or you're seriously just wasting your time.

AB EXERCISES THAT ACTUALLY WORK

Stop with the hundreds of crunches already! You see, you can crunch until the cows come home and still have a muffin top folding over your jeans. The reason? When you're doing those hundreds of daily sit-ups you are actually extinguishing all of the oxygen from your muscles; essentially you are suffocating them as opposed to strengthening them. This doesn't mean that crunches are pointless. But there are techniques you can do to make your ab routine more effective and efficient, giving you better results in less time—as little as five minutes a day!

If you want to make the most of your ab routine, you've got to amp it up. How? Change it up. Try these.

Yoga Boat Pose (see photo on page 201)

This simple hold that looks like a V position, with the bottom of the V being your butt balancing on the ground, engages the core for an enduring burn. Hold still for 100 seconds or as long as you can.

Pilates 100

Pilates is a known core-strengthening workout. This seemingly simple move fires up the abs thanks to a combination of pumping the arms and 45-degree legs. Place your body in the boat pose (V-position), balancing on your butt. Unlike the boat, where you hold still, with Pilates 100 you are going to pump your arms up and down off the ground just a few inches 100 times.

Russian Twists (see photo on page 201)

Balance on your butt with your knees bent and pressed together, and your feet elevated off the floor. Bend your elbows, clasp your hands together in front of your chest, and rotate your lower body slightly to your right as you rotate your upper body slightly to your left. Alternate from side to side. Amp up this exercise even more by holding a 3- to 5-pound weight!

◀ Yoga Boat
Pose

201

◀ Russian
Twist

Plank *(see photo on page 190)*

Yes, this yoga pose, also known as the "top of a push-up," is a surprisingly intense full-body-strength practice, placing particular focus on the abs. Hold still for 100 seconds or as long as you can. You can work slightly different muscles by bending your elbows and placing your forearms on the ground, balancing on your forearms instead of your hands. This is called the Pilates plank *(see photo on page 207)*.

X-Plank

Same position as the plank but with your legs spread wide. Hold still for 100 seconds or as long as you can.

Knee to Nose *(see photo on page 203)*

Start in plank position, lift one leg off the ground, bring that knee as close as you can to your nose without moving your head, then extend your foot back to the starting position. Switch legs. Repeat back and forth 10 times on each leg.

Knee to Shoulder *(see photo on page 203)*

Start in plank position, lift one leg off the ground, bring that knee across your body as close as you can to your opposite shoulder, then extend your foot back to the starting position. Switch legs. Repeat back and forth 10 times on each leg.

Knee to Elbow *(see photo on page 203)*

Start in plank position, lift one leg off the ground, bring that knee up as close as you can to the elbow of the same side, then extend your foot back to the starting position. Switch legs. Repeat back and forth 10 times on each leg.

DIET

Diet is 70 percent of ab appeal. Change your diet if you really want to see a difference in your stomach. How? Eat five to six small meals a day, watch the sodium and the soda, stay away from white rice, bread, and pasta. Here are some more tips:

Eat Fat for Flat Abs

The Mediterranean diet is all about loading up on "good fats," like olive oil, fatty fish, avocado, nuts, and seeds—all of which have been shown to prevent belly fat from bulking up.

◀ Knee to
Nose

◀ Knee to
Shoulder

203

◀ Knee to
Elbow

Fat-Burning Foods

Food isn't just for the purpose of filling or fattening you up. It can also help you to fight fat. Yes, some foods are considered to be fat burning because of their ability to break down, burn, or flush out fat, actually liquefying the sticky stuff and making it less likely to latch on and bulk you up. They heat up the body while helping to increase the metabolism or keep fat from being absorbed by your cells and flushing them out before they have a chance to bind to your body. A few fat-burning foods include grapefruit, Greek yogurt, fresh ginger, Szechuan peppercorn, cayenne pepper, and cinnamon bark.

ANOTHER TRICK? BREATHE

Both a form of stress release and a secret ab toner, proper breathing is a major component of achieving flat abs. First create a neutral spine. Pretending your core is a corset, pull your rib cage down, engage your abs by pulling your belly button in, and exhale on every contraction.

Simple right? Now get busy cutting that fat. You've got a tongue-wagging-worthy six-pack waiting to be revealed!

204

Because There's Always Time for a Quickie

No time to work out? That's no longer an excuse. Believe me, I get it that your life is packed to the gills with the often-exhausting task of making it in the real world on your own. But now, more than ever before, is when you need to make a commitment to move your ass. It's not just to burn off that "Freshman 15," it's to stay sane. Seriously. Doing something wholly for yourself, especially exercise, is the ultimate stress reliever. Even if you can't find thirty to sixty straight minutes to dedicate to getting your body in shape, you can still move your butt enough to make a difference. Just break up your workout and slip it in throughout your day. Studies have shown that even short exercise spurts help to increase blood flow, burn calories, and trim fat. Even one intense minute is *some*thing. Seriously.

More than slimming your physique, exercise is the ideal midday boost, particularly in the midst of a crazed afternoon. It's been shown that exercise helps focus the mind and increase productivity. Instead of (or in addition to) my 3 P.M. coffee break, I like to do a Quickie workout—anything from one to twenty minutes depending on how much time I have. And the great thing is that by just inserting a Quickie into your day, you can instantly amp up your metabolism, helping you burn more calories even after you've finished working up a sweat.

You seriously have no time to squeeze in even the quickest of workouts? You can burn calories and tone your muscles by adding a little oomph to your daily routine with these one-minute blood-flow boosters:

1-MINUTE QUICKIE: JUMPS

- **10 Jumping jacks**

- **10 Tuck jumps** *(see photo below)*. Jump up and tuck your body like you are doing a cannonball into the pool. Just remember to land standing straight up.

- **10 Air jacks** *(see photo below)*. Like a jumping jack, but when you jump up you are extending your limbs out in an X. When you land back on the ground you are bringing your feet together and hands back down to your sides.

- **10 Skips**. Do these just like when you were a kid.

Tuck Jumps   **Air Jacks**

1-MINUTE QUICKIE: LUNGES

- **10 Forward lunges** (alternating legs, 10 on each leg)

- **10 Side lunges** (alternating legs, 10 on each side)

- **10 Reverse lunges** (alternating legs, 10 on each leg)

1-MINUTE QUICKIE: BOOT CAMP

- **20 Jumping jacks**

- **10 Seated dips** *(see photo on page 207)*. You can dip off your sofa, a sturdy chair, a park bench, or any sturdy surface that is approximately as high as your knee. Stand with your back to the sturdy surface. Bend your knees, keeping your back straight, and place your hands on the edge of the surface with your fingers folded over the edge. Your butt should be ½ inch from the edge, your thighs parallel to the ground, and your calves perpendicular to the floor. Slightly bend your elbows, lowering your butt a few inches. Straighten back up. Repeat.

- **10 Wall or angled push-ups.** You can do angled push-ups off your desk, the back of your sofa, your counter, or anything that is sturdy enough to hold your weight and is higher than your waist. The slower you go and the closer your chest is to the ground, the harder the exercise is. (Or do regular push-ups if you can.)

- **10 Squats.** Make sure to stick that butt out.

1-MINUTE QUICKIE: TOTAL-BODY TONER

- **Plank** *(see photo on page 190)*. (20 seconds)

- **Single-leg plank.** Get into plank position. Keeping your body straight like a board, lift one leg up off the ground so that you are balancing on both hands and one foot. Switch legs. (20 seconds each leg)

- **10 Mountain climbers.** Get into plank position. Now bend your right knee and bring that foot up to the outside of your right hand. Switch legs. Alternate legs (10 on each leg). Amp it up with jumping mountain climbers! Instead of simply placing your foot next to your hand, keep both hands firmly on the floor and jump both feet several inches (and as much as a foot) up in the air, landing with your right foot next to your right hand and your left leg extended straight back in the starting position. Then switch legs by jumping both feet up into the air and landing with your left foot planted next to your left hand. Alternate legs, jumping from one to the other. (10 reps on each leg should take 20 seconds)

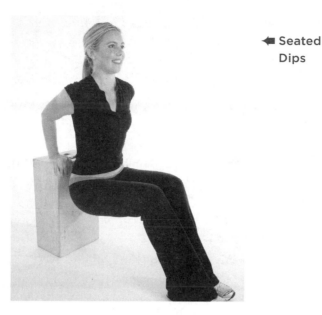

← Seated
Dips

1-MINUTE QUICKIE: SEXY ABS

- **20 Russian twists** *(see pages 200-201)*.

- **Yoga boat pose** *(see pages 200-201)*. (20 seconds)

- **Pilates plank** *(see page 190)*. This is the same as the plank, except you
  are bending your elbows and balancing your weight on your forearms
  instead of on your hands. (30 seconds)

STILETTO QUICKIE (QUICKIE AT WORK)

When your boss is running five minutes late, or while you're
waiting for your frozen meal in the microwave for seven
minutes, or for an e-mail to finally come through . . . *move
your body!* Studies show that people
who work out multiple times a day,
as opposed to chunking it
into one long workout, actually burn more calories and
lose more weight than those
who do one longer workout
and don't move much the rest
of the day. Just because you're
wearing stilettos at work, or you just like to hang
around the house all dolled up, doesn't mean that you
can't slip in a Quickie, calorie-burning, muscle-toning workout
without breaking a sweat. In fact, the elevated heel on your stilettos just

might help your cause when it comes to toning your calves and sexing up your legs. Below are my fave Stiletto Quickies. Do each as a daily 100 (100 seconds or 100 reps). If you want, do them in a circuit, stringing together several Stiletto Quickies in a row to create a longer workout that targets more areas of your body.

In a Chair

- **Seated side crunches** (100 reps per side). Put your hands together behind your head, open your elbows out to your sides, bend at your waist from side to side to get into your obliques (your side abs).

- **Seated jump rope** (100 seconds). Spin your arms as if you have a jump rope in your hands to get into your chest, biceps, and shoulders.

- **Seated upper-body spinning** (100 seconds). As if you're holding on to the pedals of a bike with your hands, sit up straight, hold those imaginary pedals, and pedal as fast as you can! Do 100 seconds forward, then reverse and backpedal for 100 seconds.

- **Seated bicycle crunches** (100 reps per side). As if you're laying on your back doing bicycle crunches (bringing opposite knee to opposite elbow), but do the same motion sitting up, hands behind your head, elbows out to your sides, rotating your torso from side to side as you bring your knee up to your opposite elbow.

- **Bounce and circle** (100 seconds). Put one arm straight in front of you and the other arm straight out to your side. Now bounce the front arm a few inches up and down and do little controlled circles with the side arm. Repeat this continuous move for 100 seconds, then switch arms and repeat for another 100 seconds. This tones your arms, shoulders, and chest.

- **Butt squeezes** (100 seconds). Squeeze your butt cheeks. Clench them tight! Hold for 10 seconds. Release briefly. Hold again! Repeat 10 times.

- **Ab squeezes** (100 seconds). As if you're being punched in the stomach, exhale fast and squeeze all of the air out of your stomach as you flex your abs. Flex them tight! Hold for 10 seconds. Release briefly. Hold again! Repeat 10 times.

Standing

- **Stand up, sit down** (100 reps). Literally stand up and quickly sit down. As soon as your butt touches the seat, stand up again. Up and down 100 times!

- **Standing side crunches** (100 reps per side). Lift one knee up to your side and bring the elbow of the same side down to meet your knee as you squeeze your side abs (obliques). Release the foot down, and just before it touches the floor, bend your knee and bring it up again. It's kind of like a train conductor sounding the horn, but you are also getting your leg in on the action. Repeat 100 times, then switch legs and repeat!

- **Circle with the arms, circle with the hips** (100 reps per side). Stand with your legs about 3 feet apart. Move your hips in a circle. At the same time, circle your arms in front of you in the same direction as if you are creating a big circle with your hands on the kitchen counter. Rotate one full circle in that direction, then switch and do one full circle—hands and hips—in the other direction. Rotate back and forth 100 times.

- **Butt lifters** (100 reps per side). Stand with one foot straight back, with just your toe touching the floor. Now lift that straight leg up just a couple of inches and place it back down. Pulse your leg back up and down and repeat 100 times. Switch sides.

- **Saddlebag slayers** (100 reps per side). Same as butt lifters but with your leg out to your side.

Quickie Workouts in Bed (No, Not Sex!)

Some people take issue with the idea of working out in bed, saying, "The bed is only meant for sleep and sex!" I used to be a believer in that bed sanctity, too, but the fact is that exercising in bed is a great place to get in a few minutes (even an entire hour) of serious calorie-burning, muscle-toning, body-sculpting, fat-trimming activity. And the best part about it is, even the laziest of the lazy have no excuse not to. I mean, you're already lying there; may as well move your body a little bit, right?

Think about it, how many times have you gotten into bed only to realize that you "forgot" to work out that day? Or what about when you wake up in the morning and you just can't seem to motivate yourself to get out of bed because it's too cold beyond the covers? Stop hitting snooze! Really, those snoozing minutes aren't great sleep anyway. If you can't motivate yourself to get your butt out of bed quite yet, start doing butt squeezes instead. Then how about a leg lift, and some arm circles? Suddenly you're pumping fresh blood and oxygen through your muscles, into your brain, and you can't help not only to be wide awake and warm, but you've already burned some calories. Talk about the right way to start the day!

Here's how you can get in both your cardio and resistance workouts without ever touching a foot off the bed:

When it comes to cardio, I'm not about to suggest that you run in place, do jumping jacks, or situate your recumbent bike on your bed. That would be just silly. But you *can* stay in bed and move several muscles at once, engaging both the upper and lower body, in order to get the blood circulating quickly, getting the heart rate up, and therefore doing a cardio exercise. In addition to searing off loads of calories, these cardio exercises will also warm you up and are ideal when you first get in bed at night and your covers are still chilled.

When it comes to resistance, keep in mind that a single pound of muscle can burn 30 to 50 calories per day. So what does this mean for you? The more muscle you have, the more calories you will naturally be burning, even when you're doing nothing but sleeping. Translation: increased metabolism! When it comes to doing resistance exercises on the bed, there are two ways to go about it: (1) *slow,* controlled movements and (2) *faster,* focused movements that hone in on a single muscle group, getting deep into a specific section and working it until it fatigues. Think: Pilates, yoga, and isometric (static/not moving—example:Plank) exercises, but instead of doing them on a mat on the floor, you are doing them on your bed (the harder the bed, the better)!

Before you get started, think about why you're working out today (it will help focus your attention and deliver better results faster). You're not just sweating for the sake of sweating, but for energy, to blow off steam, to trim your thighs, firm your butt, perk up your boobs, sweat out the toxins from the night before, or simply burn loads of calories and therefore fat. So think about it. What's the point? OK, now choose your Quickie.

SKINNY STOMACH QUICKIE WORKOUT IN BED

- **Pilates 100** Place your body in the boat pose (see page 201), balancing on your butt. Unlike the boat, where you hold still, with Pilates 100 you are going to pump your arms up and down off the ground just a few inches 100 times.

- **Russian twists** *(see pages 200-201)* (30 reps). Balance on your butt with your knees bent and pressed together, and your feet elevated and off the floor. Bend your elbows, clasp your hands together in front of your chest, and rotate your lower body slightly to your right as you rotate your upper body slightly to your left. Alternate from side to side.

- **Plank** *(see photo on page 190)* (100 seconds). Hold the top of the push-up and don't move!

- **Side plank** *(see photo and instructions on page 191)* (100 seconds . . . each side). This one is for your obliques (side abs).

- **Side plank twists** *(see photo below)* (10 twists each side). From the side plank position, round your top arm at the elbow in the shape of a half circle (like you are giving someone one of those lame half hugs). Rotate your upper torso just slightly down toward the bed as you bring that top rounded arm in front of your body and slowly press it through the space between your supporting arm and the bed (like you are threading a needle). Slowly and without losing your balance, return that rotated arm straight, with your hand reaching up toward the ceiling, returning your body to the side plank position. Repeat 20 times (if you can), then switch sides. Now you're really targeting those obliques!

- **Butterfly crunches** (30 slow and controlled 4-second crunches). Spreading your knees apart takes the work out of your legs and butt and wholly focuses the entire move on your abs.

- **Sit-up stay** (60 seconds). Similar to the boat pose (pages 200–201), balance on your butt with your knees bent and feet on the floor. Sit up straight, then hinge your upper body back a couple of inches until you feel your ab muscles engage. Hold there.

◄ Side Plank Twist

- **Leg Raise** *(see photo on page 213)* (10-second holds). Lay on your back with your legs pressing together straight in front of you. Now exhale with your abs flat and lift your feet up 6 inches off the bed. Hold there. Lower and repeat.

SEXY LEGS QUICKIE WORKOUT IN BED

- **Seated leg lifts—quads** (20 reps each leg). This might seem easy. It's not. Sit up straight with your legs extended straight in front of you. Engage your core and, without bending your knee, lift one leg up a couple of inches off the bed. Hold it for 2 seconds and place it back on the bed. Alternate between each leg.

- **Side elevated single-leg lifts, upper—thighs** *(see photo on page 213)* (10 reps each side). Both legs will start pressed together and elevated off the bed, but the top leg will be the one that is moving. Exhale completely before the first lift, then inhale and quickly exhale with each lift. You'll need the continuous flow of oxygen to power you through this one.

- **Side elevated single-leg lifts, bottom—inner thighs** (10 reps each side). This is the same as the side elevated single-leg lifts, upper, except that this time the top leg is staying still and the bottom leg is doing the work, dropping down a couple of inches to almost touch the bed, then lifting back up to touch the top leg. Again, remember the exhale.

- **Foot warmers—fat burner** (repeat until you are exhausted and can't do even one more). Lie on your back, bend your knees, place the bottoms of your feet gently on the bed, engage your abs, and as if you are cross-country skiing, skim your feet atop the sheets—fast! The friction will warm up your feet *and* burn lots of calories, slimming your legs.

- **Flutter kicks up and down—butt, hamstrings** *(see photo on page 213)* (10 reps up and down). Do quick little leg crosses back and forth at the ankles, working your way up to the ceiling and back down to almost (but not) touch the bed, then back up. Place your hands under your butt to help take pressure off your lower back.

BETTER BOOBS QUICKIE WORKOUT IN BED

- **Baby front and side arm circles** (100 each direction). These baby arm circles focus on the muscles beneath your boobs, firming, toning, and uplifting them to perky perfection. First, stretch both arms straight

212

◀ Leg Raise

◀ Side
Elevated
Single-
Leg Lifts

213

◀ Flutter
Kicks

out in front of you, then make teeny circles with each arm, 100 in each direction. Second, stretch your arms out to your sides and repeat the move.

- **Shadowboxing** (50 reps each arm). Kneel on your knees and, as if you are in a boxing match, punch! Alternate from one arm to the other, moving fast and with aggression! Actually pretending to punch someone makes you do it with even more vigor, flexing those muscles to the max.

- **Speed-bag boxing** (1 minute forward, 1 minute backward, as fast as you can). Imagine a boxing speed bag! Not sure what that is? Bring your fists, one above the other, up to chest level, your arms bent and elbows extending out to the sides. Keeping your fists close together (but not so close that you will knock them together), rotate them around each other in little circles. Your forearms and fists are the only body parts moving. It's speed over strength here that forces your muscles to engage and stay that way for the entire duration of this exercise.

- **Seated upper-body spinning** (1 minute forward, 1 minute backward, as fast as you can). As if you're holding on to the pedals of a bike with your hands, sit up straight, hold those imaginary pedals, and pedal as fast as you can!

- **Reverse plank dips** (15 reps). This is like plank position (see page 190), except that your body is flipped over so that you are facing the ceiling, balancing on your hands and heels. Now slowly, keeping your body straight like a board, bend both elbows simultaneously just a few inches. Then straighten them back up. Repeat. If you feel strain in your elbows, skip this one.

- **Platform venus** (10 seconds). Flip back onto your stomach with a pillow under your stomach. Lay facedown with your body straight and clasp your hands behind your back. Slightly lift your arms back behind you, using this lift in your arms to create an arch in your back. This is a major chest and back stretch.

CALORIE BURNING QUICKIE WORKOUT IN BED

- **Foot warmers** (repeat until you are exhausted and can't do even one more). Lie on your back, bend your knees, place the bottoms of your feet gently on the bed, engage your abs, and as if you're cross-country skiing, skim your feet atop the sheets—fast, fast, fast!

- **Crocodile roll** *(see photo on page 215)* (repeat 20 times back and forth). Lay on your stomach completely stretched out, arms to legs, so you are as long as possible. Now, keeping your body straight, roll onto your back, and back to your stomach. Repeat and reverse the roll. Seems easy, but wow, it's amazing for the back and waist—a total body burner.

- **Swimming** (100 seconds, fast, as if you're trying to swim away from a crocodile). Similar to the starting position of the crocodile roll, but this time alternate lifting your arms up and down as you kick your legs, alternating from one leg to the other. Do this fast! It seriously works the hamstrings, butt, back, and arms.

- **Leg lifts, arms raising** *(see photo below)* (50 reps each leg). Lay on your back, abs in, butt engaged, thighs pumping toward the ceiling. Raise your opposite arm up to try to meet the foot, then alternate. Pump so fast back and forth that you can feel the wind.

215

◀ Crocodille Roll

◀ Left Lifts, Arms Raising

- **Elbow to knee** (50 reps on each side). Lay on your back, hands clasped behind your head. Exhale and engage the abs as you bend one knee and bring it up to your stomach while simultaneously bringing the opposite bent elbow across your body to meet the knee (or as close as you can get). Alternate sides. It's like a bicycle sit-up but without the circling.

OTHER NONEXERCISE WAYS TO WORK OUT IN BED

Play

Burning calories doesn't always have to be so serious! Now it's time to have a little fun (and still work up a serious sweat)!

Tickle Wars

Definitely best done with a partner or child, but whatever floats your boat. . . . Tickle wars get the heart rate up two ways: (1) as a natural reaction to touching sensitive nerve receptors, you can't help but flinch and laugh uncontrollably out loud (a proven calorie burner—averaging 50 calories every 15 minutes); (2) the whole idea of a tickle war is that you're usually moving really fast as you squirm around trying to get the best possible tickle position!

Jumping on the Bed

First make sure your mattress has springs (unlike memory-foam mattresses, which won't have the same effect). Now, Mom (or you) may not condone it for fear of damaging the mattress, falling off the side, breaking the bed frame, or getting the comforter dirty . . . but jumping on the bed has a similar cardio effect to jumping on a trampoline. In fact, some studies have shown that it's similar to working out on a treadmill, burning an average of 9.5 calories per minute.

Massage

Massage doesn't just feel good, it's actually good for you! In fact, both participants can benefit from the mind/body calming practice.

Getting a Massage

Massage has been shown to directly relate to weight control or loss because of its ability to improve circulation, helping in the interchange of oxygen and nutrients between the blood and tissue cells, which increases muscle recovery and strengthening. More than addressing the muscles, massage is believed to be able to burst fat cells, forcing them to be absorbed away instead of bunching up on your thighs or elsewhere.

216

Giving a Massage

If you've ever given someone a serious massage, you know that it takes work! You are engaging your muscles in order to relax his or hers, working your hands, arms, back, and core. Giving an average one-hour massage can burn 260 calories.

Foreplay

Kissing can seriously get your heart pumping and your blood flowing. Yes, kissing can burn an average of 70 calories an hour. A vigorous make-out session (no sex included) can scorch 95 calories an hour!

Sleep

More than just a pretty-making mechanism, sleep is your body's mode to boost itself up while slimming itself down. Yes, while you're enjoying those eight hours of shut-eye, your digestive system is pumping hard to process your food, metabolizing carbohydrates and breaking down fats. Some studies have shown that sleep deprivation may be linked to weight problems. Why?

Cortisol. Cortisol is a hormone responsible for regulating the metabolism of sugar, protein, fat, minerals, and water. A lack of sleep may lead to elevated cortisol levels, which makes the body less efficient at breaking the fats down.

Insulin. Insulin, another hormone, controls blood sugar and promotes fat storage. Because sleep deprivation has been associated with increased levels of insulin, weight loss can be more challenging when you're not sleeping enough.

Mile-High Quickies

There was a time when air travel was luxurious. Yeah . . . not anymore. Between layovers and delays, lack of leg room and no peanuts, it's easy to get antsy, angry, and over it all really fast. Help combat the mental and physical frustrations with a mile-high Quickie—no not "that" kind. Sure, exercise is great to tone, trim, and strengthen, but it's also known to combat fatigue, minimize frustration, and keep blood flowing (which can fight off blood clots that form from sitting for too long). I'm definitely not suggesting that you get up and start sashaying through the aisles, knocking elbows and tripping on sleepers' feet on your way. But get your workout in, in your seat.

When it comes to the types of mile-high Quickies you can do, there are two distinct phases: discreet and less discreet. It's up to you to decide how obvious you want to be.

217

DISCREET

- **Floor presses.** Press down on the floor as hard as you can. You will feel it in your legs, butt, even your abs. Hold for 10 seconds, then let go. Repeat at least 10 times.

- **Butt squeezes.** Squeeze your butt cheeks tight like you are trying to crack a nut between them. Hold for 10 seconds, then let go. Repeat at least 10 times.

- **Stomach crunches.** As if you're being punched in the stomach, exhale all of your air out fast as you squeeze your ab muscles. Imagine tying your rib cage together tightly like a corset. Hold the exhale for 10 seconds, then let go. Repeat at least 10 times.

LESS DISCREET

- **Knee-up hold and lift.** Engage your abs, press one foot down on the floor, and lift the other knee up several inches off the floor. Hold there for a few seconds, then pulse up 10 times. Release your foot back down to the floor and switch legs. Repeat, alternating legs, 10 times on each leg.

- **Double-leg knee-up hold and lift.** Same as above, but with both knees simultaneously. Place your hands firmly on the seat cushion to help you engage your abs. Repeat 20 times.

- **Hovering.** Place your hands firmly on the cushion of your seat with your wrists pressed against the sides of your thighs. Now press your hands firmly down onto the seat so that your butt is hovering slightly above the seat. Engage your abs, slowly lift your feet onto your toes, find your balance, then lift your feet completely off the floor, placing all of your weight on your hands. Hold for 5 seconds if you can. Release your feet back down to the floor. Repeat 10 times if you can.

Mile-high Quickies are a great way to keep your blood circulating on long flights, burn a few extra calories, and make your flight time go by a little bit faster!

QuickieChick's Cheat Sheet

1. Different motivators make us work out. For some it's "Hey, fat ass," others "Hey, gorgeous." And then there are those who make the decision on their own regardless of outsider input. Decide if negative or positive affirmations get you going, then put one (or many) of the motivators to use to whip your fat/beautiful/soon-to-be-skinny ass into shape.

2. Forget about 1/5/10/15 minutes or miles. Numbers are rigid and stressful. Setting a goal of running for just one song is a great way to motivate you to move for even longer. But if you can't possibly get through another, that's OK, too; you've already achieved your goal.

3. You can fake a perfect body the night of a big date by drinking lots of water, restricting carbs, eating fat-burning foods, and doing cardio.

4. Some foods, like grapefruit, jalapeño, and apples actually burn off fat.

5. Increasing your potassium intake by eating foods like avocado, papaya, spinach, and yogurt have diuretic qualities that counterbalance bloating foods like salt and alcohol.

6. You can get a full-body cardio and resistance workout while watching TV by doing moves like marching in place (basically power-walking in a box) or holding the top of a push-up (plank). Some of the most effective resistance moves require no moving at all. Instead, you engage the muscle, then hold it in that one spot until it fatigues.

7. Exercises that engage multiple muscles can actually increase your metabolism, helping you burn more calories and drop fat faster.

8. Getting a massage feels great. But give one and you will burn calories and tone your muscles.

9. If all you have is a minute, you can (and should) work out. Just do a quick interval session including jumping jacks, tuck jumps, and air jacks to increase your heart rate and get your blood pumping.

10. A great way to sneak in exercise is to do it in bed. You can do 5-minute ab, butt, leg, even arm workouts without ever setting foot on the floor, slipping on sneakers, or even changing into more, ahem, appropriate exercise attire.

219

8

Beauty, Hair & What to Wear

FACT: You don't need to spend wads of cash in order to look (and therefore feel) fabulous! It's almost insane to drop generous amounts of money on the newest whatever just to watch it go on sale two weeks later—truly a crushing moment when you realize that you haven't even yet removed the tags! You can still do yourself up with some seriously fab beautifying products, accessories, and statement-making fashion without dropping major dough (which you don't have anyway). But before we get into the QuickieChick tips, let's learn a little something about your fashion and beauty beliefs.

QuickieChick Quiz

QUIZ

1. **If a product is "natural," that means . . .**

   A. It's organic.
   B. The entire process from the soil to the product is completely void of chemicals.
   C. Once picked, the plant ingredients were not sprayed with pesticides.

   The answer is C. With natural products, once the ingredients are picked out of the ground, they aren't tampered with, but chemicals could still have been used in the soil. Only certified organic products keep the process chemical free from the moment the seed is planted in the ground.

2. **I will start using antiaging products when . . .**

   A. I notice wrinkles.
   B. I get a little older.
   C. I'm already using antiaging products.

   The best answer is C. The most effective way to fend off the visible signs of aging on your face is by being proactive and taking a preventative approach. Once your skin has gone slack and your connective tissues have weakened (wrinkles/cellulite), it's harder to reverse the damage. The same goes for dark spots and blotches, which are much easier to fight off than to fix. A simple antiaging skin-care regimen might add 3 minutes to your day—max. Or you could wait until you are visibly aging and start dropping serious funds on age-reversal treatments (that might not be so effective and may look fake—like on those older women who look as if they are "trying to look young"). That could be avoided in the first place just by taking a few moments out of your day.

3. **It takes me _____ to get ready to go out.**
   A. 20 minutes, tops. I pride myself on my ability to get ready fast!
   B. 45 minutes to 1 hour. Depends on whether I have to blow-dry my hair or not.
   C. Hours . . .

   Really, ideally, your answer would be B. Pancaking on the makeup won't go unnoticed. In other words, unless it's for a photo shoot (in which case you want to paint your face perfectly), if you spend tons of time "putting on" your face, then go out and stand a few inches away from someone; they will notice. Lots of makeup actually ages your appearance. If you happen to have any fine lines or wrinkles, the makeup will get into those creases and accentuate them! Plus, it's a serious turnoff for guys when a chick takes ages to get ready, and it's not so much fun for friends who *always* have to wait for you. It's also not so Quickie. . . . However, priding yourself on your ability to get ready in a jiff might not be the best, either. Yes, if you are going out casually and you really don't need to be put together, that's fine. But if you are trying to make an impression, take the time to blow-dry your hair instead of going out with it still damp, check that your makeup looks good, and spend a moment to put together an outfit that says something. Your appearance is the visual presentation of you, your visual biography. What do you want to say about yourself when you go out?

4. **If I literally have 2 minutes to get ready, I . . .**
   A. Throw on my go-to outfit that I know looks good no matter how bloated I am, apply a quick layer of mascara, and put my hair in a cute ponytail.
   B. Impossible. I'd rather not go out.
   C. Put on sweats and sunglasses. Who cares what I look like?

   A is my answer. I have a go-to super-cute short-skirt, long-sleeve, hot pink cotton dress that perfectly flatters my body. It's comfortable, versatile, and I always get compliments when I wear it. Mascara is my must. I have big eyes and I know that they are a focal point for me. If I highlight my lashes even more, my eyes will distract from the rest of my face (in case I have a pimple or am a tad pale from lack of sleep). A ponytail makes me look cute but relaxed, without having to brush my hair and brush out the cowlick that I have on the back of my head. Chickadees, answer B is not OK. You have to be able to look good on the go. Figure out what your go-to outfit would be. C—really? Try just a tad bit harder.

5. My style icon is (and though I love her style, I don't necessarily feel confident enough to pull it off myself) . . .

    A. Reese Witherspoon—I love the classic, elegant, put-together look.
    B. Angelina Jolie—sexy, seductress, beautiful!
    C. Nicole Richie—hippie, boho, casual, cool, comfortable—love it!
    D. Jessica Biel—strong, athletic chic, discreetly sexy.

There's no right answer here! It's time to think about what styles you like and why. Maybe it's a combo of several based on your mood. Maybe you haven't yet figured out a style that perfectly suits you, so it's time to play around with different outfits and test your comfort. Do you act differently in different styles? Do certain styles play up a specific side of you?

Take Care of Your Skin Now (Before It's Too Late & You're Suddenly Old—Trust Me)

"If I knew then what I know now . . . " I hate to say it because it is so cliché. However, there are a few things that I really wish I hadn't been so dismissive of during my "I know everything" late teens and early twenties.

WHAT I DID TO TAKE CARE OF MY SKIN

Thankfully, I did listen to most of the biggie things, like these:

No Sunbathing

I've never been a sunbather (which I really only avoided thanks to my tendency to come down with sun poisoning or a heat rash). Sunbathing is bad because the UV rays penetrate the skin and dramatically increase your chances of skin cancer. And it doesn't just happen on your face. Be cognizant of your hands, chest, and back of your legs, too. Beyond cancer, sunburns sap your skin of essential moisture, weakening connective tissue and speeding up the signs of aging—sagging, wrinkled, dimpled (cellulite) skin. Of course some sun is good for you, naturally boosting the mood and upping your body's immunity, but you only need it in small doses.

No Tanning Beds

Tanning beds, we've been told time and time again, are very, very bad. Studies have shown that the ultraviolet radiation they put out are about as lethal as arsenic—yes, poison. They are on a par with cigarettes in terms of cancer risk. In fact, the study showed that people who start self-tanning before the age of thirty increase their chances of skin cancer by 75 percent!

Eye Cream

I have been a long-time eye-cream addict (because I became a beauty writer at twenty-three years old and *had* to test products in order to write about them). I gently dab it under my eyes using my pinky finger. (Smearing and pressing with the pointer finger applies too much pressure, stretches the skin, and can cause bags—another beauty editor insight.)

223

Silk Eye Pillow

I sleep with a silk eye pillow (because I have a hard time sleeping and need the darkness combined with the weight). Silk contains naturally occurring amino acids and helps with warding off the signs of aging.

WHAT *DIDN'T* I DO THAT I *WISH* I HAD?

Neck

I didn't moisturize my neck. Oftentimes it's your neck that expresses your age, not your face. Your neck is often just as exposed as your face. The skin is similarly sensitive, and it has the tendency to show age more readily if you've forgotten about it when applying those serums, creams, and antiagers you so diligently apply to the skin on your face.

SPF (Sun Protection Factor) Sunscreen

I didn't wear sunscreen during everyday outdoor activities (including on my one-hour daily walks). Now I have more freckles and more negative freckles (areas of pigment loss that appear as white spots) on both my face and hands.

Frowning

I didn't attempt to not frown so much, causing deep "Grand Canyon" (as my mom affectionately calls them) wrinkles on my forehead.

But, really, the notion of antiaging has never sat quite right with me. If the whole idea is *anti*aging, then why don't we start before the signs of aging appear, as opposed to suddenly launching an antiaging regimen full-throttle after the signs have already begun to emerge? Yes, genetics certainly play a part in the aging process and how it affects your specific face (my mom was carded until she was thirty, and I, now at thirty-four, am still carded, while friends of mine from college were served drinks, no questions asked, at twenty!). But there is also something to say about learning how to care for your skin from your mother . . . or me—someone older who has gone through it and regrets a few decisions made and *not* made.

WHAT ANTIAGING REGIMEN DID MY MOM INSTILL IN ME?

Antiaging Began at Eighteen

I began using eye cream at the age of eighteen and face cream at twenty.

Beautiful Breakfast

I sprinkle flaxseed on my soymilk-soaked cereal or oatmeal in the morning. Soymilk is derived from super-nutritious soybeans, which are packed with protein, fiber, and—when fortified—calcium. Beyond beauty, soymilk contains no cholesterol, while dairy milk contains 10 milligrams per cup. In fact, studies have shown that people who regularly consume soy products (including soymilk) have significantly lower LDL (bad) cholesterol levels than those who choose not to eat soy products. And that flaxseed that I generously sprinkle atop my cereal supports my cardiovascular system. Yup, flaxseed is rich in alpha-linolenic acid, an omega-3 essential fatty acid needed for blood pressure regulation, and lignans, healthy compounds with antioxidant-like properties.

Fitness for My Face and Body

Exercise is a regular part of my daily life, not just because it keeps me fit, but because it keeps my metabolism kicking, my blood flowing (and therefore my heart healthy), and my joints moving. Studies show that thirty minutes of exercise a day will keep you looking and feeling younger. My parents instilled in me the importance of exercise when I was six years old, as I laced up my first pair of figure skates and took to the ice.

Water to Stay Supple

I drink at least eight glasses of water every day, which is a known natural beautifier, keeping skin supple and glowing.

Fruits and Veggies

I indulge in ample servings of fresh fruits and vegetables to make sure I am getting a large variety of antioxidants and nutrients to nourish my skin and insides.

I Oil My Skin

In addition to serums and lotions, I rub oil on my skin, argan oil in particular. I know, if pizza grease or salad dressing drips down your chin, you frantically grab a napkin and rub it off, as you imagine that oil clogging up your pores and your skin bubbling with pimples. With "oil free" proudly stamped on countless lotions, the skin-care industry has done a great job of making us fear oil. You see a tiny shiny spot on your face and you think, *"Oh no, I have the oily skin condition!* as you grab those little oil wipes and dab away until your skin is powder dry. But the fact is that your skin needs a certain amount of oil, and your incessant need to strip it of its oil is actually making your pores work harder to produce more oil . . . and that can be the culprit of developing a blemish "oil" problem. Certain facial oils absorb easily into your skin and nourish skin cells while helping release stuck impurities. Argan oil is rich in vitamin E and essential fatty acids, grown organically in Morocco, and coveted for its skin-hydrating, nourishing, toning, and firming benefits.

It's Called a Beauty Routine, Because It's a Regular Routine

I have a consistent beauty routine that I don't skip morning or night no matter how tired, rushed, or hungover I might be. Translation: *ALWAYS WASH YOUR FACE BEFORE BED!*

Expert Insight

Josie Maran

Josie Maran, a supermodel who has been ogled at within the pages of *Sports Illustrated Swimsuit* issues, on the cover of *Glamour* magazine, and as a GUESS model—a career that began when she was twelve years old—knows something about beauty. She also has her own beauty line called Josie Maran Cosmetics, which features one ingredient in particular: argan oil.

Josie's 5 Beauty Musts

1. Using easy multitaskers, such as Tinted Moisturizer and Argan Color Stick

2. Getting lots of sleep

3. Drinking plenty of water

4. Curling your eyelashes

5. Using Mascara

Aging: The Reality Checklist

Enlarged Pores

Fight them with: Egg whites. Yes, the "egg-white face-lift" is said to tighten and lift the skin, temporarily (it's a preventative measure). Whip up egg whites and apply to your face as a mask. Let sit for fifteen minutes, then rinse off with lukewarm water. (*Don't* use hot water or you'll have scrambled egg all over your face!) Why does it work? Egg whites contain proteins that, when they dry, tighten the skin and help shrink pores. Another idea? Cucumber. Cut a cucumber into thin slices and place them on areas of your face where your pores are enlarged. Let them sit for ten minutes as you relax. Why? Cucumber contains amino acids that cool and refresh the skin and tighten pores.

Dry, Sallow, Dull, Bumpy Skin

Fight it with: Nivea Skin Refining Scrub (or any other exfoliator). Or rub a small handful of dry short-grain rice against your face for two minutes. Why? The rice is smooth enough to not break the skin, yet coarse enough to loosen dead skin cells and encourage cell turnover. The technique has been used by Japanese women for centuries. Another idea? Pumpkin pie filling. The stuff that comes out of a can is usually 100 percent pureed pumpkin, which happens to be filled with alpha hydroxy acids, which are naturally

Makeup Must Haves

Zoe, 21, Internet Radio Host: "Makeup essentials I don't leave the house without are blush, mascara, and ChapStick. Any drugstore mascara and ChapStick works well for me, but I usually splurge on NARS Orgasm blush, which complements pretty much any skin tone. If I'm feeling kind of pasty, which happens pretty often with such pale skin, I'll put a translucent shimmer under my eyes and on my cheekbones, which usually livens up my skin. For an easy at-home remedy for pimples, take a packet of yeast, mix it with a little water, and put it on any blemish overnight. It reduces swelling without drying out the skin.

exfoliating enzymes that eat away dead skin cells, leaving your complexion looking instantly refreshed, revitalized, and glowing! Just scoop out a tablespoon and smooth it onto your face. Leave it on for five minutes (it might tingle), then wash it off! Save the rest of the filling in a Tupperware container for later.

Note to Self

Reorganize to Rejuvenate

Tools

Which antiaging techniques could you incorporate into your beauty regimen?

_____

_____

Starter Sentence

I am going to keep these products

_____

_____ ,

in these places

_____

_____ ,

all the time for easy access.

Brown "Age Spots"

Fight them with: Wear SPF lotion, even when driving, taking a walk, or running errands. Too late? Place a small drop of lemon juice or 100 percent cranberry juice directly on the dark spot. Filled with vitamin C, these antioxidant-stocked juices have been shown to treat and improve the appearance of uneven skin pigmentation.

Wrinkles on Your Forehead and Down the Side of Your Cheeks

Horizontal and vertical wrinkles are from frowning, and vertical wrinkles going to your chin line are from smiling.

Fight them with: Ginseng tea bags. Soak the bags in warm water, pat them until they are moist but not dripping wet, then lay them on your forehead and cheeks. Why? The ginseng helps relax those strong facial muscles, causing them to temporarily calm down, releasing the wrinkles.

"Crows Feet"

These wrinkles on the outside of your eyes, fanning out, are from smiling.

Fight them with: Organic green seedless grapes. Cut a few green seedless grapes in half and rub them on your face, letting the juice soak into your skin for a good twenty minutes before rinsing it off, for a visible reduction in wrinkles! Why? Used as an active ingredient in many major wrinkle creams, green seedless grapes are full of antioxidants as well as dead-skin-ridding acids that help visibly reduce the appearance of fine lines and wrinkles.

Wrinkles Along Your Top Lip

These crease up into the skin above your lip, making your lipstick look less defined as it begins to smear into the vertical lines from pursing your lips.

Fight them with: Exercises! Yes, I am serious. There are exercises you can do with your lips that strengthen the muscles around your mouth and decrease the appearance of lines.

1. Put your lips together and pucker them. Lift your lips up toward your nose. Relax, pucker again, and repeat.

2. Part your lips just slightly. Pucker your lips and push the pucker away from your face. Try and move your top lip toward your nose. Hold for 10 seconds, relax, and repeat.

3. Smile! It only makes sense that you smile in order to combat frown lines. In this exercise, you are going to smile as wide as you can while keeping your lips together. Then, contract the smile and make a pucker face. Hold this position and smile again. Repeat 10 times.

Bags, Circles, and Generally Tired-Looking Eyes

Fight them with: Two metal spoons that you left in the freezer overnight. In the morning remove them, let the iciness naturally defrost off, and gently apply the backs under your eyes. Why? The cold spoons will help to redistribute and remove the water-retention that causes puffiness.

Random Black Hairs

These can appear particularly along your mustache area and chin.

Fight them with: Wax, tweeze, or laser them off. I once had a guy tell me that the little pieces of peach fuzz made him feel like he was kissing a guy. That was the last time that peach fuzz was ever found on my face! Now I'm kind of obsessed with tweezers and keep them everywhere—at my desk, in my car, in my purse, and of course in the bathroom.

"Turkey Neck"

A baggy, speckled neck shows your true age, even if your face swears it's under age.

Fight it with: Apply your face products down a little bit farther so you incorporate your entire neck, too. You can buy special neck/décolletage tightening creams or just use your normal facial moisturizer. Why? Your neck skin is fragile just like your facial skin. If you don't cleanse, moisturize, and protect it with SPF lotion, it will show the signs of aging faster than the skin on your face. Soon the connective tissues will slacken (due to age), and the skin will start to droop.

Jowls

These occur when your skin drops slightly below your jawline, particularly if you have a round and full face.

Fight them with: Facial exercises—a full-face workout. Strengthen your entire face and minimize tension in your jaw and your temples with this workout:

1. Sit comfortably.

2. Open your mouth as far as you can.

3. Stick out your tongue.

4. Open your eyes wide.

5. Hold this funny face for several seconds.

6. Completely relax your eyes, mouth, and jaw.

7. Repeat at least 5 times

A Double or Less-Defined Chin Line

Fight it with: Facial exercises—the double-chin toner:

1. Lift your eyes and neck to look up at the ceiling.

2. Still looking at the ceiling, stretch your neck to look up to the right.

3. Return to looking up straight.

4. Look up to the left.

5. Return to looking up straight.

6. Lower your head to neutral.

7. Repeat 5 times.

DAILY FACE-CARE REGIMEN

Every Morning

1. Wash your face with water.

2. Exfoliate with a gentle exfoliating scrub or mask (every *other* day)

3. Pat skin dry.

4. Apply a serum or lightweight moisturizer.

5. Apply a lightweight SPF lotion specifically for the face (the body creams can be too rich and can clog pores, causing breakouts).

6. Apply under-eye cream.

Every Evening

1. *Wash your face before bed no matter what!* Use whatever cleanser is best for your skin type (e.g., a milk-based product for delicate skin, a clarifying one for acne).

2. Pat it dry.

3. Apply a vitamin C or antioxidant serum or toner (depending on skin type and needs).

4. Apply a heavy moisturizer.

5. Apply a rich eye cream.

Dollar Beauty

Your M.A.C and Stila cosmetics addictions, not to mention the luxury of getting a quick blowout from your hairdresser before an event, are draining your budget. But you're on a whole new dating plane. You have job interviews. And, quite frankly, you're stressed. The LAST thing you need right now is to feel less than stunning. I get it. My mother always told me, no matter what's going on—whether you're going through a horrible breakup, you were just fired, or you just feel emotionally and mentally battered—make yourself look pretty (think about how amazing you feel when you step out of the hair salon). It will always make you feel good, and you can *always* do it. I promise. These beauty deals for one, five, and ten dollars at most major drugstores or online retailers can make it possible.

UNDER $10

SPF Sunscreen

Neutrogena UltraSheer Dry-Touch Sunblock SPF 45

Gently moisturizes skin without leaving that layer of oil most sunscreens do. This sunscreen is great for those who easily break out. $10

Mascara

L'Oréal Original Voluminous Mascara

Pumps up lashes. The thick brush lengthens and darkens lashes in just a couple of strokes. $7.29

COVERGIRL Lash Blast Luxe

The ultrathick brush gives you long, thick lashes in just a few strokes. $7.99

Fake Eyelashes

Ardell DuraLash Naturals

Fake lashes can be as much as $12 at specialty stores. The neutral-colored lash line in DuraLash Naturals makes them look like your own lashes. $8

Facial Cleansing Cloths

Olay Daily Facials Express Wet Cleansing Cloths, Sensitive Skin

These wipes remove even the most stubborn of makeup and leave your skin feeling incredibly fresh. Great for after a long night of partying, when you want face cleansing to be quick and easy. $4.99

Blush Stick

Max Factor Lipstick, Ms. Understood

This multitasking stick comes in a fierce pink and can be dabbed on your cheeks to quickly brighten up your face. $8

Nail Polish

Essie Nail Polish

One of the few low-cost nail polishes that actually stays on well. $7.99

Eye Pencil

Revlon ColorStay Eyeliner

This pencil doesn't run, smudge, or crease and glides on the lid easily in one stroke. $6.79

SPF Lip Balm

Neutrogena Revitalizing Lip Balm, SPF 20

This balm deeply moisturizes your lips so you don't have to reapply all day, and the added SPF will keep your lips from cracking. $8.99

Oil Blots

Clean & Clear Oil Absorbing Sheets

These wipes reduce oil buildup throughout the day and help you avoid those nasty shiny spots. $5.99

Bodywash

Olay Plus Ribbons Moisturizing Body Wash, Luscious Embrace

Infused with jojoba butter and crushed orchid extract, this stuff leaves your skin clean, moisturized, and smelling insanely good! $5.59

Body Oil

Neutrogena Body Oil, Fragrance-Free

Your skin absorbs this light oil quickly without leaving you with a greasy film. You'll feel moisturized and silky smooth. $8.39

UNDER $5

Hand/Body Butter

Queen Helene Cocoa Butter Hand and Body Lotion

Made with lanolin and cocoa butter to moisturize without leaving you greasy. Added bonus: It can help fade scars. $4

Eye Shadow

L'Oréal Paris Eye Shadow, Plum Royale

The violet hue is surprisingly neutral, so it can be worn with almost any color and stays on all day. $4.25

Nail Shiner/Buffer

Ms. Manicure High Gloss Shiner & Buffer

This four-sided buffer provides a great, quick alternative for girls who don't have time or money to get a manicure. $3

SPF Tinted Lip Gloss

Kiss My Face Organic Lip Balm, SPF 15

All-natural ingredients and blissful scents combine to make your lips baby-skin soft. Made from beeswax, canola oil, shea butter, and aloe vera, the balm keeps your lips moisturized without leaving that goopy feeling of lip gloss. $4

Face Powder

NYC Color Wheel Mosaic Face Powder

The mosaic combines four neutral tones to give your face a natural-looking flush. Serving as a bronzer and a blush, it's an even bigger beauty bargain. $5

Bodywash

Caress Evenly Gorgeous Exfoliating Body Wash

Removes dead skin cells and leaves you smelling like brown sugar. The bodywash also makes shaving a smoother process. $3.50

Shower Gel

Essence of Beauty Shower Gel, Citrus Coconut

Who doesn't like to smell like a tropical vacation? The coconut and lime leaves in this shower gel will leave you smelling like a piña colada, while the almond oil, honey, and aloe vera combine for a moisturizer that relieves sun-damaged skin. $5

Shampoo

Herbal Essences Drama Clean Refreshing Shampoo

The berry-tea and orange-flower extracts make you want to stay in the shower longer. This is just one of my favorites, but there are dozens of scent options in this line. $4

Nail Polish

COVERGIRL CG Boundless Color Nail Polish

Mix and match any solid colors with a sparkly topcoat to get a salon look. $4

Deodorant

Dove Ultimate Go Fresh Cool Essentials Clear Deodorant

You already know Dove's reputation for giving you ultrasmooth skin. This deodorant combines that with a refreshing cucumber-and-green-tea scent that helps keep you cool. You'll be odor-free all day, without any irritation or annoying marks on your clothes. $5

Hair Things

Scünci No Damage Firm and Tight Elastics

Leaving out the usual metal piece, these elastics won't leave kinks in your hair or break it. The elastics come in an array of colors, so you can blend them with your hair or match them with an outfit. $3

UNDER $1

A few of these were finds at my local 99¢ Only Store, which you may be able to find at yours, too, or at other discount stores. I found all of these for one dollar. You might not find the exact same loot, but at least you can see that there are serious finds for a buck.

Lip Gloss

NYC Liquid Lip Shine, Cherrywood

This is great for girls just opening up to the idea of a little red tint, and it stays on for hours.

Eye Shadow

L.A. Colors, 6 Color

This six-color eye shadow is highly pigmented and actually sticks to your lids. It comes in different shade packs including neutral tones, pinks and purples, or greens and blues.

COVERGIRL Eyeslicks

These give a nice light shimmer to your eyelids and usually cost $3 to $5 in a drugstore. Get a pack of two for $1 at a 99-cent store.

Cosmetic Wedges

An item I often forget to buy but that is so necessary. Usually $3 to $5 at Target, you'll find a pack of a dozen or more at a 99-cent store.

Foot Scrub

Sally Hansen Salon Ultra Smoothing Foot Scrub

Exfoliators tend to be expensive; this 5.4-ounce tub is $10 at a CVS.

Fake Eyelashes

An easy way to glam up an outfit, but normally $3 to $6 at a costume shop.

Lip Gloss

NYC Lip Sliders

These give color and moisture to your lips without leaving them sticky. Colors include Sugar Coated for a neutral tone and Sugar Kiss for pink lovers.

Hair Things

Goody Ouchless Headbands

These make face washing infinitely easier, and they're missing the metal piece so you won't be left with dents in your hair. Get a pack of seven at a 99-cent store.

Hair Brush

Goody Touch of Style hairbrush with Comfort Handles

The cushy grip is usually only found on expensive brushes. This particular brush runs about $7 at Walmart.

Hand/Body Lotion

Prescription Care Lotion, Dry Skin Formula

Brand-name moisturizers are often no different from your generic alternatives when it comes to deeply moisturizing your skin. This lotion packs vitamins A and E into a generous 15-ounce bottle. Usually an 8-ounce bottle is $5 to $8 at a drugstore.

Deodorant

Lady Speed Stick

Obviously, deodorant is something you go through pretty quickly, but it can cost up to $10 per stick at a regular drugstore. The 99-cent stores carry most of the trusted brands like Speed Stick and Clear Stick.

Acne Wash

Generic Oil-Free Acne Wash

The bottle looks almost identical to the Neutrogena version, and that's because the ingredients are almost identical.

Face Oil

Beauty Drops Vitamin E Beauty Oil

A lot of skin specialists are advocating oil instead of cream for your skin. It's more natural to your skin and actually gets absorbed into the pores rather than sitting on the surface.

Razors

Disposable razors—generic brand

If you're already someone who refuses to shell out $12 on a reusable, sturdy, but totally overpriced Gillette razor, you may as well not overpay for your throwaway's either. You can get a pack of eight for $1 at a 99-cent store.

SHOP BY LOCATION

Ross Stores

Perfect for pretty packaged beauty products. Plenty of items that go to Ross were originally intended for stores like Macy's and JCPenney. If you're buying a gift, or if you just like your beauty products to come in prettier packages, Ross is a great place for bath-and-body gift sets of lotions, perfumes, body washes, and soaps in decorative boxes and baskets.

Target

Target is best for makeup. You usually can't afford to skimp *too* much on things like mascara, eye shadow, foundation, blush, or eyeliner. Many of the generic brands wear off quickly. Target has a lot of brands that haven't *quite* gotten their names out there as "high end" yet, so they're reasonably priced, but nearly the same quality as larger brands.

99¢ Only Store

This is a great place to get the basics. You will find many of the necessities that you need to stock your bathroom with and tend to buy a lot of, like generic cotton swabs, disposable razors, makeup-applying wedges, deodorant, hair things, floss—anything that really doesn't vary by brand and that you use up quickly.

T.J.Maxx

Sometimes, you want the brand stuff so you can pretend for a second that you're not on a budget. When you want to treat yourself, T.J.Maxx has items like Jaqua Shower Syrups for $10, Lucky Chick Mandarin White Orchid Sugar Body Scrub for $5, and GapBody Lotion for $6. Yes, the brands from stores your mom used to take you shopping at on the weekends when money wasn't an issue (or at least it was *much less* of one). Don't worry—just because you may feel like a completely disoriented mess on some days during this transitional time doesn't mean you have to look like one.

A lot of girls give up on the idea of looking as pretty as they used to when they had hours to do their (expensive) makeup before that oh-so-convenient noon class. They just accept a slightly haggard look as part of being a stressed, rushed, and tight-for-money grown up. But glamming yourself up is one of the *few* ways you can still treat yourself during a time when you're cutting out a *lot* of luxuries. And it will give you a very-needed ego boost. Now you know how to get that ego boost on a budget.

Be a Natural Beauty

126—The number of chemicals the average woman smears on her skin every day (thanks to unnatural skin care)

60 percent—The amount of those chemicals found floating in the bloodstream

If you eat organic food, plant trees, wear bamboo clothes, and drive a hybrid, why would you stalwartly stick to your chemical-filled makeup and skin-care routine, incessantly spreading toxins onto (and therefore into) your body? Have you ever even looked at the ingredients list on your face cream, blush, or nail polish? Maybe you should. You'll be shocked, I'll tell you that.

Note: Yes, I did just list lots of mainstream products in the last section, many of which are not organic. However, this is about information. I am giving you lots of different types of info so you can make educated choices based on your specific needs, wants, and beliefs. I'm all about personal preferences and individual decisions. Once you know what's out there, it's up to you to decide what to do with the info.

A CHEMICAL COCKTAIL IN A REALLY PRETTY SHADE

Your skin is like a sponge, soaking up anything that you smooth on your face, slather into your hair, and rub onto your body. Since you take such pride and care in what you put *in* your body, it is time you pay more attention to what you put *on* your body. Don't forget, your skin eats, too. Feed it well. You wouldn't choose to eat, drink, or even lick a chemical cocktail, so stop forcing your skin to.

The fact is that your average blush, lipstick, and powder are chemical cocktails in really pretty shades. Why do you think so much animal testing goes on? Because many of the chemicals can be toxic when they touch the skin, leaving rashes, burns, and worse. Believe me, having been a beauty writer doing lots of product testing, I have experienced the thrill of slathering on the most "amazing," "revolutionary," "luxurious" creams, serums, and potions on my skin as part of my pre-bedtime ritual, only to wake up and be terrified by my swollen, rashed, one-eye-sealed-shut reflection in the mirror. Never a fun way to start the day.

MAKE GREEN CHOICES: OPT FOR ORGANIC

It may be time to green your beauty routine by switching out your toxic stash with organic or all-natural options. But that's where it gets slightly tricky.

"ORGANIC" VS. "NATURAL"

"Organic" and "natural" are not one and the same. Many skin-care companies make a "commitment to the earth" by using "natural" ingredients, but that doesn't mean that the end product is all natural; it simply may mean that they used some herbs, essential oils, or other natural ingredients.

When perusing the seemingly endless aisles of beauty products promising to preserve your youth, plump your cheeks, or soothe your skin, *do not forget* that the terms *organic* and *natural* are not of equal earthliness. If a product is touting the term *organic* it is for a good reason. The certification process is time intensive (at least three years), expensive, and regulated by the United States Department of Agriculture. Certification requirements include the following:

- Farms growing plants, herbs, fruits, and vegetables must do so without the use of prohibited chemicals, fertilizers, and pesticides.

- Livestock must be raised without the use of prohibited antibiotics and hormones.

Only products that have met the very high standards are permitted to flaunt the USDA "organic" seal of approval.

Because not all skin-care companies are able to abide by the organic rules, due to some ingredients that are impossible to harvest organically (e.g., many SPF products), the USDA has divided organics into three categories:

- **100 percent organic**—USDA certified. The USDA seal may be used.

- **Certified organic**—It contains at least 95 percent organic ingredients. The USDA seal may be used.

- **Made with organic Ingredients**—It is made from at least 70 percent organic ingredients. The USDA seal may not be used.

I know . . . it's confusing.

"Natural," on the other hand, is not "organic." "Natural" products are not federally regulated, leading to a lot of truly unnatural imitations. But the honest definition of "natural" is "Made with botanical ingredients without the use of additives or preservatives." Note the active, yet likely unnoticed, phrase "made with" as opposed to "grown with." Unlike their "organic" counterparts, the herbs and plants in "natural" products aren't necessarily grown in chemical-free soil. "Natural" only comes into play after the botanicals are picked. In fact, the soil isn't considered when labeling the product "natural." Which is why reading the label—just like you might read the nutrition label on food items—is essential.

If you are looking to clean and green your skin-care routine, 100 percent organic is the greenest choice. But anything naturally created is great, too.

Pretty Ugly Beauty Secrets

Unfortunately, some chemicals have become so commonplace that when analyzing the ingredient list, we recognize the chemical name and think it's actually good for us, just because we recognize it. But that may be only because it is listed so often and in so many products—not that we have any idea what it actually is, does, or where it came from. A few of the regulars to watch out for include:

Fragrance

That lotion/shampoo/cleaner smells so great! Kind of like . . . hmmm, I can't pinpoint it. Gardenia? No. Rose? No. Cedar? Oh, that's right—chemicals! Despite the fact that essential oils, extracted directly from flowers, plants, and herbs, emit the most intoxicatingly beautiful scents NATURALLY, the majority of skin- and hair-care companies (even the "natural" ones) inject a little squirt of "fragrance" into many of their products. What "fragrance" really means is chemically created scents—some of the top allergens in the world!

- Look out for fragrance in practically everything—deodorant, shampoo, décolleté cream, body lotions, etc.

Parabens, Methylparaben, Propylparaben & Butylparaben

Dead bodies are doused in preservatives like parabens, synthetic preservatives that minimize microbial growth to slow decomposition. But they have also been identified as estrogenic, meaning they mimic natural estrogen, which in some women can promote breast cancer. So why exactly does the beauty industry find it OK to inject its products with the same ingredients?

- Look out for parabens in many brands of tanning sprays, shaving gels, personal lubricants, moisturizers, etc.

Placenta

It sounds downright revolting, but human and cow placenta—the same pouch that supports the growth of babies when in the womb—is extracted and used in some skin- and hair-care products! More than gross, the hormone-saturated sack is so potent it can potentially stimulate breast growth in infants!

- Look out for placenta in some brands of skin toners, hair-repair products, eye creams, and face masks.

Mercury, Methylmercury, or the Mercury Preservative Thimerosal

Remember those cool silver-fluid-filled thermometers that suddenly disappeared from store shelves in the 1990s? That was because that silver stuff was mercury, a highly toxic heavy metal that has been proven poisonous to the nervous system and possibly even cancer causing.

- Look for mercury in some brands of mascara and even eyedrops!

Lead

You know how you aren't supposed to eat paint? There's a reason for that—lead. This lethal metal was once used in most house paints, lead-glazed pottery, lead crystal, batteries, pipes, oh, and many of my once-favorite beauty products. That is until the government got smart and set up regulations and standards minimizing its consumer use. Except—get this—when it came to hair dye. High or chronic doses of lead can decrease fertility, increase blood pressure, and cause cataracts and memory loss.

- Look for lead in some brands of hair dye and even some hair gels.

Animal Parts, also Disguised as Emu Oil or Mink Oil

Oil from animals isn't as easily extracted as oil from flowers and plants (known as essential oils). One common way to obtain the oil is by scraping the fat from the back of the animal, killing the animal in the process, then rendering it into oil.

- Look for emu or mink oil in some brands of sunscreen, shaving cream, hair spray, shampoo, soap, etc.

Nano-ingredients, also Known as Fullerenes, Nano-capsules, Nano-Metals & Buckyballs

Nano-ingredients are untested, manipulated microingredients, like teeny, tiny bits of metal that easily penetrate deeper layers of skin, not to mention cells in the lungs, brain, and other organs. Carbon fullerenes have anti-

Makeup Must-Haves

Bianca, 22, Production Assistant: "I live in a really dry, cold climate, so I can't live without a daily moisturizer with SPF." Beyond the SPF, Bianca's beauty musts are to "wear color, put your hair back, and go for the fresh-faced look instead of hurrying your makeup." Nobody wants to look like a doll with caked on makeup.

bacterial properties, but they also have been shown to cause brain damage when tested on fish.

- Look out for nano-ingredients in some brands of SPF, concealer, and smoothing makeup.

Petroleum By-Products and Derivatives, Coal Tar, Mineral Oil, Polyethylene Glycol (PEG), Propylene/Butylene Glycol

The average chick hears "petroleum" and thinks *gas*. I think *skin care*. Sadly, petroleum for your car and petroleum by-products for your face come from the same factories! More than just dirty, these by-products are often contaminated by cancer-causing toxins like 1,4-dioxane, hydroquinone, ethylene oxide, formaldehyde, nitrosamines, PAHs, and acrylamides.

- Look out for petroleum by-products in many brands of hair relaxers, cleansers, anti-itch ointments, styling gels, etc.

Sodium Lauryl Sulfate (SLS) or Sodium Dodecyl Sulfate (SDS or NaDS)

You haven't had your mouth washed out with soap since you were in elementary school, when you accidentally used the F-bomb when your mom was in the room. Or so you thought. Sodium lauryl sulfate is a common foaming ingredient in things like floor cleaners, car-wash soaps, oh, and in skin-care products like shampoo, shaving cream, and, lest we forget, toothpaste. Amusingly, the frothy ingredient is also used as a skin irritant during clinical studies. More than a minor irritation, its protein-denaturing properties have shown to break down and disable cell membranes—not a good thing when it comes to your skin.

- Look out for sodium lauryl sulfate in many brands of toothpaste, shampoo, shaving soap, face wash, etc.

Fight Cellulite & Wrinkles with These Skin-Smoothing Foods

Now that you know the dirt that lurks in your once-adored skin-care stash, and the damage it can do to your health and—ahem—beauty, it's time to lighten the mood and talk about beauty ingredients you *should* be using, ingredients with purpose—food ingredients.

If you are anything like me, you have a drawer brimming with beauty essentials that promise to do everything from banish wrinkles to smooth cellulite. And while many serums, creams, and sprays really do work to keep flaws at bay, you may be able to save a whole bundle of money by focusing less on buying expensive skin-care products and more on food.

SMOOTH CELLULITE

Caffeine

Yes, just like the stimulating stuff we drink to perk up our minds in the morning, caffeine (a known diuretic) gets fluid flowing, pulling excess water out of the cells. The eye-opening bean is also a natural topical stimulant, encouraging increased circulation and cell turnover, while redistributing fat cells and decreasing the appearance of cellulite. Scrub used coffee grounds on your skin in your morning shower to help smooth the appearance of cellulite. Now that's something to wake up to!

Seaweed & Algae

The ocean is rich with healing minerals, which is why you will often find oceanic ingredients, such as seaweed and algae, in treatments at spas. Thankfully, the ocean's bounty is now bottled as lotions, serums, and scrubs, and one of the many benefits is that they temporarily firm and tighten the skin, while slightly plumping the surface area and therefore filling in the dimpled spaces that cellulite creates.

Lecithin & Fatty Acids

Eating ingredients that include lecithin (such as egg yolks) and essential fatty acids (flaxseeds, fish and nut oils) help repair cell membranes and minimize fat's ability to squeeze through connective tissue, turning into cellulite.

Cayenne Pepper

The fiery spice heats up food with only a dash, getting your blood flowing, making you sweat, and even upping your metabolism. Now it's being used in the beauty industry for its same stimulating effects. When rubbed into the skin, cayenne increases circulation, quickens cell turnover, and has

242

been shown to successfully minimize the appearance of cellulite and stretch marks.

REDUCE WRINKLES

Papaya

This antioxidant-brimming, vitamin C–plumped fruit helps fight wrinkles and maintain skin's supple texture. When either rubbed on the skin or eaten, the multitasking fruit even helps increase collagen production, improving skin's strength and resiliency.

Blueberries

The diminutive berry is power-packed full of age-defying agents. Blueberries contain more than a dozen vitamins and minerals but are most adored because of the wrinkle-busting antioxidants and anti–inflammatory phytochemicals they provide. And, yes, frozen blueberries are just as nutritious as fresh, so eat up!

Mushrooms

Mushrooms are more than edible fungi; they have also been shown to have immune-enhancing, cancer-preventing, and anti–inflammatory properties. When incorporated into skin-care products, the fungi function as wrinkle-reducing, puffiness-placating, hyperpigmentation-equalizing, and moisture-replenishing ingredients.

EXFOLIATE DEAD SKIN

Walnut

When ground, walnut powder gently exfoliates and detoxifies, which in turn encourages cell turnover and leaves skin looking fresh and pinched-cheek pink.

Pineapple

Fruit enzymes found in pineapple act to eat away dead skin cells, detoxifying pores and leaving the skin naturally glowing. It may sting, but when incorporated into skin-care products, this acidic fruit is a stellar exfoliator.

Milk

Milk is known to do your body and your beauty good, and it is being used in a slew of skin-care products to increase moisture, stimulate circulation, brighten dull skin, slough off dead skin cells, and reveal younger, smoother-looking skin. The naturally occurring alpha hydroxy acids gently yet deeply exfoliate, dissolving dead skin cells, revealing the supple, younger-looking skin beneath. While the old cells are being turned over, milk does double duty, as the proteins act as humectants, drawing moisture to the skin's surface—a much more effective moisturizer than those that you simply rub on your skin.

FIGHT AGING

Green Tea

Green tea is a powerful anti-inflammatory antioxidant proven to prevent photo damage, improve elasticity, repair and strengthen the skin, and naturally shield from UV damage. Originating in China more than four thousand years ago, this age-old healing medicinal is still used in modern skin-care to pacify the soul and restore the body. Drink up and save the bags, squeezing the excess tea into your favorite moisturizers.

Plantain

Popular in Asia and in Europe for its medicinal properties (and in South America for its fabulous flavor), the bananalike plantain possesses astringent, antioxidant, and restorative properties that help protect skin and hair from free-radical pollutants. Plantains have humectant qualities giving them the ability to naturally draw out and bind to moisture, helping turn dry, brittle hair soft, and scaly, wrinkled skin supple. Place them on your face and eat them for both the delicious rich taste and beauty benefits.

Wild Alaskan Salmon

This delectable protein is the richest dietary source of the age-defying omega-3 fats, along with a superpotent antioxidant called astaxanthin. Omega-3 fats are the body's most powerful natural anti-inflammatory agents and optimize blood flow—fundamentals of healthy, exuberant skin.

Spinach/Kale

These leafy greens are a dietary must for fabulous skin. They provide more nutrition per calorie than any other food and are the reigning antioxidant champions of all vegetables, not to mention being loaded with phytochemicals called carotenoids, which dramatically increase the SPF of your skin.

Dark Chocolate

Nature's sweet treat may also be youth's "magic bullet." Studies show that cocoa is extraordinarily rich in potent antioxidants called flavonols, which increase blood flow by as much as 40 percent! The higher the cocoa content, the better, so eat up the extra dark!

Pomegranate

The fruit has been revered for its potent powers since ancient times. The juice extract and seed oil from this ruby fruit is steeped in potent antioxidants and skin-cell energizers. Topically, pomegranate extract is especially effective in protecting cells from free-radical damage by inhibiting the formation of harmful enzymes that cause cells to grow out of control. Pomegranate has also been proven to have the ability to protect skin from the sun, boosting the efficiency of your average SPF sunscreen by 20 percent.

Olives (& Olive Oil)

A known antioxidant powerhouse, this "good fat" fruit is rich in antioxidants, coenzyme Q10, and vitamin E, known to fight free radicals and promote cellular energy production without clogging pores. Eat up, and slather the oil on your skin!

HEAL AND SOOTHE

Marigold/Calendula

The common "pot marigold" and the prized therapeutic calendula are one in the same. Topically, the brightly colored petals are hailed for their healing and antiseptic properties, diffusing inflammation, reducing infection, and accelerating recovery time. Naturally antibacterial, fungicidal, and antiviral, calendula is used as an antiseptic remedy for cuts, burns, and even unsightly varicose veins. When the sun rages and your skin burns (or turns into a heat rash, like mine), turn to calendula to quell the pain.

Rose

Revered for its healing qualities, the seventeenth-century English physician Nicholas Culpeper wrote about the red rose's ability to strengthen the heart. History aside, ask any chick what a red or even a pink rose represents, and the answer is love. But roses aren't just about romance either. Rose is the perfect remedy for apathy. It helps enrich life and increase enthusiasm and motivation.

Witch Hazel

Witch hazel is a mild astringent and skin tonic that has been shown to reduce inflammation from an array of irritants, including bug bites, razor bumps, rashes, and hemorrhoids.

Aloe Vera

The succulent plant that rampantly grows in desert climates like Southern California and Arizona has long been used as a backyard remedy for cuts, scrapes, and burns. Now the sticky stuff residing within its prickly skin has been bottled and infused in beauty products to help accelerate cell growth, balance natural pH levels, and soothe the skin. You can also drink it to benefit from its detoxifying and digestion-enhancing benefits.

Luxury for Less

Tools

When was the last time you felt completely relaxed?

_____

_____

What sort of treatment/activity embodies luxury for you?

_____

_____

Take Note

Read the ingredients in your beauty products! Notice any refrigerator/garden ingredients that you have at home?

_____

_____

Starter Sentences

This is my new regimen for saving money and still looking fabulous:

_____

_____.

I am BUYING these beauty ingredients to make my own gorgeous-making products on the cheap:

_____

_____.

1-Ingredient Facials and At-Home Spa Treatments

I am a spa fanatic, but the one-hour treatment, plus the twenty minutes on either side to get there, simply takes too much of my day to rationalize it. Instead, I choose to raid my fridge for twice-weekly refrigerator facials. Refrigerator facials are fast, inexpensive fixes using ingredients that you already have in your home or garden and which can reveal radiant skin in mere minutes without a trip to the beauty boutique. Essentially, you're getting a $150 spa treatment out of a $1 tomato, lemon, and potato. Now that's budget beauty!

You don't have to actually go to a spa to attain the benefits of spa-ing. In fact, all you have to do is light a candle in your bathroom, pull a few products from your refrigerator and medicine cabinet, snip an herb or two from your garden and—voilà—spa!

A few of my favorite one-ingredient refrigerator facials are:

- **Potato** (the potassium minimizes dark circles). Puree a raw potato and place one teaspoon of the potato under your eyes and leave it for five minutes. Wash off.

247

- **Full-fat plain yogurt** (firms/moisturizes). Smear it all over your face; leave on for five minutes. Wash off.

- **Honey** (exfoliant/cleanser). Smear it all over your face; leave on for five minutes. Wash off.

- **Horseradish** (stimulates scalp). Mash, add *small* amount to conditioner; leave in for five minutes. Wash out.

- **Tomato** (antiaging and antioxidant). Squeeze a small amount of juice out. Brush it on your face; leave on for five minutes. Wash off.

- **Lemon** (skin lightener/balances hyperpigmentation). Mix a *small* amount of juice with face wash. Apply to skin; leave on for five minutes. Rinse. Or apply a small amount of juice directly to dark age spots. Leave on.

- **Milk** (moisturizing/exfoliating). Use it to wash your face, or soak in it in the tub. (Hey, Cleopatra dit it!)

AT-HOME SPA TREATMENTS

Here are quite simply the easiest at-home spa treatments around (no appointment required):

Steam to Soothe and Detox

Steaming is an incredibly simple, yet utterly indulgent spa treatment that de-stresses, detoxifies, and moisturizes.

Fill a pot with hot water. Add lavender or rose petals and buds to the pot. Allow the ingredients to steep in the hot water for 5 minutes. Place your face about 6 inches above the pot, drape a towel over your head to trap the steam, and steam for 5 to 10 minutes. The moist heat opens your pores, cleanses, soothes, and moisturizes your skin. Afterward, pat your face with a cool washcloth to close your pores and refresh your face, bringing you back to your senses.

Raw Potato Eye Mask to De-Puff and Brighten

Looking a little worn down? Are your eyes strained from too many hours staring at the computer screen? Apply a little potato to your eyes and you'll brighten up in no time!

Peel and grate a raw potato, then mix it with your favorite eye cream or a dollop of plain Greek yogurt to make a creamy mask. Put the mixture over your delicate eye areas and leave on for 15 minutes, then rinse.

Crystallized-Honey Foot Scrub to Exfoliate

If your soles are in dire need of a quick soothing buff, turn to nature's nutrients.

Combine equal parts of olive oil, crystallized honey, and rice or oat bran in a bowl. Stir the ingredients until thoroughly combined. Rinse your feet with warm water, then apply the mix to your feet and work it into your feet with your hands for 5 minutes (the consistency is a little rough). Pay special attention to your heels and the balls of your feet. Wash off the sticky concoction to reveal silky smooth and callous-free feet!

Frozen Grapes to Soothe a Sunburn

If you ever miss a spot or forget to apply sunscreen, be sure to stop the heat from doing further damage as fast as possible with frozen grapes.

Wash a handful of red grapes and place them in the freezer and leave them for about 3 hours until frozen. Using a fork, mash the frozen grapes to a thick pulp (kind of like a slushy) and apply directly to your sunburn. Leave on for 5 to 10 minutes, allowing the antioxidant-rich grapes to cool your skin while simultaneously working to fight sun damage and premature aging. Rinse off with cool water, and stay out of the sun!

From Rat's Nest to Sexy Hair

Love the feeling of the hot sun baking down on your skin and the ocean salt drying your hair into that sexy, beachy do? What about the dry-as-hay feel after that salt- and sun-soaked day? Oh, and don't forget the scent of chlorine that you just can't seem to wash out after a day spent in the pool? And then you go to the salon to further fry your porous locks, as your colorist crosses her fingers that she doesn't remove your hair along with the blond color foils. But it's not just summer's wrath that can wreak havoc on your hair. What about the shockingly (literally) dry strands that static-cling during the ultradry fall and winter months? Or spring showers that leave your hair full of frizz and on the fritz no matter how many straighteners you shellac on? Before your hair becomes a tangled mass, try these lock-taming techniques;

EASY HAIR RESCUING TRICKS

Drink Plenty of Water

Among the many obvious benefits of drinking water, it is also one of nature's most effective and inexpensive moisturizers for skin and hair. Tote your own reusable container filled with fresh water to drink throughout the day.

Cut the Cocktails

One of the reasons that having too many cocktails results in hangovers is due to dehydration. Alcohol also dries out skin and hair. It's just one of many good reasons to avoid overindulging.

Keep Things Loose

Pull hair back in a loose ponytail using soft hair ties. Avoid metal clips and tight rubber bands, which can put stress on hair and cause breakage, especially when hair is wet.

Apply Protective Sunscreen to Hair and Scalp

UVA and UVB rays can damage hair, leading to split ends, breakage, and loss of a healthy shine (not to mention increasing your odds of melanoma on the scalp), even during the winter. Protect your hair and your scalp with a UV sunscreen.

Avoid Sea Salt and Chlorine Like the Enemy

Rinse off your hair after taking a dip, as both sea water and chlorine can dry it out, leaving it brittle and lifeless. Besides, who wants to walk around covered in that chemical chlorine scent?

Use Leave-In Conditioner or Rinse Hair with Tap Water

Prepping the hair with a leave-in conditioner or even just rinsing with tap water before taking a dip prevents chlorine and sea salt from harming the cuticle, leading to breakage and split ends. Yes, just a simple tap-water rinse helps to saturate the follicles first, leaving little room for the salt or chlorine to soak in.

Avoid/Minimize Hair Dryers and Flat Irons

Air-drying is the most hair-friendly method for drying your hair. If you can't just air-dry your hair, let it dry halfway on its own, then use the hair dryer to finish the job. It's a much more gentle way to dry your hair, leading to less breakage and minimizing drying and thinning. Of course, you still want to look good, so doing a quick curling or straightening brush-over at the end isn't a bad thing. Don't let your hair leave you looking unpolished.

Avoid Color Treatments or Perms

Thankfully, the perm craze is over, but color treatments are very much in full swing—which are damaging enough as it is, but add the elements of hot sun, dry wind, or freezing cold and you are potentially creating havoc on your hair. Instead of dying hair with chemical colors, try natural hair-lightening tricks like squeezing fresh lemon juice on your locks before a day in the sun. Can't cut your coloring habit? Ask your colorist to occasionally do moisturizing treatments, locking in oils and minimizing breakage and split ends.

Use a Wide-Toothed Comb for Wet Hair

Wet hair is especially fragile and can easily break or tear. A wide-toothed comb will reduce breakage. If you hear your hair ripping with each brush-through, be more gentle, go slowly, or spray on a detangler first.

Treat Your Hair to a Nutrient-Rich Homemade Hair Mask

You don't have to go to a salon and spend an arm and a leg on expensive hair-nourishing treatments. Instead, try a refrigerator hair mask to help heal and rejuvenate your hair without spending a dime (not to mention much time).

Brunette Hair: Avocado Moisture Hair Mask

Mash up one or two very ripe avocados, depending on the length and density of your hair. Shampoo and lightly towel dry. Apply avocado mask to hair, and massage into scalp, too, then wrap hair with a warm towel. Let sit for 15 to 20 minutes. Shampoo again and condition as usual. Avocados are naturally extremely moisturizing.

Blond Hair: Banana Moisture Hair Mask

Follow the same directions as with the Avocado Mask but use bananas for blondes. Why? Avocados are green and can possibly stain blond hair. Bananas are also naturally extremely moisturizing.

Beauty Buffet

Bonding with girlfriends is an essential component of a happy and fulfilled life. It doesn't matter how perfect your relationship with your guy is, how ideal your career has shaped up to be, or how pretty your house, car, or clothes are; believe me when I tell you that the secret to a wholly happy woman is girlfriends.

One way to bond with (or even woo, if you don't have enough) girlfriends is by throwing an utterly over-the-top, way-too-girly-for-words party. I call mine a Beauty Buffet. Even the most tomboyish of girlfriends can't help but openly giggle with Valley Girl enthusiasm at one of these events.

So enough of the idle chitchat, let's get to the deets:

Beauty Buffet

Defined: An afternoon bash during which hoards of beauty products are lavished upon girlfriends who are simultaneously guzzling champagne and sampling bite-size nibbles.

Here's how. OK, I am an extreme example of a Beauty Buffet host, since I also happen to be a beauty writer and, as part of my job, I receive literally hundreds (very likely thousands) of the "hottest new" beauty products to sample and write about every year. After I'm done slathering my own face with them (not to worry, they aren't all dipped into; very often I am sent duplicates), I invite all of my friends over (plus a few ladies who I would like to get to know better) for a Beauty Buffet.

I cover every flat surface with beauty products organized by category—hair care, makeup, face lotions, body lotions, specialty (eczema, acne), anti-aging, etc.—then I let the girls go crazy!

For those of you who aren't beauty writers and don't have the luxury of being sent bundles of the best beauty products to try for free, this is how your party might go:

1. **Invite.** Send out a Beauty Buffet evite to all of your girlfriends. You can also ask each girlfriend to invite one of her girlfriends from another circle; it's a nice way to make new friends. Let's face it, it's a lot harder to find quality girlfriends now that we are in the real world and not surrounded by a selection of options from the playground or schoolyard.

2. **Everyone contributes.** Ask each woman to come with all of her unwanted beauty products in hand. We all have products that we tried once and didn't like. Not to mention the loads of freebies and gifts-with-purchase that we just tossed into a bag and never looked at again. Those products may not have worked with your skin type or tone, but one woman's trash is another's treasure!

3. **Make it festive.** On the day of your Beauty Buffet, clear all the surfaces in one room and cover the tabletops, counters, and stools with pink, red, white, or even animal print tablecloths. Add candles, framed photos of girlfriends, disposable cameras (or a digital camera if you have one), little signs designating the product category for each location, and, of course, your own beauty products.

4. **Bubbles and nibbles.** Bring out the bubbly, fruit tarts, cheese and crackers, or whatever little nibbles you want to offer.

5. **Organization is key.** As the ladies arrive, have them place their products in the categorized areas.

6. **Peruse and mingle.** Don't let anyone take products yet! The mingling hour is when everyone will get a chance to go around and take mental notes as to what they want. Before you let the ladies loose, ask them to give a little description of the products they brought, what they think is appropriate for each skin type or complexion, as well as why it didn't work for them.

7. **GO CRAZY.** Then let the product-picking frenzy begin!

Note: To avoid any one woman from becoming uncontrollably greedy and dumping a table's worth of products into her purse (à la Halloween candy when your neighbor would leave a bowl outside the door), let each lady select two products. Once everybody has their chosen two in hand, start round two, then three, then four, until all products are gone and the girls are exhausted.

At the end of the day, if you still have leftover products, donate them to a women's charity. And be proud of yourself for making this world a prettier place—even if just superficially (hey, feeling pretty goes a long way).

Are You a Label Whore?

Let's be honest, why do we really spend twenty dollars on a tube of lipstick, two hundred dollars on a pair of jeans, and two thousand dollars on a purse just so that we can strut around in an outfit that costs as much as a used car or a first-class flight to Italy?

Let's face it, you're dressing to impress—just like the old adage goes.

So if the point is to make a statement, stand out in a sea of monotonous clothes, and make all other mere fashion-mortals salivate over your style savvy, there are more effective, less savings-sacrificing ways to have the same stop-them-in-their-tracks effect.

Take my favorite purse, for example. It looks, essentially, like one of those wooden mats that shape sushi into rolls, but it's black. The bag itself is made with recycled chopsticks. In place of leather straps are dark, tea-stained, re-purposed wooden handles. Jingsi, a street vendor in Beijing, was selling it for five dollars—a price that I felt wholly offended by (which happens when you get into that bargaining mind-set). I offered three dollars and made the deal. Best three dollars I ever spent. The same concept goes for fab finds retrieved from secondhand stores like Goodwill (I have an amazing leather bag that cost four dollars from Goodwill), and even yard sales (yes, one person's once-fave can be your current obsession).

My point? Don't be a label whore. "Whose shirt is that?" Mine. Style savvy isn't necessarily dictated by the designer but by how well you put the look together and how fabulously you pull it off. Whether picking up handmade shoes sewn together by a group of local women in a small African village, buying an Indian tunic made from barkcloth (a material made from the inner bark fibers of trees), or supporting local artists and being the first to sport a camo mini made of recycled car upholstery, own your style. If you have to carry a Prada or Chanel in order to really get that gooey feeling inside, I feel your pain. . . . I have a closet full of them—and the credit card bills to prove it. But you likely will get more attention and feel better about yourself if your style is dictated in other ways than the designer labels.

Style is personal. It expresses your personality. What's yours?

"That's My Style"

Plenty of chicks say "That's just not my style" when a friend tries to dress them and puts together an outfit that they would *never* wear. Or maybe just one they haven't attempted to pull off *yet*. Where did this idea of personal style come from? Yourself! And you can change it.

It's easy to get into a style rut. Your brain works a certain way and resorts to the tried-and-tested items—low-cut jeans, empire-waist dress, no bright colors on the bottom. Whatever they may be, we all have "rules" when it comes to fashion. But sometimes we see someone—a friend, a stranger, a model in a magazine—who totally breaks our rules, and we *love* it. It's time to train your brain to break your rules. Slowly but surely, you'll have very few rules, and the world of fashion will be your playground. No store will be off-limits. Then the only rules you'll have to set will be dictated by your budget. But we'll discuss that later.

What's your style, *today*?

BOHEMIAN

The most important thing when it comes to dressing bohe-mian is details, details, *details*. The boho-chic shopper spots a unique piece that she loves—in a thrift store, at a yard sale, from a street vendor—and grabs it. Bohemian isn't a store-bought look. Some stores sell trendy, classy, and even trashy clothes. But no one is going to store-feed you a pre-made boho outfit. For this style, you really just have to take the reins—which, for those of us who depend on the salesperson or a style magazine to dress us, can be intimidating. But it can also be *liberating*. So first things first: Accessories are key. Scarves with interesting prints, stacked rings, large cuff bracelets, layered necklaces, funky belts, feather earrings—if you have it, *add* it to the outfit.

As a general rule, nothing boho-chic is particularly tight, clingy, or sexy. The classic, clean ultrafeminine lines are nowhere to be found here. Boho clothes are flowy and easy to move in.

Bottoms

Sarong skirts

Maxi skirts

Ripped jean shorts

Ripped jeans

Bell-bottoms

High-waisted wide-legged jeans

Prairie skirts

Tops

Plain T-shirts

Solid-colored tank tops

Vests (knitted, denim, suede, embroidered, floral)

Bandanna tops

Ponchos

Tunics

Ruffled blouses

Off-the-shoulder tops

Dresses

Maxi dresses

Shifts

Tunics

Sarong dresses

Low-waist dresses

Empire-waist dresses

Prints & Colors*

Earthy tones—forest green, brown, brick red, navy blue, yellow, orange

Ethnic, tie-dyed, and floral prints

Psychedelic

Paisley

Jewelry

Long beads

Large stone rings

Stacked rings and bracelets

Large cuff bracelets

Feather earrings

Long-chain necklaces with large pendants or vintage brooches

Rope bracelets and necklaces

Wooden bracelets

Gypsy bracelets (string of small coins)

Leather wristbands

Accessories

Belts

Skinny suede belts

Waist belts with unique buckles—e.g., Native American emblems or turquoise stones

Waist sashes

Cowboy belts

Knitted belts

Bags

Satchel bags

Hobo bags

Messenger bags

Long-strap pocketbooks

Woven bags

---

*Stay away from bright colors, especially neon's, silver, or gold. If you can't find that color in the wilderness, you probably shouldn't find it in your boho outfit.

Hats

Fedoras

Slouchy berets or knitted hats

Knitted beanies

Head scarves

Floppy hats

Shoes

Simple flip-flops

Gladiator sandals

Sandals with tasseled ankle straps

Cork-bottom platforms or wedges

FIFTIES HOUSEWIFE

Those clean, ultrafeminine lines that are nowhere to be found in the boho look are the building blocks of the fifties housewife outfit. The "waist" on a dress or skirt falls where the actual waist does on a woman—that's *above* the belly button and the smallest part of your torso. Fifties housewife attire emphasizes the hourglass figure, with full-belled skirts, tight waistlines, and fitted tops. No question about it, the fifties housewife style is *girly*. So if you're an urban feminist who tries to androgynize your body, you might want to skip this style. But if you're headed to the polo fields, cooking a romantic dinner for two, or if you just want to feel like a woman (not to get too Shania Twain on you), this is the style for you.

Fifties housewives mainly wear . . . you guessed it . . . dresses! While patterns and materials will vary, the basic structure will always be a fitted top, tight waist, and either a full skirt or a pencil skirt.

Tops

Shell and cardigan combos

Short-sleeved sweaters

Crew neck, fitted three-quarter-length-sleeve sweaters

Back-buttoned blouses

Sweetheart necklines

Bottoms

High-waist cigarette pants

High-waist pencil skirts

High-waist pleated skirts

High-waist full skirts

Prints & Colors

Polka dot

Plaid

Floral

Baby hues

Gingham

Jewelry

Cameo brooches

Anything shaped like a ribbon

Pearls

Simple and delicate rings (plain bands or a small pearl/jewel/ decorative pieces)

Amethyst

257

Accessories

Belts

Belts should emphasize the hourglass figure. Thick or skinny belts in solid colors. Standard square buckle or round, loop-through buckle. Have one in a few colors that work with everything, like white, black, brown, a bold red, navy blue.

Hats (This is where you can go a little wild. Fifties women wore elaborate hats!)

Floppy hats

Hats rimmed with flowers

Berets

Velour caps

Bags

Long, sleek clutches in patent leather or satin

Envelope clutches

Long-chain clutches

Structured, mini totes with hard walls

Shoes

Kitten heels

Peep-toe heels

Patent-leather Mary Janes

Ballerina flats

PROFESSIONAL

If the look you're going for is "professional," as in power suits, there are a few general rules that should be followed: no denim, no cleavage, and no sequins. Look at it this way: If your mom wouldn't let you out of the house wearing it, don't wear it to work. I know, one of the best new liberties you can take now that you're living away from home is wearing whatever you want! Well . . . you can't, at least not all the time. But the good news is you don't actually have to set aside a budget explicitly for "work" clothes. A lot of clothes that pass the business-meeting test could also be worn to a lunch with friends, cocktail party, even a bar. I'm going to give you ideas for pieces that can break out of the restraints of traditional "professional" clothes while still being professional.

Tops

Plain scoop-neck, crew-neck, or V-neck T's—yes, they can be worn under a blazer.

"Pirate tops"—essentially, white or crème chiffon tops with billowy fabric along the neckline and/or with buttons

White button-up, in cotton or silk. These will never go out of style.

Button-ups in funky prints or strong colors that can later be paired with jeans, heels, and bold jewelry

Lace camisole—Worn under a blazer, these aren't too provocative for the workplace, but still allow you to look feminine.

Cardigans—Depending on the dress code, you may be able to skip the blazer and top off your outfit with a cute, colorful cardigan. Three-quarter-length sleeves look less stiff and can be worn with jeans, too.

Bottoms

High-waist pencil skirts—Get one with a back, exposed zipper for a vintage look, one with belt loops to accessorize, and a soft and elastic one that just slips on for bloated days.

Wide-legged pants, high-waisted or low-rise—Wide-legged pants are a classic women's professional piece. They look great over stilettos or boots.

Boot-legged pants

Dresses

Structured, fitted one- or two-toned dresses that reach the knee—Avoid spaghetti straps, but thick tank-top straps are generally fine.

The "shirt dress"—This is essentially a button-up shirt with a skirt attached to it, usually connected by a belt.

Wrap dress, knee length or longer—Careful with the cleavage on these. Wear a camisole underneath if necessary.

Jewelry

Honestly, whatever you want. Jewelry tends to be the only part of your outfit that you have complete (or at least lots of) freedom with in a workplace where a dress code is enforced. Add some of your personality to your outfit with your favorite jewelry. Probably not the time to whip out your giant warrior cuff, spiked "collar" necklace, or those chandelier earrings you wore when you dressed up as a Fembot. But have fun with it.

Accessories

Belts

Skinny or thick belts with standard square buckles or round buckles in leather, patent leather, shiny plastic, or suede.

Hats

Stay away from hats if you're working indoors. Teachers didn't like you wearing them in the classroom as a kid, and your boss probably won't appreciate them in the office now. At most, headbands will be appropriate. Headbands also allow you some stylistic freedom with your work outfit, so let these show your style—with jewels, embroidery, even standout pieces like feathers or flowers.

Shoes

Knee-high or ankle-high leather boots
Mary Janes
Kitten heels

Closed-toe pumps (some companies do allow open toes; ask before assuming)

Plain or decorative ballerina flats

Loafers

Bags

Neutral-colored, black, gray, or white totes

Shoulder totes

Clutches and long-chain clutches

Prints & Colors

Mostly solid colors like grays, neutrals, blacks, browns, and crème

Pinstripes

Bold colors in small splashes (like on jewelry, shoes, or belts)

Floral, striped, or otherwise patterned blouses

PREPPY

This doesn't necessarily mean straight out of a J.Crew catalog (though there's nothing wrong with that either). A lot of preppy items mix well with other styles. But in general, if it looks good on a yacht, at a "luncheon," or at the polo fields, it's probably preppy. Prep up your look as little or as much as you want with these:

Tops

Argyle vests or button-up cardigans

Plaid blouses (long-sleeve or short) tucked under vests

Thick horizontal-striped sweaters/shirts

Polo shirts (of course) in bright and baby hues

Cardigans with emblems embroidered over breast-pocket area

Bottoms

Short or knee-length pleated skirts

Pressed wide-legged trousers

Cigarette pants (not denim)

Plaid shorts

Plaid miniskirts

Light-colored jeans (baby pink, baby blue, yellow)

Dresses

Pleated skirt dresses with tank tops or polo tops

Structured tank or short-sleeved dresses, knee-length, in baby or bright hues

Simple floral or solid strapless dresses with waist sash

Colorful tweed (think Jackie Kennedy)

Polo dresses

Jewelry (These will match the fifties housewife closely.)

Pearls (single strand, single pearl, earrings, or stacked strings of pearls)

Charm necklaces or bracelets

Sleek, colorful watches

Simple silver or gold hoop earrings

One or two delicate, feminine bracelets (real or fake pearls and beads in baby hues)

Accessories

Belts

Thin, cotton belts in plaid or stripes

Designer belts with brand symbols (Louis Vuitton, Lacoste, Calvin Klein)—You can find these at vintage stores, on eBay, or at discount stores at a fraction of the original cost.

Thick leather belts in solid colors

Hats

Paperboy hats in plaid

Boating hats

Tennis hats

Short-rim fedoras

Big-brim hats (think Audrey Hepburn)

Shoes

Keds or TOMS

Ballerina flats

Riding boots

Loafers

Mary Janes

Wedges

Bags

Vintage designer totes

Long-chain clutches

Barrel bags

Straw bucket bags

Plastic water-resistant totes in baby or bright hues

HIPSTER

You'll find this style widespread, but particularly in big cities. Compared with other styles, this one is a little more difficult to pin down, mostly because the hipster look is a combination of many, many styles. You can find an item from pretty much *any* style in the hipster chick's wardrobe. The tiny twist that turns the look hipster is pairing items in unexpected ways. The hipster chick outfit is always *almost* feminine, but then a more masculine item will set it off. Some even call it an androgynous look. There is a reason that you never know if you're in the male or female section of American Apparel. Since the hipster style encompasses all of the other styles, I'm not going to list specific items for this style. Instead, I'm going to suggest different ways to pair some of the items I've mentioned under the previous styles.

Staples of the Hipster Style

Thick-rim glasses

Skinny jeans in *all* colors

Oversize cardigans

Graphic T's

Combat boots

Ripped jeans

Leggings

Plaid shirts

Denim vests

Hipster Combos

A high-waist, bell-shaped skirt with Converse sneakers

A frilly blouse with ripped jeans

An oversize biker jacket with a minidress and heels

Combat boots and a floral dress

A sexy camisole with Aladdin pants

Ripped jean shorts over leggings

Plaid shirts with miniskirts

Graphic T's with pleather pants

Sequined miniskirts with oversize sweaters

Corsets with cuffed jean shorts

Brightly colored high-waist skirt with razor-back tank top

Oversize cardigans with a graphic T and miniskirt

Blazer with funky pins over a camisole with jeans

T-shirts with cut-out sleeves over leggings

Sweater dresses over funky print tights

SHAMELESSLY SEXY

Disclaimer: It's best to wear this type of outfit either with a boyfriend or out with your girlfriends. Don't put on a shamelessly sexy outfit and head out to a bar by yourself.

If you're anything like me, you *do* worry about crossing that line between sexy and trashy. You shun visible bras, skin-tight skirts, and plunging necklines. You're constantly checking yourself while you get dressed for the night, asking, "Is this too slutty?" But also, if you're anything like me, you notice once you hit the town, there are girls dressed ten times more provocatively than you are. And suddenly you wish you would have taken a few more liberties in flaunting what you've got. Well, maybe it's about time you *do that*.

Yes, you're going to turn heads, and not always in a good way. Some girls will think you look skanky. Some guys will think you're an easy lay. But you know what? Sometimes—just for yourself—you need to flaunt it if you've got it. People think you look slutty? So what. You know you're not. You're young. You've probably still got perky boobs and a minimal amount of cellulite. You can cover up when you're old. Sometimes, we put SO much time into trying to put together the cutest, most-stylish outfit. We find the best way to show off our wardrobe. What if, sometimes, you want to find the best way to show off your body? After all, you spend so much time getting it fit, it's time to show that healthy gorgeous body off! Here's how to dress sexy without going too far over the slutty line:

Tops

Corsets—yes, every girl should have at least one. They play up the hourglass figure, hold in your stomach, and perk up your boobs.

Backless tops

Sequined strapless top

See-through lace tops. Pair with same-color or nude bra

Slinky satin camisole—braless if you're feeling daring

Low-neckline, off-the-shoulder, long-sleeve top

Tank tops with seriously low side cutouts. The side boob cleavage deserves as much attention as the cleavage—it's sexy, too!

Skin-tight, slightly sheer turtleneck—Yes, the skin is covered up. But they show off your shape really well, and that little bit of mystery is always sexy.

Bottoms (Obviously, these are all pretty fitted.)

Pants with bold designs—zebra, plaid, psychedelic—Whatever pants you found in a store but thought *When am I going to wear these?* Wear them now.

Snug pencil skirts

Skirts with exposed back zippers

High-waist short-shorts

Mini schoolgirl skirt, plaid and pleated

Sequined or leather miniskirt

Colors & Prints

Metallic, neon, black, red, hot pink, silver, gold, *any* animal print, chain links, sequined

Jewelry

Just like the workplace jewelry, go wild with jewelry here. You're already wearing a loud outfit. As a general rule, though, if you're wearing solid colors, wear jewelry that is more elaborate with bold colors. If you're wearing crazy prints, keep jewelry simple, like rhinestone necklaces, thin bangles, teardrop earrings.

Accessories

Shoes

Anything platform

Peep-toe pumps

Strappy stilettos

264

Knee-high or over-the-knee boots in bold colors, elaborate designs, or just fab spike heels

Shiny patent pumps

Animal print pumps

Bags

The only word you need to know when it comes to clubbing purses is *clutch*. You're dancing, right? So you don't want anything swinging around or something bulky. You can hold clutches easily in your hand while you dance. If you just don't want to hold your purse, get a long-chain clutch. These dangle pretty low, usually around your hips, so they don't get in the way while you dance. Not clubbing or dancing? The general rule is that smaller (though not childish) is sexier. You don't want a huge bag that distracts the eyes from looking at your sexy outfit. Just a punch of color or flash is perfect! Try bags in these materials, prints, and colors:

Sequined

Quilted patent leather

Royal blue, hot pink, bright red, neon orange, silver, gold

Snake, leopard, or zebra print

Tasseled

More than anything, when it comes to fashion, don't be afraid. Take chances with styles that you might not be used to rocking. There have been so many times that I have ventured out in an outfit that wasn't "my style" and I ended up getting loads of compliments the entire night, showing me that "my style" or not, it looked damn good! On the other side of the coin, you might wear something that ends up not looking great. And that's OK, too. Not all fashions look great on all bodies or suit all personalities. The good news is that no one is taking your pic and publishing it in a "what not to wear" magazine article. Try, try again!

Shop in Your Own Closet

I am going to reintroduce you to a method that you may remember from eighth grade. It worked then, and it works now: Shop in your own closet! Turn on some good trash TV—or eighties music—anything that will put you in a good mood. Do not drink. Believe me, I have shopped in my closet after a few, and it's never a good thing. Here are the five essential steps to follow (each step is important, so don't skip any!):

CLEAR OUT

Throw open your closet doors, pull out your drawers (even those belonging to bras, socks, and panties), and take stock of *all* that you've got. Section by section, category by category, go through your clothes and determine which pile they belong in: "definitely yes" (which can stay neatly hung in your closet or folded in the drawer), "definitely no" (which will be put in a pile on your bed or the floor, and donated), "definitely, maybe"(this pile has potential).

TEST

The only way to determine which item goes in which pile is literally by trying on every single piece of clothing that you own. If you skip this essential step, you will end up keeping lots of crap that doesn't look good on you—never has, never will. I have allowed way too many clothes to take up prime closet space because in my whacked-out head I thought that they actually might look good on me someday. After years of taking up space, I finally buckled down, tried them on, and—shocker—definitely no!

Once your piles are determined, put on one "definitely, maybe" skirt and pair it with (I'm not kidding you) every top in your closet. The reason for trying on every top is because you have to force yourself out of your rigid style lines. You will be surprised by how amazingly some of the most unexpected combos come together. Now keep up this trend with every other skirt, pants, shorts, slacks, etc. in your closet until each item has been tried with every other item. For all of those "definitely no" items? Either get a few girlfriends together and do a "shop in your girlfriend's closet" swap party, have a fab garage sale, or donate them to a charity.

WRITE

Whenever you find a good fit, write it down. No joke. Take a photo of yourself if that helps, too. This way, next time you are having a preparty "I have nothing to wear!" meltdown, you can simply turn to your lists and photos for some "definitely yes" outfits.

SHOP WITH PURPOSE

If, after all of this sorting and trying on, you still honestly believe that you don't have anything to wear, *do not* rush out and drop a grand on yet another outfit that will likely eventually end up in your no pile. Shopping under such desperate measures rarely leads to good things. Instead, write a list of the items you need and shop with purpose! Would a black pencil skirt pair perfectly with five tops that you already own? Or maybe gray skinny-leg pants? Use this opportunity to create ten outfits from two purchases by filling needed holes in your wardrobe. Once you have that list of needs, only then can you go shopping and find those essential wardrobe builders that you can multipurpose!

Come on, ladies, get creative! I bet you can unearth fifteen new outfits from the depths of your closet. You'll come to find that what's seemingly all used up is good as new!

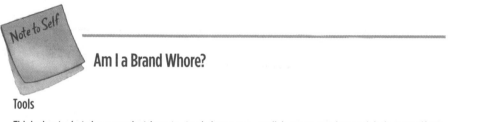

Am I a Brand Whore?

Tools

Think about what shops you just *have* to stop in because . . . well, because you just can't help yourself. It's beautiful, it smells nice, the dressing rooms are huge, the selection is always perfect.

_____

_____

Explore the stores you never go in. What is it about them that turns you off?

_____

_____

Starter Sentence

I have a weakness for this store

_____

_____ ,

but, realistically, I could shop at these stores, too

_____

_____ ,

and find equally cute clothes for less money.

Chic on the Cheap: Where to Shop, Save & Look Fab

Just because you're trying to save money doesn't mean you have to stop shopping cold turkey. In fact, you can stumble upon some pretty fab finds without depositing yourself into a poorhouse mentality (or making much of a dent in your bank account at all). Here's how:

Flea markets are *great* places to buy just about everything, including clothes. You've got a mix between gently worn (sure, some items maybe not so gently, but you can sift through that) and, at some of the best, up-and-coming designers peddle their wares at flea markets to get their start. There are, of course, also lots of vintage (and some just old) shoes, but make sure they aren't wrecked before you buy them. If you do buy used, one bit of advice: Wash it before you wear it.

Consignment stores—both online and storefront—could be your best bet when it comes to cheap, fabulous, high-quality *couture*. Yes, slightly worn couture still counts as couture, but better because the second time, it's seriously inexpensive (or at least less expensive)! Little known fact: Celebrities and television shows often use their couture and name-brand clothes only once, then they're over it. So, what do they do with all of those one time-worn paparazzi-documented duds? They sell them for a quick buck to consignment stores. And that's where you come in.

How Do You Dress Well Without Spending a Lot of Money?

Summer, 24, Art Gallery Assistant:

1. **Resale boutiques!** "My clothing budget is pretty tight, but there's a line between buying brand new and hitting up Goodwill. A good resale shop will cull through the dross and lay out an attractive selection." If you're designer savvy, it's *the QuickieChick way* to afford those names and good cuts. "Best of all is bringing in the nice items you've held on to for too long, making some money off of them and using those earnings to buy something new for you. Not quite a closed economic loop, but definitely an improvement. Frankly, it can be a lot more fun than simply buying the monotonous rack items at bigger box stores. The pieces I get the most compliments on are inevitably my consignment shop finds."

2. **Learn some basic sewing skills.** "Seriously, ladies: I know it's not for everyone, but if you do pick up some sewing skills, they're invaluable. I design and sew a great deal of my clothes from scratch, or just by refitting other pieces that I would have gotten rid of because of the fit, the neckline being too boring, etc. Even just learning to hem can make you refigure a skirt you often pass over or a pair of jeans that are otherwise the perfect fit."

Shop in a friend's closet. Sure, first glance, this might sound like a strange idea. But before you poo-poo the idea, think about all of the unworn clothes that hang in your closet that have never ever been worn! Not many? What about those that you wore once, twice, maybe even ten times, but you're now over them, overweight, or on to a new style phase? Here's the concept: Get your girlfriends to each scour their closets for items that they are no longer interested in. Then throw a party, asking each person to be responsible for one food or drink item (wine, appetizers, chocolate . . .) and of course bring her unwanted clothes, shoes, accessories, even beauty products. Now trade!

QuickieChick's Fashion & Beauty Obsessions

SOLE SOCIETY

As much as you may scavenge thrift stores and even spend hours "shopping" in your closet, sometimes you just *can't* pull together an outfit that you feel "wow" about. There's an easy fix for that: a fabulous shoe. It can make a drab outfit pop. It can make you feel like a million bucks when you're wearing less than fifty bucks. Shoes can truly *make* the outfit. Personally, I like when the shoe stands out a bit, makes a statement, says something about who you are. I love shoes; I'm totally obsessed. My closet is filled with them! And while my obsession can at times be slightly out of control, I'm not breaking my bank. That's thanks to solesociety.com, a membership-based shoe haven for chicks who like to get a monthly shoe fix without breaking their budget. It's actually a great way to build your shoe closet, signing up to buy one style a month (or you can skip a month if you need/want to). Their shoes look straight off the runway, have incredible designs, colors that pop, and somehow are seriously budget-friendly. It's a totally intuitive Web site where you fill out a "style profile" and then they suggest shoes they think you'll like based on your style personality. And they're usually right! They are seriously awesome.

HAUTELOOK

I hate realizing that a sale *just* ended at my favorite store. And it happens way too often. I don't get as peeved by it though when I realize I can just shop on hautelook.com. The online store works with different brands every day to give shoppers insane discounts, sometimes 75 percent off, on top beauty, lingerie, clothing, lifestyle, accessory, and even travel brands. I check it obsessively, since each sale (generally organized by brand) lasts just a few days and then that deal is gone. But I always know another good one will come along. I'm not going to lie: I get pretty excited every day to see who they are featuring. I'm so excited that most of my go-to going-out dresses are from hautelook.com. I'm obsessed.

SKINNYJEANS

These bad boys aren't like any pair of jeans that you have strut before. First of all, they really are called *SkinnyJeans*. And they got that name for a reason: They make you look *skinny*! The cut, design, pockets, inseams, wash, and fabric combo creates the appearance of slimmer thighs, narrower hips, longer legs, and a perkier butt. I mean . . . can you say dream jeans? But it's not just one-size-fits-all style. Choose NiteWash (deep indigo) for going out on the town, DayWash (medium blue) for daytime, obviously, and colors for when you want to show off a little personality in addition to your rockin' body! I gotta admit, I love WhiteOut. There is just something sexy and standout about white jeans. They take guts to pull off, but you will be happy you did. More than making you look skinnier, Skinny-Jeans make you *feel* skinner, and that comes with an instant confidence boost. Now *that* is sexy! And I *love* that the Web site, Skinnyjeans.com, suggests you "Do a pilé in your SkinnyJeans to get them on right and tight!" How fab is that?

NATUROPATHICA'S ROSEMARY LEMON CLARIFYING MIST

I hate feeling "blah." Everyone does. Dull. Tired. Like I haven't slept, haven't exercised, haven't even showered. And it can take a lot of work (or caffeine) to get myself out of that funk. That's why I seriously love Naturopathica's Rosemary Lemon Clarifying Mist. You just close your eyes and spray it directly onto your face for an instant eye-awakening, mind-enlivening refresher—which also happens to be great for your skin! I keep it on my desk for those moments when taking a nap is simply not an option, and in my purse for when my skin feels icky at a crowded bar or after a long and draining meeting.

BURT'S BEES EYE CREME

I know that women live way longer than they used to. But wrinkles didn't get the message, and they still pop up way earlier than you're ready for them. Not that anyone's ever ready. Your career is blooming (hopefully) and stressful (likely), which leads to a menagerie of more smiles (successes), more frowns (frustrations), plus less sleep (giving skin less time to rejuvenate). You don't want lines along your skin to advertise it. Believe me, I've been there and fought not to show it! My secret weapon all along? Eye cream! Specifically, Burt's Bees Royal Jelly Eye Creme. It's like my personal guard between the skin under my eyes and the rest of the world. I delicately dab it on at bedtime (because if I wore it during the day people would think I was crying: It's that rich and doesn't really soak in), and it totally slows down the progression of those lovely lines.

KISS MY FACE SUNSPRAY LOTION

I really don't like having greasy hands. It's kind of a pet peeve. Cooking oil, hair product, whatever it might be—I can't stand the feel of grease. But, obviously being the wrinkle maniac I am, I need to wear sunscreen. Kiss My Face SPF 30 Sunspray Lotion is one of my favorites because I don't really have to touch it—it sprays on—and even when it's on my skin it doesn't feel the least bit sticky. It pretty much dissolves instantly. And it smells *so* good. Chicks, save your skin's youth and don't leave home without it slathered all over you (top of your hands included!).

ORANGE OIL

I frantically flip the pages of every beauty magazine that claims to know the "best" skin-care products. But no matter what the dermatology industry comes out with, I'm always loyal to my orange oil. It's the best remedy for blemishes I have *ever* used. And that's probably because it's anti-inflammatory, so it calms down those puffy pimples; antimicrobial, so it seriously zaps bacteria and fights off those little microbial growths; and it just smells so freaking good. By the way, guys think so, too. So if you're ever spending the night with one, for god's sake, please don't put those white sticky dots of pimple cream all over your face. Dab on some orange oil, and your guy will think you just put on perfume. Plus, orange oil is a natural aphrodisiac. Talk about multitasking skin care!

QuickieChick's Cheat Sheet

1. **It's not really "antiaging" skin care if you wait until the signs of aging have already set in.** Start taking care of your skin now. Sunscreen, moisturizers, and scrubs are your best friends.

2. **Natural and organic are not the same.** Look for the USDA organic seal of approval.

3. **Find beauty products in your kitchen.** Remember coffee grinds, egg whites, olive oil, pomegranate: These all have skin-fortifying and repairing powers.

4. **Refrigerator facials.** You don't need to spend a bundle on facials. In fact, the most natural facial can be found in your kitchen with potatoes, honey, and milk.

5. Your hair is as sensitive as your skin! Remember, avoid chlorine and salt water, keep ponytails loose, avoid overdoing it on the cocktails, and apply a protective SPF sunscreen to your hair and scalp.

6. A great way to bond with girlfriends and score awesome beauty products for FREE is a Beauty Buffet. Invite all your girlfriends over, have them bring a few products, and let the swapping and gossiping begin!

7. Shopping in your closet. If you're female, odds are you have too many clothes. Make a night of shopping in your closet. Try on every single item. Make yes, no, and maybe piles. You'll be amazed at what you rediscover.

8. If after shopping in your closet you *still* don't feel you have enough outfits, **don't forget about flea markets, consignment stores, and thrift shops.**

9. Don't follow trends; it's exhausting and never-ending. **Define your own style.** Let your clothes speak for you.

10. Like cooking, style can be about spice, flare, little extras, and accessories. It's OK to sometimes **explore outside your comfort zone.** You might discover something you really like!

Who Are You . . . Really?

SINCE YOU WERE A LITTLE GIRL, you have been introduced to specific activities, exposed to particular experiences, and given the opportunity to learn certain subjects in an attempt to shape the person that your parents, teachers, and other influential people believed were best for you. You were shuttled from ballet (to be imbued with poise and grace) to tennis camp (to learn how to play well with others). You took the requisite history classes (to understand how happenings in the past affect our present) and math classes (to stretch your mind to think in numbers). You engaged in extracurricular activities like babysitting (to learn about money and responsibilities) and cross-country family trips (to expose you to an array of lifestyles and expand your depth of experience beyond your hometown). Don't think that those specific experiences were accidental. They were critical components, building blocks, to the person whom you were being groomed to become.

But who are you really, at your core, in your gut? What is your passion? What enlivens your mind, makes your heart rush, and flushes your cheeks from sheer enthusiasm? Just because you did something on a regular, ongoing basis and you were good at it, doesn't mean that you did it because you liked it. In fact, chances are that over time you just did it because that's what you've always done, because that's what you were taught to do. It's time to determine who you are, on your own terms.

After years of input from others as to who you "should" be, how do you figure out who you really are?

So what if you realize that this person who you want to be isn't that person you were being groomed to grow into? What if you realize that the person you have been, the people who have surrounded you, the life you have chosen really aren't part of who you actually are or who you want to become? How do you gracefully transition? Don't stress. I cannot say this enough: All of the years leading up to your "Who am I?" moment were *not* a waste. They haven't been leading you astray from your true self. Your true self has always been in there, taking note of what invigorates and enlivens it.

Postgrad Pressures

Julia, 23, Environmental Educator: "Postgrad pressure is normal: Should I be investing in building a firm career foundation, applying to grad school before I get too caught up in routines and life, or should I have some 'dream job' goal or idea of what I want to achieve?"

This questioning and realizing happens . . . a lot. And chances are it will continue to for a while. And that doesn't mean that you are lost or that anything is wrong with you. It means that you're normal and you are a thinking, processing, analyzing human. In fact, it's the question-asking that has brought you through each phase of life. You just might find that you're asking yourself different questions. So don't shy away from those "Who am I?" moments. I know, they are scary, and you might think it's just the same old song and dance as the last time you had one of those moments and that you'll learn nothing new. But, actually, each time you come closer to really figuring out the true you. Example: My first batch of "Who am I?" moments consisted of a *lot* of questions about what was wrong with my ex-boyfriends. The next "Who am I?" moments, however, consisted of questions about me: How could I do things differently in those relationships? How did I contribute to the downfalls? What was it about me that made me attracted to guys who had those issues? And what in me allowed myself to be in and stay in those unhealthy situations?

It's interesting to take note and be aware of these changes in your way of thinking. Seeing how your thinking has evolved turns those "Who am I?" moments from being scary, confusing times, to moments that make you realize how much you have grown. So allow yourself to really get into those moments. I'm not saying to harbor old issues or live in the past, or become totally lost in your head. Just take a walk, take a bath, and really think about those moments, even allowing yourself to feel them again as you think through them and try to figure out the lessons they offer. If they make you sad or terrified, call your mom, a friend, or your sister for advice. You need to fully experience these moments; they will only help you grow. As I always told my mom after yet another one of my screwups, "I'm sure there's a lesson in here somewhere; I just need to figure out what it is and try to learn from it."

It's very common for college grads to feel a bit lost when it comes to who they are and who they want to be. You have been told your entire life that you would make a great teacher/attorney/chef/professional athlete, etc. So upon graduating you pursue that career, and you come to realize

Note to Self

Transitioning from Old You to True You

Take Note

What are your aspirations? What do you want to achieve in your life?

_____

_____

What does success mean to you?

_____

_____

What does happiness mean to you?

_____

_____

What does happiness feel like and look like to you?

_____

_____

Which of your personality traits are you most proud?

_____

_____

Which of your personality traits would you most like to improve?

_____

_____

What lessons/benefits have you learned from life's letdowns/bummers?

_____

_____

that that job is not for you at all! Now what? Instead of taking it as a major blow, consider it part of the learning process. I mean, really, how could you know if you hadn't tried? Nobody just intuitively _knows_ ahead of time the exact career that is right for them. Some people may claim to know, and if that career does work out for them, great, but the truth is, they didn't _actually_ know until they tried it. Anyone has the potential to realize they've gotten into the totally wrong career. And if you find yourself in that situation, that's OK, as we talked about before; just make a mid-course

correction and try to take with you the lessons that you learned. Was there anything about the career that you *did* like? What was it about the career that you *didn't* like? Analyze the lifestyle, the hours, the people, the actual work. What about it suited and didn't suit you?

You see, life in the real world is more than just finding the "perfect job," or the "perfect-on-paper" boyfriend. It's about finding yourself, creating your identity, and defining who you are as an individual.

Unexpected Ways That You Might Change

- You may realize you prefer nerdy or reserved guys to the loud frat guys you were habitually around in college.

- You may realize one day while you're dancing on a table at a club that, hey, you hate clubbing! You would much rather be taking a salsa class or attending a book club meeting.

- You may realize that you actually love, *love*, ultra-feminine dresses as opposed to the low-rise jeans and tanks you've always opted for on nights out.

- You may realize that your parents have been right about things all along, that they are pretty cool, and maybe they can even be your friends.

- You may realize that your closest group of girlfriends are just on totally different paths than you are, and that if you really want to become who you want to become, you may need to distance yourself from them.

These all sound so incredibly nutty right now. But I *never* thought five years ago that if a totally gorgeous guy asked for my number I would be more apt to say no than yes. But you learn things as you go along that drastically shed light on your choices and how they affect your happiness. I know it's annoying, but I have to say it: You have a lot to learn. And that's exciting! The more you learn, the more you can alter your life to get closer to your idea of happiness.

Making Mid-Course Corrections

Feeling like something in your life is sort of off? Maybe you need to stop, think about who you are, where you are going, and if this career, life, person you are working to become is really you. If it's not, don't stress. We've all been there. Just make a mid-course correction. A mid-course correction is exactly that: It's stopping, analyzing, and making necessary change. Even if that change is a complete 180 and it's scary, don't *not* change, don't continue to do what you don't like, or continue walking along the path that doesn't feel right, or continue developing a persona you don't want to become just because you are afraid, embarrassed, or "you've already come so far." Believe me, you're still young; "this far" isn't so far. Imagine still doing what you're doing in ten, twenty, forty years from now. Put yourself in that place and time. Are you happy? Believe me chickadees, I've done it. I've done it in relationships: I went through with something that I knew would end in failure, but I did it anyway because of a combination of embarrassment, self-doubt, and "but I've already come this far."

I've also made the mid-course correction, nipping the mistake in the bud before the mere annoyance festered into something that made me a miserable human being. Sure, I was scared; yes, I was intimidated; absolutely, I was afraid to fail. But I did it. And you know what? I didn't fail. As soon as I spun around and got my footing on my new path . . . it was easy! Shockingly easy, considering how much I felt like I was a salmon swimming upstream in my old path. Of course, then the inevitable questions arise: "Why didn't I do this earlier?" I question my corrections: "Did I really make the right decision? Maybe I didn't give that path enough of a chance; maybe if I'd just tried a little longer, or if I had done it this way. . . . " And in some instances I reverted back, and you know what? I got the same exact outcome as the first time around. Maybe for a few months things appeared to be on the up-and-up. But once the waters settled, I was back at it—swimming upstream again. Now *that* is when the mid-course correction is embarrassing, because you have to do it yet *again* (which I have also done). But you *do* have to do it again. It's either that or make the decision to be less than happy for the rest of your life. I'd personally rather endure a little embarrassment than that fate. Trust me, I know from experience.

Here is some good news: Mallika Chopra, the founder and CEO of Intent.com, an online destination for turning your intention into tangible action—where she, her dad, Dr. Deepak Chopra, and many other influential people help inspire others through daily blog posts—says that "painful experiences, failure, challenges often turn out to be our most transformative and powerful learning experiences." In addition to running Intent.com, Mallika is the president for Chopra Media, a member of the board of directors of Virgin Comics and Virgin Animation, and also helped launched MTV in India, Michael Jackson's Heal the World Foundation, and Go Networks. How do you think she became so successful in so many fields? By stopping along each path and asking herself questions.

In order to be constantly open to taking lessons from painful experiences, Mallika suggests that you ask yourself basic questions about who you are, what you want, and what will give you peace and happiness. "In asking the questions and then setting basic intentions about who you aspire to be, you will start creating the path for self-discovery." Like what questions? Mallika asks:

- Who am I?

- Where do I come from?

- What do I want?

- How do I find peace?

- How can I serve (serve yourself, your God, etc.—however this questions resonates with you)?

Questioning doesn't make Mallika feel uncomfortable. She is a strong believer in the power of intention. "By clearly stating your intent, your aspirations, you begin the path to realize them. So to transition from your current place, begin with the intention for change, and slowly you will see the path ahead. Trust your intuition about the right pace for change."

So are mid-course corrections and changing directions actually good, helpful, and positive? Mallika says yes! "At any point in our life, we can ask ourselves if we are on the right path. Practice listening to yourself and trusting your intuition to guide you on the next steps. Knowing that you can change direction at any time is empowering to know that you are never trapped." So true!

I know . . . this is a lot, and it can be overwhelming, even disorienting, forcing you to question yourself and what you already just *know* is a good thing. Trust your intuition, your inner self's "gut" reaction—without the weight of judgment, emotion, or analysis. Some people call that "knowing" an "aha" moment, a click, a "voice in your head," a feeling that "it's just right" or "it's just wrong." Listen to that feeling.

After All of That Hard Work . . . Why Does Everything Suddenly Feel Too Easy?

What's interesting is that once you listen to your intuition and you are on the right path, once you are doing what you are "supposed" to be doing, once you have found your "calling"—whatever you want to call it—things just seem to click, they fall into place, the right people are somehow presented to you, and, oddly, everything feels almost too easy. And that's how you know that it's right. You sit there thinking, *I know this isn't supposed to be so easy; I know I should be trying more frantically, flailing around each corner. Why is this path so effortless?* You want to know the answer? It's because you actually already flailed around and tried frantically. Remember all those "Who am I?" moments you made yourself go through? This time when everything feels easy, it's happening because you worked really hard, put in the time, energy, and legwork, until you finally found the beat, got into the groove, and it all just seemed to flow into place. The funny thing is, you might still be working as many hours as before, but you just don't notice it because it doesn't feel like work anymore. And that is what's great about doing what you love to do.

Not feeling like you're on the exact right path quite yet? Haven't found that click? That's OK. Stop, reassess, look at the path you have been on, and see the future it's leading to. Are you on track? Did you somehow get side-tracked? Or maybe you just realized that this path you have always dreamed about isn't actually your passion anymore. Know that you are allowed to make mid-course corrections. I did. And it wasn't only OK, those corrections turned out to be great! Because I didn't simply turn around and blaze a new path in a new direction; I blazed that new path with a better understanding of who I am, what I'm looking for, plus a bunch of life lessons in my pocket to help make me stronger along the way. Once I was able to get on the right path, it suddenly clicked! It was like the lights switched on in a huge room, and doors were opening for me that I didn't even know existed. And *that's* when work no longer feels like work.

Remember: This isn't a destination; it's a journey, a journey that is boiled down into rich little moments—Quickies. And that's what the point of life is—being completely present and enjoying the moment and knowing that putting your all into every second will make the next one better, while seeing the positive in the negatives, the benefits in the bummers. It's living in and learning from the now, while paving a path for tomorrow, and occasionally taking a peek into the rearview mirror to appreciate the view of the past and how far you have already come. Every Quickie might not be perfect, ideal, pretty, or convenient. But have fun, learn, be honest and true to you, allow yourself to let go, let loose, get out of your rigid box, explore new things, and follow your passions . . . because life needs more Quickies.

279

Index

285

288

About Laurel House

Laurel House is a Fit Lifestyle Expert, personal trainer, and nationally recognized print and online magazine writer (*Women's Health, First for Women, Men's Journal, Elegant Bride, Fit, Spa, Fit Yoga, Playboy,* Yahoo!Shine, PlanetGreen.com, and DailyCandy.com). Beyond writing, Laurel has appeared as an expert on television morning shows including *Weekend TODAY, The Daily Buzz, Better.TV, KTLA Morning News,* CBS, Fox, NBC, and *ABC Morning News* shows both locally and nationally, and her YouTube videos have been seen by over six million viewers. She is also known as the "QuickieChick." No, not the late-night booty-call kind of quickie! Her "quickies" are all about making the most of every moment—whether it's a saddlebag-burning "Quickie Workout in Bed," a metabolism-boosting "Bites with Benefits" meal, or how to get a $150 spa-quality skin peel out of a $1 tomato and lemon with an "At-Home Refrigerator Facial." So don't tell her that you don't have time . . . because there's always time for a quickie.